0

CHINOOK CRASH

By the same author

The Loch Ness Monster: The Evidence
The UFO Mystery Solved
The Rise and Fall of Jesus

CHINOOK CRASH

The crash of RAF Chinook helicopter
ZD576 on the Mull of Kintyre

by

STEUART CAMPBELL

Pen & Sword
AVIATION

First published in Great Britain in 2004 by
Pen & Sword Aviaton
an imprint of
Pen & Sword Books Ltd
47 Church Street
Barnsley
South Yorkshire
S70 2AS

ISBN 1 84415 074 7

Typeset in Sabon and Univers by
Phoenix Typesetting, Auldgirth, Dumfriesshire

Printed and bound in England by
CPI UK

Pen & Sword Books Ltd incorporates the Inprints of Pen & Sword
Aviation, Pen & Sword Maritime, Pen & Sword Military, Wharncliffe
Local History, Pen & Sword Select, Pen & Sword Military Classics
and Leo Cooper.

For a complete list of Pen & Sword titles please contact
PEN & SWORD BOOKS LIMITED
47 Church Street, Barnsley, South Yorkshire, S70 2AS, England
E-mail: enquiries@pen-and-sword.co.uk
Website: www.pen-and-sword.co.uk

Contents

Acknowledgements

I am especially grateful to defence analyst Malcolm Spaven for his many comments, help and advice, especially on RAF operations and procedures. I also acknowledge the help and/or advice given to me by the following: Stephen Breen; Dr Lynda Clark QC, MP; Russell Ellacott; David Harrison; Michael Jones QC, LLB; Ralph Kohn; Hector Lamont; David Murchie; Michael Tapper; Ann Tyler and Wing Commander T.K. O'Donnell.

I also acknowledge the help of Court Reporters William Hodge & Pollock Ltd for supplying me with a digital copy of their transcript of the FAI proceedings and thank The Scottish Court Service for permission to quote from it. I thank the Ministry of Defence for their general assistance and for permission to reproduce the Military Air Accident Summaries in Appendix One and I thank Paladin Invision for supply of a frame from their documentary about the crash.

Parliamentary copyright material from the House of Lords Select Committee Report (HL Paper 25(i)) is reproduced with permission of the Controller of HMSO on behalf of Parliament.

The maps on pages 175 and 189 are based on Ordnance Survey material and reproduced with the permission of the Ordnance Survey on behalf of the Controller of HMSO under licence no. 100042276. The chart on page 175 is also reproduced with the permission of the DGIA. Unauthorized reproduction infringes Crown Copyright and may lead to prosecution of civil proceedings

List of Diagrams

Flying in itself is not inherently dangerous, but it is mercilessly unforgiving of human error.

Slogan on a US Marine Corps fighter squadron bulletin board.*

* Quoted by astronaut John Glenn in 'Touching the Void', *Scotland on Sunday* Spectrum Magazine, 4 April 2004

Glossary of abbreviations and acronyms

AAIB	Air Accident Investigation Branch
ACM	Air Chief Marshal
ADR	Accident Data Recorder (in effect an FDR)
AFCS	Automatic Flight Control System
AM	Amplitude Modulation
AOC	Air Officer Commanding
AR&TF	Aircraft Recovery and Transportation Flight
A&AEE	Aircraft and Armament Experimental Establishment
BD	(RAF) Boscombe Down
CA	Controller Aircraft
CCF	Combined Cadet Force
CFIT	Controlled Flight Into Terrain
C-in-C	Commander-in-Chief
CO	Commanding Officer (same as OC)
CVR	Cockpit Voice Recorder
CW	*Computer Weekly*
DASH	Differential Air Speed Hold
DDCI	Draft Defence Council Instruction
DDU	Distress and Diversion Unit
DECU	Digital Electronic Control Unit
DERA	Defence Evaluation and Research Agency (formerly DRA)
DGIA	Defence Geographic and Imagery Intelligence Centre
DRA	Defence Research Agency (now DERA)
DTLR	Department of Transport, Local Government and the Regions
FADEC	Fully Automated Digital Engine Control
FAI	Fatal Accident Inquiry
FRC	Flight Reference Cards
FDR	Flight Data Recorder
FM	Frequency Modulation
GMT	Greenwich Mean Time (same as UT)
GPS	Global Positioning System
GS	Ground Speed
GSDI	Ground Speed and Drift Indicator
HCS	Horizontal Course Selector
HMA	Hydro Mechanical Assembly
HOC	House of Commons

HSDE	Hawker Siddeley Dynamics Engineering
HUMS	Health and Usage Monitoring System
IAS	Indicated Air Speed
ICF	Initial Contact Frequencies
IFR	Instrument Flight Rules
ILCA	Integrated Lower Control Actuator
IMC	Instrument Meteorological Conditions
IRA	Irish Republican Army
IT	Information Technology
JATOC	Joint Air Tasking Operations Centre
LCT	Lower Control Actuator
LCTA	Lower Cyclic Trim Actuator
LFA	Low-flying Area
LFC	Low-flying Chart
MALM	Master Air Loadmaster
MOD	Ministry of Defence (UK)
MTBF	Mean Time Between Failures
NAO	National Audit Office
NERC	Natural Environment Research Council
PAC	(House of Commons) Public Accounts Committee
PPM	Parts per million
PTIT	Power Turbine Inlet Temperature
OC	Officer Commanding (same as CO)
QNH	A code indicating atmospheric pressure corrected to sea level datum
RadAlt	Radar Altimeter
RAF	Royal Air Force (MOD)
RNS	Racal Navigation System
ROC	Rate of Climb
RPM	Revolutions per minute
RUC	Royal Ulster Constabulary
SAS	Special Air Service
ScATCC	Scottish Air Traffic Control Centre
SHF	Support Helicopter Force
SRAFONI	Senior RAF Officer Northern Ireland
TACAN	Tactical Air Navigation System
TANS	Tactical Area Navigation System
TETRA	Terrestrial Trunked Radio
TL	Textron Lycoming
UT	Universal Time (same as GMT)
VFR	Visual Flight Rules
VHF	Very High Frequency (radio)
VIP	Very Important Person
VMC	Visual Meteorological Conditions
VOR	VHF Omnidirectional Radio
WP	Waypoint

Introduction

Just before 18:00 on Thursday, 2 June 1994, an RAF Chinook helicopter crashed in thick fog on the Mull[1] of Kintyre in Argyll (Scotland). Twenty-nine people were killed almost instantly, making it the RAF's worst peacetime accident and the worst loss of life in a single RAF accident since 1972. It was also the tenth aircraft to crash on the Mull since 1941 (Pike 2002). Apart from the loss of life, the Ministry of Defence (MOD) lost an aircraft worth £11 million and has had to pay about £15 million in compensation to the relatives of the deceased, that to the dependants of the pilots being cut by half on the basis of the latter's 'contributory negligence'.[2] The Government has agonized over the crash; over its cause, the huge loss of life and the blame heaped on the pilots, and hopes that the controversy will die down. Meanwhile, the grieving families of the pilots refuse to let it die down; they want the RAF's inquiry reopened and their sons exonerated.

The crash was also a disaster for the Government's counter-intelligence operations. The twenty-five passengers were top security specialists involved in planning secret tactics against the IRA[3] in Northern Ireland, the origin of the flight. They included senior police officers from the Royal Ulster Constabulary (RUC),[4] British Army officers and officials from the Northern Ireland Office, including members of the intelligence services. There were five majors, one colonel, three lieutenant colonels, two detective inspectors, one detective chief inspector, four detective superintendents, two detective chief superintendents and an assistant chief constable. The latter was Assistant Chief Constable Brian Fitzsimons, head of the RUC's Special Branch and responsible for

1

tracking down the Brighton bomber Patrick Magee. They were all on their way to attend a security conference at Fort George near Inverness, an annual event. The four crew who died included pilots Flight Lieutenant Jonathan Tapper (28) and Flight Lieutenant Richard Cook (30). Tapper was the captain, acting also as navigator. A cairn commemorating those who died was subsequently built on the site of the crash (see plate 1). The Queen sent a message of condolence to the families and colleagues of the victims and Prime Minister John Major praised the latter's skill and determination in their work of national importance.

The accident caused a full-scale rescue operation coordinated by RAF Pitreavie in Fife. It sent two Royal Navy helicopters from HMS *Gannet* at Prestwick, one of which collected an emergency medical team from Glasgow's Southern General Hospital. One helicopter landed at the landing pad by the lighthouse ready to evacuate casualties. Pitreavie also sent a Nimrod aircraft and a helicopter from RAF Kinloss, the latter carrying a mountain rescue team. Another helicopter was sent from RAF Boulmer in Northumberland. Campbeltown lifeboat was called out, as were Strathclyde Fire Brigade and fire tenders from the RAF base at Machrihanish. Strathclyde police also attended. Unfortunately, differences in the way the RAF and Strathclyde police control crash sites led to tension between them.

The accident has been the most extensively examined air crash in the history of British military aviation. Following the initial official investigation, it has been re-investigated by various parties at various times over a period of at least eight years.

The RAF immediately convened a Board of Inquiry[5], while an inspector from the Air Accidents Investigation Branch of the Department of Transport (AAIB) began work at the crash site. The latter finished his report in January 1995 and the Board reported in March 1995. Neither of these documents was made public at the time, but it was announced that the pilots were responsible; two senior air marshals, reviewing the Board report, accused them of 'gross negligence', a verdict that had not been declared before. This was based on the RAF Manual of Flight Safety[6], which declared that 'only in cases where there is

2

absolutely no doubt whatsoever should deceased aircrew be found negligent'; it lists several categories of negligence.[7] Although not as a consequence of this accident, the Manual was amended in 1997, directing that, although Boards of Inquiry may assess any human factors involved in an accident, they 'should not consider, nor make any statement about, blameworthiness'. This followed the example of the International Convention on Civil Aviation, which requires accident investigators to find causes, not to apportion blame.

Meanwhile, as required by Scottish law, the local procurator fiscal[8], based in Campbeltown, began his own investigation. This necessitated the holding of a public Fatal Accident Inquiry (FAI) to be held before a sheriff.[9] This was held in Paisley Sheriff Court over eighteen days in January and February 1996. It was the first opportunity that the public had of hearing the details of the accident, what led up to it and the subsequent investigation. However, the FAI failed to explain the accident; the sheriff even rejected the MOD's own explanation.

Because they were unable to accept that the pilots were responsible and being convinced that there must have been something wrong with the aircraft, the pilots' families have persistently campaigned for re-examination of the incident by the MOD, or for a new public inquiry. In particular, because doubt still exists about the cause of the accident, they want the accusation against the pilots withdrawn or modified. In April 1998, the families of the pilots even instituted litigation in the Court of Session[10] against the Lord Advocate[11] representing the MOD. When compensation was agreed in March 2000, this case was withdrawn.

For their part, the air marshals have no doubts and stoutly defend their verdict. It can be argued that in no case will there be *absolutely* no doubt and that it was unwise of the RAF to adopt this philosophically indefensible position. It is ironic therefore, that Boards of Inquiry now only have to try to explain accidents. Likewise, this book is not concerned with who was to blame and to what extent; it is concerned with explaining how the accident occurred.

*   *   *

3

Many members of the UK Parliament have been drawn into the controversy on the side of the families, with ninety of them signing a call for the RAF's inquiry to be reopened. There have been some sixty or so letters to ministers, about 200 questions in Parliament, including two to Prime Minister Tony Blair[12], debates in both Houses of Parliament and discussion in three parliamentary committees. The crash has been considered by ten ministers from two governments. After publishing the Board's report, the AAIB's report, the Sheriff's Determination and the oral and written evidence submitted to it, the House of Lords Select Committee reported in January 2002. Although it could not point to any specific mechanical defect that caused the accident, the Select Committee concluded that it could not endorse a verdict of gross negligence against the pilots. The MOD disputed that conclusion and refuses to reconsider its verdict.

Because of the controversy, the matter has become a cause célèbre, exciting the mass media, with newspapers giving it a great amount of space. It has been claimed that prominent newspapers and magazines published 500 articles on the subject in less than two years and that there have been 100 reports on television and radio. On 27 January 1997, Channel Four's *Cutting Edge* programme broadcast David Harrison's documentary about the crash and the inquiry[13], an updated version of which was broadcast on 3 June 1998. During the three years from November 1997, Harrison produced a series of reports about the controversy on Channel Four News. On Thursday, 30 Nov 2000, BBC TV's *Newsnight* programme broadcast an interview with Air Chief Marshall Sir William Wratten, one of the RAF chiefs who accused the pilots of gross negligence. A Scottish Sunday newspaper described it as 'one of Newsnight's clashes of the year, with both Paxman [the interviewer] and Wratten outsneering each other . . .'[14]

Unfortunately, most journalists have little understanding of the technical matters involved, or of RAF and legal procedures. Consequently, their reports contain numerous errors and misperceptions, usually leading to false conclusions. Worse, alleged scandals and cover-ups are newsworthy regardless of the truth. The result can be that the public, dependent on mass media reports, is misled. The large amount of press coverage devoted to the families' campaign and its criticism of the MOD leads the public to believe that they (the families) must have a strong case; truth tends to be measured by the number of column inches, or programme time on TV.

The matter even reached the Church of Scotland General Assembly. On 21 May 2003, after the families had asked the Kirk to intervene on their behalf and a speech by the Revd John Paton, a minister from South Argyll, the Assembly voted unanimously to urge the MOD to 'revisit' the disaster. In subsequent correspondence between the Kirk and the MOD, the latter accused the former of prolonging the grief of the families. When this was revealed in a report to the 2004 Assembly, there was dismay and outrage.

Possibly as a result of the sheer volume of criticism and the publicity given to the families' case, there is widespread refusal to accept the MOD's conclusion. This has been exacerbated by a growing distrust of the UK Government for many other reasons. The criticism flourished because of the absence of any logical reason why the pilots continued their track when they entered cloud, breaking RAF rules in the process. There is a general conviction that they must have been distracted or have had some kind of mechanical or computer problem that prevented them changing track. The absence of any evidence for such a malfunction has not deterred many from assuming that such a malfunction existed. People cannot believe that highly qualified pilots could make a simple navigation error. The pilots' fathers in particular campaign on the basis that their sons would never make such an error.

The MOD claims that the pilots' mistake was to select an inappropriate rate of climb over the Mull (it also points to the breaking of RAF rules in not climbing to safety altitude[15] when they entered cloud). This assumes that the pilots knew where they were and what lay ahead of them and it ignores any navigation errors. It will be shown that the cause lay, not in a faulty climb rate, but in faulty navigation. Moreover, it will be shown exactly what the fault was. Even in a case of CFIT (Controlled Flight Into Terrain), it is necessary to explain how the error came to be made.

Where an incident is the subject of one or more inquiries, especially in the latter case, a window is opened on persons and procedures that is normally closed. In this case, the FAI and the subsequent release of the Board's report give us a fascinating insight into RAF operations. Not only is this interesting in itself, it shows up surprising defects in personnel and machinery. The subsequent controversy over blame also has its own fascination, demonstrating as it does the refusal of many to accept official explanations and/or their failure to understand the complex issues involved. The fact that the controversy has reached the highest levels of government in the UK makes the matter even more interesting and important.

Some have pointed to the comments by former Secretary of State for Defence, Sir Malcolm Rifkind, who reported the result of the Board to the House of Commons in 1995. Four years later and out of Parliament, after he heard about a claim by the MOD against the manufacturers of the Chinook and its engines, he joined in the criticism of the MOD by declaring that these facts should have been revealed to the Board. It is claimed that Rifkind's comments reinforce the case against the MOD and undermine its conclusion. However, this is not the first time that Sir Malcolm has changed his mind on a controversial issue. With his Party in opposition, he was bound to be critical of the Government. He has no special knowledge of the subject and his view is of no more value than that of anyone else. Indeed, it may be of less value; in a later newspaper article, he claimed that the FAI had found that the finding of negligence was *'unsafe'* and should not be maintained.[16] As a lawyer, Sir Malcolm should have known that FAIs cannot rule on blame and that the sheriff in this case did not do so.

The accident has been much discussed on an Internet site ('Still Fighting Back') operated by the Professional Pilots' Rumour Network (PPRuNe), where most of the comments support the families and call for the exoneration of the pilots from the charge of negligence. This has resulted in the creation of a dedicated website called 'Battle for Justice' (subtitle 'Chinook Crash'!).[17]

Although most military pilots support the families in their campaign, some accept that the crew made a mistake and that they are culpable.

When no obvious and generally accepted explanation emerges for a well-publicized aircraft accident, almost any explanation appears to fill the void and desperation drives many to adopt unsustainable hypotheses. Necessarily these include irrational explanations, such as that the Chinook fell foul of a UFO or a top-secret US plane called Aurora, which allegedly flew into or out of RAF Machrihanish, ten miles (sixteen kilometres) from the Mull. Some believe that Machrihanish is also where alien spacecraft were dismantled. Terrorist activity has also been proposed. While there is no evidence for any of these explanations, they will persist in the absence of a logical one.

Apologies

While most of the world has adopted the (SI) metric system, aviation seems to be stuck in the imperial past or at least mixing metric and non-metric units. Distances are usually measured in nautical miles (nm), but metric units occasionally appear. Height (altitude) is usually measured in feet (ft). Likewise, speed is measured in knots, nautical miles per hour, abbreviated here as 'kt'. As scientists, meteorologists use SI metric, but seem to use some imperial mensuration when communicating with aviators.

I apologize for having to go along with this mensuration mixture. However, for the benefit of metric-oriented readers, I will give metric equivalents of imperial or other non-metric quantities the first time they occur, but not subsequently. A nautical mile is the average length of one minute of arc on a great circle of the Earth and is defined internationally as 1,852metres (m), equivalent to 1.15 statute miles. Consequently, a knot is equivalent to 1.15 miles per hour (mph), 1.85 kilometres per hour (kph). Some quantities are given as received, in metric units with no imperial equivalent. Climb rates are usually given in feet per minute (fpm) for which the metric equivalent is metres per second (m/s), also used for some wind speeds.

I also apologize to any female readers who might be annoyed by references to pilots only as male. This appears to be an RAF habit that I find I have to follow when quoting RAF personnel. Otherwise, I allow for pilots of either sex.

Terminology

Throughout this book, 'track' describes the path followed over the ground and 'heading' describes the direction in which an aircraft is pointing.

Chapter One

The Watchers and Listeners

On Thursday, 2 June 1994, the British news media were mainly concerned with who was going to become leader of the Labour Party following the premature death of John Smith. In Northern Ireland, at RAF Aldergrove, just after 17:00, an RAF Chinook helicopter with the designation ZD576 sat on Bay 6. This helicopter would itself be the subject of the next day's headlines.

At 17:07, Belfast International Airport Ground Movement Control received a message from the Chinook's captain: *'Aldergrove Ground. Good evening, Foxtrot four Juliet four zero'*. The controller acknowledged by asking the aircraft to pass its message. The captain replied: *'Foxtrot four zero* [the abbreviated form of his call sign]. *Requesting start Bay 6. We'll be looking for a non-standard departure, outbound zero two seven degrees, low level'*. The controller replied: *'Sorry? Say again the heading'*; the heading, to the north-north-east, was unusual for a military Chinook and the words 'non-standard' indicated an unusual mission. The captain explained: *'Zero two seven. We're initially going to do a* [going to?] *DA2 and then outbound on the heading'* (he was going to move to another part of the airfield before departure). The controller replied: *'Understood. Start is approved. Temperature plus one four QNH'* (the air temperature was 14 degrees C and the atmospheric pressure — which pilots use to set their altimeters to give the correct reading – was 998 millibars). The captain replied: *'998 and clear start Tango— correction: Foxtrot four zero'* (the captain inadvertently started to use another call sign, and had to correct himself). Further exchanges involved the atmospheric pressure for another part of the aircraft's planned route. The captain then requested and was given permission to 'hover taxi' to a position north of tower DA2; he was also given the wind direction and strength. Later, at 17:40, the controller heard: *'Foxtrot four zero. Request a departure DA2, non-standard outbound, heading[18] zero two seven, low level'* (they were ready to depart on track 027 and they would be flying at low level). The controller replied: *'After airborne DA two, will be a left turn out'* (on departure the Chinook will need to turn left to gain its track). Evidently not wishing to turn left, the captain replied: *'What will be best for you? We can go right if possible.'* The controller replied: *'As I said, hold position. Expect a one-minute delay. I'll call you shortly.'* If the captain wanted to go right, he would have to wait, probably for another aircraft movement. The captain replied: *'Holding POI[nt] — Foxtrot 40.'* The time was now 17:41. Then, from the aircraft: *'Tower; Foxtrot 40's visual with landing traffic'* (the crew had seen the traffic for which they had to wait and were gently urging the tower to let them go). The tower replied: *'40 Roger. The aircraft is a Cessna 150 about to cross the 17 threshold. He will be doing a touch and go for further right-hand circuit. Once he has passed clear, take off behind him with a right turn out on to your desired track at low level. The wind is 170 at 10.'* The captain acknowledged by replying: *'Behind the landing traffic clear, take off outbound zero two seven Foxtrot 40'* and, at 17:42, *'Foxtrot 40 is now lifting and departing.'* Finally *'One two zero decimal zero* [a radio frequency shift acknowledgement]. *Good day. Foxtrot four zero.'*

That evening Sinead Swift (25) was on duty as an air traffic controller at Belfast International Airport, which also covers RAF Aldergrove. More precisely, she was the Approach Radar Controller, who also deals with departures. At 17:43 she received the following message from the Chinook on the 120.0MHz frequency: *'Approach, good evening, Foxtrot four . . .* [unintelligible, but probably *'Juliet four']* *zero's outbound, zero two seven, low level.'* The captain was informing her that the aircraft was departing on a track of 027 magnetic at low level, i.e. below 500ft (151.4m). Sinead understood that the flight would be under Visual Flight Rules (VFR), i.e. the pilots would navigate by sight of the ground, but with some instrumental support.[19] The track '027' was to the north-north-east, towards Scotland's Kintyre peninsula. Sinead replied: *'Foxtrot four zero, roger, report at the zone boundary. There's a Lynx helicopter inbound from the north-east. He's high-level VFR.'* This was an instruction to the aircraft to report when it reached a distance of 9nm (16.6km) from the Airport. It should also watch out for another helicopter approaching on a reciprocal track, but above 500ft. At 17:44 the Chinook captain replied: *'Call . . .* [unintelligible] *zone boundary, Foxtrot four zero.'* Later she received another message: *'Foxtrot four zero, visual with the incoming traffic.'* The Chinook's crew had spotted the incoming Lynx. Sinead acknowledged the message and noted that radar showed the Chinook on its track of 027 degrees magnetic at a distance of 7nm from the Belfast VOR.[20] She next heard from the aircraft at about fourteen seconds after 17:46, when she received the following message: *'Approach, Foxtrot four zero at zone boundary, VFR, operational, good day.'* The Chinook was now 9nm from Aldergrove on track for Kintyre, was still flying VFR but was switching to a military 'operational' frequency. Normally it would have made no further contact. However, because Sinead did not hear the message clearly or was distracted by something else, she asked the Chinook to repeat its message. At about twenty-five seconds past 17:46 the repeat was: *'We're now at zone boundary, going en route, good day.'* This was the last message she received from the aircraft, and she signed off with: *'Bye, bye.'*

Almost immediately, the captain called RAF Strike Command Integrated Communications System (81 Signals Unit). This is an organization that listens to HF radio; all around the world, RAF Strike Command aircraft call them to monitor operations and pass messages—their call sign is 'Architect':

Chinook: *'Hello Architect, Architect. This is Foxtrot four Juliet four zero on 4's —over.'*

81SU: *'Station calling. This is Architect. Can you say again the call sign? Over.'*

Chinook:	*'Hello, Architect. You are fair readable. This is Foxtrot four Juliet four zero on fours* [?]. *We departed EGAA* [Aldergrove] *en route to Inverness and request a listening watch this frequency-over.'*
81SU:	*'Roger Foxtrot four Juliet four zero. This is Architect. Anything further? Over.'*
Chinook:	*'Foxtrot four Juliet four zero. Got twenty-nine POB and will be . . .* [unintelligible] *listening watch to EGAA Ext 30370. Over'* (The captain was reporting that he has twenty-nine people on board, including the crew).
81SU:	*'This is Architect. Can you say again? Over.'*
Chinook:	*'Foxtrot four Juliet four zero. Request relay to EGAA Ext 30370. Operations normal, and we have 29 POB.'* (The captain wanted Architect to pass this message to an RAF office at Aldergrove).
81SU:	*'This is Architect. Roger. Ops. normal and 29 POB. Will relay. Anything further? Over.'*
Chinook:	*'Foxtrot four Juliet four zero. That's no-over.'*
81SU:	*'This is Architect. Roger. Listening. Out.'*

The Chinook was now flying over the Antrim countryside, allegedly hedgehopping irregularly. Evidently, the crew did not fear any IRA attack. Observers on the ground near the flight path commented on how low it was flying and estimated it to be at about 100ft (30m). It made a great noise, causing the ground to vibrate and terrifying both people and animals. Horses at Glenravel belonging to dentist Hugh McCann panicked and had to be taken in.[21] The crew were probably deviating from a direct track to find a low-level route through the Antrim hills.

From her house in Carnlough on the Antrim coast, a little to the east of the direct track, Ann Tyler (38) had a view of the harbour to the north. Beyond that, she could normally see the Mull of Kintyre thirty-six kilometres away across the North Channel. On that day, the Mull could not be seen and visibility was one and a half to two and a half kilometres. Ann's house also had windows that face in the opposite direction, towards the south and south-west.

Between 17:45 and 17:50, she was upstairs with her daughter when they heard the noise of a helicopter. Looking south, she saw a twin-rotor helicopter coming towards them along the valley. It was flying so low that it was below trees on the far side of the valley. It made a lot of noise, and a sound with which she was not familiar. She thought that there was something wrong with it. As the helicopter flew over the house, Ann crossed the landing to watch it fly towards the sea. It seemed to be flying parallel to the ground, which fell towards the harbour. She assumed that it was participating in a military exercise, although such an aircraft was unusual; the helicopters she normally saw had only one rotor.

She later spoke to many local people who had also seen and heard the helicopter and she heard their accounts. They reported that its vibration shook ornaments about and that some fell off shelves. It skimmed chimney pots and the tall trees of an old people's home near the harbour and its downdraught blew clothing about. One person waved to the pilot and some children, looking down on the helicopter, waved to the passengers. Many thought that the sound was wrong and they all commented on how low it was; it was last seen flying out to sea 'skimming the waves'.

The Chinook followed the coast beyond Carnlough towards Garron Point, where priests at a conference at Garron Tower College on the cliff top ran out to see it fly just below them and turn out to sea.[22]

Instrument maker Mark Holbrook (37) was sailing his ketch *Serini* in the North Channel off the Kintyre coast that evening, heading for Campbeltown. His friend Ian McLeod accompanied him. From about 17:00 to 17:30 they spent some time opposite the Mull of Kintyre lighthouse changing sails. They could see the lighthouse's white perimeter wall, but above it low cloud obscured the hillside. After they set off again, away from the coast, they encountered a group of trawlers, apparently fishing. This caused them to manoeuvre to avoid their trawls. About 17:50, Ian went below to listen to the weather forecast[23] and, about five minutes later, Mark became aware of a helicopter approaching. As Ian returned to the deck, Mark remarked on this additional distraction. It was almost too much, that as he manoeuvred among six or so fishing vessels, a helicopter should fly past. They wondered if it was out on a search. They were about 2nm (3.7km) south-west of the lighthouse, evidently near the track of the Chinook.[24] Mark estimated that the aircraft was about ¼nm (400m) from his boat and flying at a height of between 200 to 400ft (61 to 122m). With visibility about 3–5nm (5.5–9.2km) he could clearly see the Mull and identify the lighthouse as a lighter patch, but low cloud still hung over the upper part of the Mull. When Mark later tried the VHF radio to tell Campbeltown coastguard that he was delayed, they told him not to use the (radio) channel for an hour. He eventually arrived in Campbeltown about 01:30 the next morning.

Kintyre (its name means 'land's end') is a large peninsula that stretches southwards from Tarbert in Argyll, past the Isle of Arran towards Ireland. It is connected to the Scottish mainland only by a narrow isthmus at Tarbert where, in 1093, a Viking king claimed the peninsula by dragging a boat across it.

Today its inhabitants are connected to the rest of Scotland only by one trunk route on the west side and a poor single-track road on the east side. Campbeltown, its major town near the southern end, is 214km by road from Glasgow and eighty-three kilometres from Lochgilphead, the next major town.

For the safety of shipping, there are three lighthouses around the end of the peninsula and one of these is located on the steep west side of the Mull facing out across the North Channel. This is the Mull of Kintyre lighthouse, in one of the most isolated spots on an isolated peninsula. Above the lighthouse, at The Gap, there is a car park and viewpoint, from where, on a clear day, one can see Rathlin Island or even the mainland of Northern Ireland.

Today the lighthouse is automatic, but in 1994 it was operated by two lighthouse keepers, who lived there with their wives, assisted by two men from Southend, a village some twelve kilo-

14

metres away to the east. The Principal Keeper was Hector Lamont (57) and his assistant was David Murchie (54). Considering how isolated the lighthouse is, it is surprising how many people there were in the area that evening — ten whose names are known and two whose names are not. They include the lighthouse keepers and their wives, Anthony Gresswell (42), Mary Green (42)[25], Alan Crabtree (54) and his wife Shirley (53), Russell Ellacott and Tony Bracher. All these witnesses gave statements to the police and some of them gave evidence at the FAI. They all reported on how, although it was fairly clear but misty down by the light-house, or below it, visibility became worse with height and that, at The Gap, there was drizzle and very thick fog. They were all surprised that a helicopter was flying in such bad weather and noted that it was very low. Except for Shirley Crabtree, who thought she saw a whirling rotor blade and a white light, none of them actually saw the Chinook. Although they had heard the sound of the helicopter stop, the Crabtrees, just below the impact area, did not realize that there had been a crash until they came across debris and fire higher up. They had not heard the sound of the crash. Eventually Hector gave them a lift to The Gap.

At 17:55, David Murchie was in the sitting room of his house adjoining the lighthouse waiting for Hector to return to relieve him at 18:00. Hector and Esther had gone to Campbeltown on a shopping expedition. The lighthouse and most of the Mull were shrouded in a thick fog, which drifted to and fro in a light wind. He told the FAI that visibility was only 20 yards (18.3m). Even the sea was invisible 250ft (76.2m) below. This fog is a common phenomenon in the area in summer as the water vapour in the warm air being blown in from the Irish Sea cools and condenses as it is forced to rise by the land around the Mull. The only sound was that of the station's fog signal, an 'air chime' located on cliffs just over one kilometre south of the lighthouse. Then he heard something else—the sound of an approaching helicopter.

David had been in the lighthouse service for eighteen years, four years at this lighthouse. Before that, he had been fourteen years in the City of Glasgow Police. However, he was no stranger to aircraft; he had flown small planes and had a special interest in helicopters. In fact, when a member of the Lothians Flying Club, he had built a gyrocopter. He had also built and flown many model helicopters. From the distinctive double beat of its twin rotors, he knew that what he could hear was a Chinook, the work-horse of the North Sea oil industry and the RAF's troop carrier.

Chinooks sometimes landed on the helipad beside the light-house and David wondered if this one intended to do so. However, he also wondered how it could do that safely in the fog. He got up and rushed around to the seaward side of the light tower. From there, he could hear the Chinook coming from the south-south-west. He was worried about two large steel pylons about 30m high close by the helipad. The pilots would be unable to see them in the fog and he feared an accident. If it was not going to land, then it should veer left and fly up the coast. But the aircraft did not change direction. He heard no change in the sound of its engines; nor did he hear the 'slap' of rotor blades that he usually heard when a Chinook prepared to land.

When the sound of the aircraft disappeared behind the engine house, David became very concerned. He could tell that the heli-copter did not have sufficient height to clear the high ground that lay behind the lighthouse. Therefore, he ran to the north-west corner of the house but, just as he got there, he heard a dull thud, followed by a whooshing noise—then silence. He knew what had happened: the Chinook had hit the hillside. His wife Margaret had gone outside by the drying green to see the helicopter, which she could hear flying very close by and low. However, because of the dense fog, she saw nothing until a large ball of flame followed by thick dark smoke rolled down the hillside towards them. David shouted to her to call the emergency services while he started climbing up the steep access road. He had only gone a few hundred metres when he saw the lighthouse Land Rover returning with Hector and Esther. He indicated to Hector to turn the vehicle around, explained to him what he thought had happened, and urged him to take him back up the road.

In this part of Kintyre, south of Campbeltown, the only major road is the B842 connecting Campbeltown to Southend. West of Southend, the roads deteriorate and, west of Carskiey, the light-house is accessible only by eleven kilometres of a narrow twisting single-track road with passing places. At The Gap car park, a panel erected by Argyll and Bute Council congratulates visitors on having negotiated 'one of Scotland's most exciting roads'. It is not just 'exciting'; in places it is frightening.

Hector and Esther were driving along that road in thick fog where Hector could only navigate by watching the side of the road. He could hardly see anything ahead and told the FAI that visibility was only about twenty yards. They had passed The Gap and were descending the steep zigzag road down to the lighthouse when Esther drew his attention to the noise of a helicopter overhead. Concerned, she asked him: *'Do you think that helicopter is going to crash?'* He replied confidently: *'No, it will be flying above the fog.'* Just then, a flash of light in his driving mirror caught Hector's attention, but he assumed that it was the helicopter's navigation light. Continuing down, they passed two tourists standing at the side of the road and arrived at the helipad, where Mary Green flagged them down and she and Tony Gresswell told them what had happened. David Murchie ran towards them and Hector turned the Land Rover around. David, Tony and Mary got in, Esther got out and Hector drove back up the road. Just where Hector and Esther heard the helicopter noise, they came across burning debris on the road and thick smoke. Visibility was now actually worse due to the smoke created by the extensive fires: apart from the wreckage, the heather was also burning. David, Mary and Tony got out to look for survivors, while Hector returned to the lighthouse to change his shoes and collect fire extinguishers and a mobile telephone. While there, he also called the fire brigade to tell them that the hill was on fire. Then he drove back up, this time accompanied by Margaret, who thought she might be able to help. Hector collected Mary and drove on up the hill, only stopping when debris blocked the road. All of them searched for survivors, but found none. David and Tony had climbed up into a scene from hell, but with no sign of life; the remains of twenty-nine people were lying among the wreckage of the Chinook. Mary realized that it had been a military helicopter when she found an identity tag. By then a police Land Rover had arrived, followed by other emergency service vehicles, fire engines and ambulances, all of which had to negotiate the winding, narrow track from Carskiey.

It was evident that Hector and Esther were very fortunate. If they had been a little later in arriving, they might have been hit by the helicopter. It had gone over their vehicle and crashed into the road behind them.

Russell Ellacott (33) from Sussex was on holiday in Scotland. He and his friend Tony Bracher were caravanning at Taynuilt and had driven in Russell's van from there that day to see what was so great about the Mull of Kintyre that Paul McCartney had written a song in its praise.[26] They parked at The Gap and saw a sign that told them that there was a deserted village further along the road and the site where a Second World War aircraft had crashed on the hillside. Consequently, they got their bicycles out of the van and cycled down to the lighthouse in search of those features. There they met David Murchie, who directed them to the sites of the deserted village and the aircraft. They had to go back uphill, pushing their bicycles, and take a track off the road. Eventually the track became too overgrown to cycle and they had to stop. Therefore, they took a short rest, left the cycles and started walking. Visibility was only 10–15ft (3–4.5m). They had only walked for a couple of minutes and were passing a ridge when they felt sudden pressure and heat. Although they never saw the aircraft, this and the sound of helicopter blades made them duck. Almost immediately, there was a thud, quickly followed by an explosion only about 100m away. A 'fireworks display' of flaming wreckage landed all round them and lay on the ridge. They were also enveloped in smoke and the smell of burning aviation fuel. In addition, a great many burning papers flew through the air and the heather and gorse were burning fiercely. The air itself was dried by the intense fires and the fog cleared up to about 20 ft (6 m).

Tony swore in shock and surprise and asked Russell what had happened. Russell thought that a helicopter had crashed and that they ought to return to the bicycles and see if there was anything that they could do. However the thick smoke prevented them getting back and so they climbed the hill to try to get above it. When the ground levelled out they came across a gruesome scene. Parts of bodies lay everywhere (they only saw one complete), one impaled on a piece of wreckage. They were identifiable by the orange survival suits they had been wearing. They came across what looked like the nose of the helicopter, intact but burning, with what looked like a body lying beside it. When they approached, there was a loud bang from the wreckage and Russell retreated in fear, stepping on human remains as he did so. At this, Russell panicked, and they ran up the hill until they came across the road, from where they could see how widespread the wreckage was. They then saw David and Hector walking up the road. It was some time before Russell's bicycle was sent back to him; the only damage was a burst, melted tyre and a little scorched paintwork. Tony never saw his hired bicycle again.

Evidently, Russell and Tony were also very lucky that day. A little slower and they would have been killed. The helicopter crashed into part of the roadway they had not long left.

Air traffic in Scotland and parts of the North of England is controlled from Atlantic House in Prestwick in Ayrshire. It now operates as the Scottish Oceanic and Area Control Centre, but in 1994 it was known as the Scottish Air Traffic Control Centre (ScATCC). This is a joint civil/military centre where there is a large operations room with mostly civilian controllers. A separate room accommodates the military (RAF) air traffic controllers, which in 1994 were known as ScATCC (Mil). The room also contains the Distress and Diversion Unit (DDU). The RAF provides a service for both military and civilian aircraft and has authority or executive control over any emergency. One of the DDU's duties is to monitor the international emergency VHF and UHF radio channels used by civil and military aircraft. In addition the military controllers monitor the Initial Contact Frequencies (ICF), used by aircrew should they require the services of ScATCC (Mil). All radar and radio communications are routinely recorded.

One of the DDU's Air Traffic Control Officers, Flight Lieutenant Hamish Miller (36), went off duty at 17:40, but was still in the building when he heard of the crash. He immediately returned to ScATCC (Mil) and impounded the relevant record-ings of the radar screens. Six radars are piped into Atlantic House. Those on the west coast of Scotland are located at Lowther Hill, forty-eight kilometres east of Prestwick and on the island of Tiree in the Inner Hebrides. Hamish made a check of the radar recordings for the period from 17:40 to 18:06 but found nothing except a slow-moving target, which travelled north in an area south-west of the Mull of Kintyre. It displayed no identification (transponder) and appeared in the half-hour after the crash. Evidently it was not the Chinook, or perhaps not even an aircraft. It is likely that the Chinook was invisible to radar because it was flying so low; it could have been concealed by high ground.

Hamish also impounded the recordings of all VHF radio communications leading up to the time of the crash. The VHF ICF allocated to Scottish Military is 134.3MHz, known to the controllers as 'Channel 10'. The tapes revealed that, just after 17:55, the following message was received on that channel: *'Scottish Military, good afternoon. This is Foxtrot four Juliet four zero.'* However, the tapes revealed no response to this greeting. Apparently, neither the controller on duty nor his two assistants sitting in the control position heard this transmission. This was the Chinook's last message; it crashed four minutes later.

Chapter Two

Inside RAF Aldergrove

RAF Aldergrove, twenty kilometres west of Belfast between Antrim and Crumlin, occupies a group of buildings mainly dating from the 1930s but with various improvements over the years. It opened in 1918, but did not become a fully operational RAF station until 1936. During the Second World War, it operated as an important Coastal Command Station and, in 1972, it was absorbed into Strike Command, latterly as part of No.1 Group. From 1981 to 2002, it hosted 72 Squadron, operating Wessex HC2s, but it still hosts 230 Squadron, which was permanently established there in May 1992. From 1969 until 1981, Support Helicopter operations were carried out by a detachment from RAF Odiham in Hampshire.

In 1963, an area north of the main runway became Belfast International Airport, with the RAF station confined to the south part of the site but with both sharing the same runway. RAF Aldergrove has been engaged as a military airhead and base for helicopter support operations since 1969, and this remains its principal function. It is the airhead for troops, equipment, Government officials and VIP visitors in and out of the Province, regularly handling Hercules, VC10, HS125 and Bae 146 aircraft.

Today, it is home to over 3,500 service personnel, MOD civil servants and their dependants. The station is the base for the Joint Helicopter Force (Northern Ireland) – JHF(NI), a mixed force of helicopters operating in support of the British Army. This consists of: 5 Regiment Army Air Corps, in which 655 Squadron operates Lynx helicopters and 665 Squadron operates Gazelles (there is also an Islander for photo reconnaissance and fixed-wing pilot training); 230 Squadron operating thirteen Puma HC 1s and an

Operations Squadron. There are also regular detachments from other Puma and Chinook squadrons. The Field Squadron is 3 Squadron of the RAF Regiment.

In 1994, there were two Chinook helicopters on the base, on detachment (roulement) from their home base at RAF Odiham, which were attached to 230 Squadron. The Chinooks were maintained and serviced by sixteen RAF engineers and technicians from Odiham under the supervision of the Senior Engineering Officer, Squadron Leader Michael Lee. Two crews of four were allocated to the Chinooks. One crew included the pilots Flight Lieutenants Tapper and Cook, who died with their loadmaster colleagues in the crash. Tapper was the senior pilot on the detachment. The other crew included Flight Lieutenant Ian Kingston (36)[27] and Flight Lieutenant Duncan Trapp (26)[28]. Trapp was a navigator, not a pilot (all the pilots were also qualified navigators). Both Kingston and Trapp gave evidence to the various inquiries.

Tapper's crew were members of the Special Forces, i.e. aircrew selected to operate aircraft in support of various Special Forces units.[29] They have to be a minimum of above average standard as compared with the rest of the helicopter pilots and be 'stable extroverts'. They undertake a long and extensive period of specialist training, during which the crew fly together on a regular basis and develop high levels of cooperation and integration with each other and a bond of trust. Tapper was basic mission qualified, while Cook was fully mission qualified. The other aircrew in a Special Forces duty (loadmasters) are expected to have a higher degree of navigational ability than standard loadmasters and to assist with navigation. The No. 2 crewman, who sits nearest to the pilots, monitors cockpit activity, including navigation, and ensures that the pilots do what they are supposed to do.

Tapper gained a private pilot's licence before he was old enough to drive. At Dulwich College, when he was sixteen and a member of the RAF section of the CCF, he won a flying scholarship, so securing a private pilot's licence at the age of only sixteen. He joined Cranwell in 1984 and won his wings in 1986. It was at Cranwell that he meet Cook and the two became friends. By the early 1990s, Tapper had accumulated more than 2,000 hours as a first pilot of helicopters, including two years seconded to the

Omani Air Force. By the time he was selected for Special Service flights, he had already flown Gazelle, Wessex, Huey and Chinook helicopters. He married in October 1989 and his first child was born in August 1993; his second was born six weeks after the crash. He arrived at Aldergrove, for his second attachment, on 22 April 1994 and was appointed senior Chinook pilot.

Cook joined the RAF in 1983, starting with training at Cranwell, and gained his wings in 1985. He served in Germany and on detachment to various parts of the world from RAF Odiham; by the time of the accident, he had nearly 3,000 hours' flying experience, 2,500 in Chinooks. He was promoted to Operations Officer Special Forces during the first Gulf War and was due to be posted to the staff of the SAS in September 1994. He married about the same time as Tapper and had a daughter. He arrived at Aldergrove, for his third attachment, on 26 May 1994. On his previous attachments, he had been the senior Chinook pilot and he was due to be reappointed to this position when Tapper returned to RAF Odiham.

Squadron Leader Stangroom, who supervised the Chinook crews at RAF Aldergrove, assessed Tapper as a well qualified, experienced, safe, sensible operator, not given to flights of unnecessary enjoyment. He was a serious pilot, who took things sensibly and safely. He described Cook the same way. He thought they were both very competent professional officers, who undertook their duties quite seriously. Kingston described both Tapper and Cook as very professional pilots, who were safety conscious. He described Tapper as an extremely capable, conscientious pilot, very honest, friendly and a very likeable person. Cook was described in a similar fashion. He was quite sure that neither would take unnecessary risks.

Planning the sortie to Scotland

On his return from flying duties about 18:30 on Wednesday, 1 June 1994, Flight Lieutenant Kingston was in the Operations Room at RAF Aldergrove with Flight Lieutenant Trapp when he received a telephone call from Helitask 8 on behalf of the Joint Air Tasking Operations Centre (JATOC). They asked if an extra

23

sortie to Inverness (Fort George) and back could be fitted into the schedule for the following day, brief details of which were explained to him. Because Tapper and Cook would be on duty the following day, he did not know what other duties they had to perform. However, JATOC told him what they were (troop movements in the morning). Apparently, he found no problem and informed JATOC that it was possible. If it was not possible for Tapper and Cook, it was certainly possible for Kingston and Trapp: although it was the latter's rest day, they could easily swap it for a sortie. Consequently, they collected more details of the sortie; they were told that there were twenty-six passengers but not that they were VIPs. They retired to the Planning Room and consulted maps; in particular, they consulted a 1/500,000-scale aeronautical chart covering Ireland and Scotland. They plotted a suitable route[30] and considered the relevant weather forecast. From the latter, they concluded that the flight would need to be under VFR. At the time, the Chinook Mk2 had a temporary icing clearance limitation on account of concern about the reliability of the engine control system; it was forbidden to fly in cloud, fog or rain when the outside temperature was below 4 degrees C.[31] Because air temperature decreases with height, there was a danger of these conditions being met if the Chinook flew too high in cloud, as it would need to do if the pilots lost sight of the ground. Then the aircraft would be in danger of ice accretion on the rotor blades and airframe; this can affect stability, controllability and ability to maintain height. On behalf of the Chinook crews, Tapper had earlier consulted Squadron Leader Millburn at Odiham about whether or not they could do an emergency flare[32] in cloud as required by RAF regulations if that took the aircraft into conditions below 4 degrees C. This was because the Chinook crews might need to climb rapidly if they came under fire in Northern Ireland. However, Tapper was also concerned with problems of individual liability in the event of accidents. At the time, he was subject to a unit inquiry following an incident (3 May 1994 at Moscow Camp in Belfast) in which a passenger waiting to embark was struck by a piece of netting picked up by the downwash from his Chinook. Changes in the nature of Crown immunity raised the question of whether or not the captain of a military aircraft could be held

24

responsible independently of the MOD. He was concerned to ensure exactly what his legal position was operating this aircraft in Northern Ireland and in more restricted conditions of the icing limitation. Millburn told him that, if they ignored the limitation, they would be reprimanded and be held personally liable for any lawsuit that followed. Tapper was also told that the same would apply if they exceeded the temporary weight limit (restricted for the same reason as temperature limit). Kingston and Trapp calculated that the temperature limitation would be exceeded if the aircraft had to climb to a safe altitude in cloud on part of the route to Inverness (under IFR[33]). They also took into consideration the weight limitation; an IFR diversion would take longer and so require more fuel. The route to Inverness was plotted as a series of three straight legs, the first of which was from Aldergrove to the Mull of Kintyre lighthouse and the latter was designated as 'waypoint A'.[34] Trapp told the FAI that this was chosen as an obvious feature, near which the aircraft could turn to follow the coast northwards. The next waypoint at Corran was designated 'B'. They also calculated that the distance to Inverness Airport (Dalcross) was 196nm (363km), and to RAF Kinloss 212.5nm (393.5km). One or the other would be needed for refuelling.

While Kingston and Trapp were discussing the sortie, Tapper entered the Planning Room and was informed about the mission. All three then discussed it, particularly how the sortie would affect the daily flight limit. Kingston and Trapp pointed out to Tapper that, with the other routine sorties he and Cook had to undertake the following day, the sortie would take them over the seven-hour limit and that he would need to ask the Duty Flight Commander for an extension to eight hours at least.[35] To avoid this problem, and because they had no duties the following day, they offered to fly the sortie. However, Tapper declared that he would get authorization for the extra hour. He accepted that, because of the icing limitation, the sortie would need to be under VFR. The surface temperature was forecast to be 10–12 degrees C; assuming a normal 2 degree C drop every 1,000ft (304.5m), the 4 degree C level would be reached between 3,000 and 4,000ft (914–1,219m). However, while the safety altitude[36] for the first leg was calculated as 2,800ft (853m)[37], the safety altitude for the third leg was 6,500ft (1,991m)[38], too high for the Mk2 Chinook. In addition, because of the fuel limitation, there would not be enough fuel to divert if the aircraft flew IFR. The chosen route was agreed as the most practical with the amount of fuel available. With two hours' more fuel, there were several route options possible to avoid the low cloud over the west coast, one of which was to go via Prestwick, across the Central Belt to the east coast, perhaps to Leuchars, and around that coast to Inverness. However, that would have taken much longer. Even so, with the chosen route, if the aircraft had to slow down because of bad visibility, there was a possibility that it would not have enough fuel to reach Inverness, or even Leuchars for refuelling. Flying by VFR on the chosen route appeared to be the only option, but it was not without difficulties.

Tapper later continued with the planning and determined that the distance to waypoint A was 42nm (77.8km) and that at an average speed of 120kt (221kph) this would take twenty-one minutes. Chinooks normally cruise at between 125 and 140kt (230/258kph); selecting 120kt allows for a 20kt (10.2m/s) headwind slowing the aircraft from 140kt.[39] He calculated the total journey time to Inverness as one hour thirty-eight minutes. Tapper also determined the coordinates of the various waypoints and the magnetic track to each waypoint; he would need these data for the on-board navigation equipment.

Some time later, Tapper approached Flight Sergeant Peter Polidano informing him that he would be carrying between twenty-five and twenty-nine passengers to Inverness the following day and that he would be the captain. Tapper expressed concern about the total weight of the passengers and their luggage and asked Polidano if it was possible to weigh each passenger and their luggage. Although the Chinook Mk1 was permitted to reach a total all-up weight (mass) of 22,700kg, the temporary weight limit on the Mk2 was 18,000kg. This meant that, with a full load of troops, the aircraft could not carry a full load of fuel (3,000kg) and was limited in range for military operations in Northern Ireland. For the journey to Inverness, Tapper needed to take on as much fuel as possible. Polidano explained that they would not normally weigh passengers and that they usually assumed 180lb (81.6kg) for male passengers or 190lb (86.2kg) if they were carrying weapons and 40lb (18.2kg) for each passenger's luggage. They only weighed passengers if they were all children or Gurkhas. Tapper accepted Polidano's estimates. Kingston told the FAI that he and Trapp had calculated that, with twenty-six passengers and their luggage, 2,400kg of fuel would give a flying time of one hour fifty-five minutes, sufficient to get to Dalcross to refuel. Although 1,000kg was usually needed in case of diversion, less than that would be available. In a Mk1 Chinook, an extra fuel tank could be fitted, but the lower weight limit for the Mk2 prohibited this. In the event, the aircraft departed for Scotland with a full load of fuel (3,080kg) and it is not clear why Tapper was concerned.[40]

After dinner, about 20:00, Trapp called into Tapper's room in the Officers' Mess for a chat and found him continuing with the flight planning. He was transferring the route and its details from the 1/500,000-scale map to a 1/250,000-scale map. The latter was taken on the flight and lost.

At the time, the Duty Flight Commander at Aldergrove was Squadron Leader Michael Stangroom (39). He commanded B flight of 230 Squadron, but he also supervised the operations of the Chinook helicopters. On the following day, Thursday 2 June, his shift started at 08:00. At about 09:00, he was approached by Tapper asking for authorization to extend his flying time that day from the normal seven hours to eight hours. Tapper considered that this would enable him to complete his sorties that day, including the sortie to Scotland. However, the tasking sheet, which Stangroom did not see at that time, but which Tapper must have seen, showed that six and a half hours had been allocated to various troop movements and four hours to the Inverness sortie, of which three were flying hours (a total of one and a half hours over the eight-hour limit). Nevertheless, they discussed the option of asking for an extension beyond eight hours, to say ten hours, although this would require the authorization of the Senior RAF Officer Northern Ireland (SRAFONI), Group Captain Rodger Wedge.[41] Stangroom was reluctant to ask SRAFONI and, in any case, because the sortie to Inverness had no operational imperative, he could see no justification for such an extension. They agreed that this was unnecessary.

At the FAI, Stangroom was asked about the flying hours limit. His attention was drawn to the fact that the Flight Authorization Sheet showed that routine sorties earlier in the day had consumed five hours forty minutes[42] and that four hours were still allocated for the flight to and from Inverness, of which three hours were in transit.[43] Since this totalled more than eight hours, he was asked for an explanation, but he could give none. He was then asked if he and Tapper had discussed the possibility of the crew staying overnight in Inverness. Apparently this was discussed, with Stangroom instructing Tapper that, if he had to divert or arrived over the eight-hour limit, he was to telephone and remain in Inverness pending a decision from SRAFONI, who could authorize his return, extending his limit to ten hours that day. Alternatively, SRAFONI could authorize the crew's overnight stay in Inverness. Stangroom had to admit that SRAFONI would not have liked to be put in the position of choosing between two unpalatable options, one of which left him with no operational Chinook in Northern Ireland (the only other Chinook, a Mk1, was out of commission). Stangroom himself would have felt let down by Tapper.[44] Had Tapper blatantly disregarded the rules and flown back without informing Stangroom, he would have faced disciplinary action. Even calling from Inverness to say that he had run out of time might have incurred a reprimand. It seems that Stangroom only agreed to Tapper's plan on the understanding (from Tapper) that the earlier taskings would take less than the time allocated and that he could therefore complete the Inverness sortie without exceeding the eight-hour limit. Stangroom had sensibly suggested that Kingston and Trapp could undertake the Scottish sortie; this would have overcome the time-limit problem. However, Tapper was eager to do it and persuaded Stangroom otherwise. Stangroom later stated that, if he had known that the total time would still exceed eight hours, he would have withdrawn his authorization and insisted on a change of crew. He could not explain Tapper's action and stated that it was contrary to his understanding of his behaviour and conduct.

Stangroom and Tapper also discussed the weather and what to do if it deteriorated. Having consulted the airport's meteorological office (he did not have the forecast with him at the time), Tapper understood that, although there was some low stratus around Northern Ireland and out across the Mull of Kintyre, it would be clear further north. It was concluded therefore, that the Scottish sortie was 'perfectly flyable'. There was also a discussion about what to do if the aircraft inadvertently entered cloud and was unable to maintain VFR. It was agreed that, if they could not regain VFR quickly, they should divert or return to Aldergrove. Diversion would have been to a principal airport (Prestwick, Glasgow or Inverness). They appear to have agreed that, if it was a small patch of scattered cloud, they may well come straight back out of it. However, if it was more solid, then they should take action to climb to safety altitude and either return to Aldergrove or gain contact with an Air Traffic Control Unit that could give them radar services.

At the FAI, it was revealed that Tapper had chosen to fly to Scotland at low level[45] to let his crew gain experience of flying low over unfamiliar territory and also to give the passengers an interesting view; they planned to fly low up the Great Glen which included Loch Ness. Low-level flying in the UK is restricted to certain times to minimize inconvenience to the public. During the outward leg, the local Low Flying Area (LFA) was open. According to Stangroom, because it would be closed, or closing, during the return leg, the return would have to be at medium level (above 150m in daylight or above 600m in the dark).[46] It emerged that, because of the cost of training crews, especially in low-level flying, the RAF maximises the use of aircraft in all circumstances to increase crew experience. This also helps to reduce costs. However, at the FAI it was suggested to Stangroom that taking twenty-five important passengers on a low-level training flight was risky and extraordinary. Stangroom disagreed, but it is evident in retrospect, that if the flight had been at a higher level, the accident might not have occurred. Only in the FAI did it emerge that an MOD CA[47] Release for the Mk2 stated that prolonged cruising flight should not take place at heights below 300ft (91.4m) unless it were operationally essential to do so. This was to provide pilots with enough height to recover from a failure of the Automatic Flight Control System, including the Differential Air Speed Hold (DASH), a mechanism which reverses the abnormally-reversed pitch control over 40kt (74kph); without it the control would operate in the opposite manner to

29

other types of helicopter—a dangerous situation which might have caused at least one Chinook accident.[48] Consequently, Tapper should not have considered a long flight at low level, especially with valuable passengers; there was no operational necessity for the low flying, although Kingston later claimed that there was.

Flying begins

Flight Sergeant John Coles (25), attached to 230 Squadron as an air loadmaster, began his shift at 08:00. After a briefing at 08:45, he and Senior Aircraftsman Turnock were given a lift in ZD576 by Tapper and Cook to another base at Ballykinler. On their way to the aircraft, they dropped Tapper off at the Line Office, where he deposited the aircraft's logbook (Form 700[49]) with engineering staff and signed for the aircraft. This particular Chinook had only arrived in Northern Ireland two days earlier, as had Cook, and it was the only Mk2 in the Province. Coles noticed that the pre-flight checks[50] took longer than usual and concluded that this was because the pilots were somewhat unfamiliar with the aircraft. Although they had both undertaken a fortnight's conversion course (from Mk1 to Mk2), it had been two months earlier. Cook had been flying Mk2s in England during May. They first flew this aircraft on a supervised test-run on the day it arrived at Aldergrove. Nevertheless, Coles told the FAI that Tapper and Cook enjoyed flying the aircraft and that because it flew so smoothly they were 'quite happy with the way it was operating'. The aircraft departed Aldergrove for Ballykinler at 09:45.

While Coles and his colleague were at Ballykinler, the aircraft was engaged elsewhere in troop movements (five return trips in fact); it returned to collect them an hour or two later. It had been delayed because the crew had called in to Aldergrove because of a problem with a gauge reading the power turbine inlet temperature (PTIT) of one of the jet engines. After Kingston and Trapp had noticed this problem the previous day, the gauges for the two engines had been swapped around. This showed that the fault was with the gauge, not with the engines. Evidently, it was still faulty. The Chinook eventually arrived back at Aldergrove at

15:25, when Coles and his colleague returned to their normal duties. Later in the afternoon, Coles was involved with the Chinook again, helping Flight Sergeant Holmes and others brief the passengers travelling to Scotland and ensuring that the aircraft had survival gear for ditching in the sea and rations for the passengers. Coles understood that the aircraft would be returning to Aldergrove that evening. ZD576 was the only serviceable Chinook and would be required for taskings in the Province the following day. There was also a requirement to return one passenger to Aldergrove from Inverness.

Corporal David Guest (27) was working that day at Aldergrove as an engineering (avionics) technician. About 15:00, he was told about an alleged problem with the global positioning system (GPS, discussed later) on Chinook ZD576. When the aircraft landed, he and Senior Aircraftsman Steven Clark (21) went over to talk to Tapper. The captain explained that the GPS was seeing five satellites and tracking seven (it could track up to eight satellites, depending how many were in line of sight at any particular time, but needed three for determining position, four for three dimensions). However, what Tapper claimed is logically impossible (Clark thought that he had misread the display and reversed the figures); a satellite needs to be seen before it can be tracked. Nevertheless, Guest examined the aerial on top of the aircraft in case it was cracked or dirty, but found no problem. He then entered the flight deck to check the connections on the GPS box and again found nothing wrong. He and his colleague then started the GPS from an auxiliary power unit brought over by Flight Sergeant (Chief Technician) Christopher Valente (40), who also joined them in the investigation. They all found the GPS working normally; it was seeing eight satellites and tracking seven. Clark later reported this to Tapper, who said *'Fine; that's OK'*. According to RAF regulations, Tapper should have formally recorded the alleged fault; instead, he told the technicians that he did not want to do that, but would do so if they found a fault.

The turnaround service for ZD576 started at 15:40. A Chinook must be serviced after eight hours' flying or as soon after that when it lands. Consequently, this service would have run out of validity at 23:40. If the aircraft was on the ground at Dalcross or Kinloss at that time, it would need to be serviced there, for which purpose the service engineers would need the log book (Form 700). Because Tapper did not take this book with him, he must have planned to return to Aldergrove that day, even though that would have meant breaking the eight-hours' limit.

When ZD576 was ready to leave (at about 17:00), the Duty Authorizing Officer was Flight Lieutenant Geoffrey Young.[51] However, he was busy with another briefing. Consequently, Tapper himself signed the Flight Authorization Sheet and deposited copies of it and a copy of his flight plan with the operations clerk at the 230 Squadron desk. Tapper was a senior captain with 'self-authorizing responsibility', giving him the choice of crew composition and flight level; he did not have to obtain flight authorization from duty officers, although it was usual to formally outbrief[52] them. Tapper and his crew were then driven to the aircraft. After a normal start-up with no problems, they re-positioned the aircraft to Air Movements Dispersal (DA4), where the passengers boarded and their baggage was secured along the centre of the aircraft's cabin floor. At 17:42, the helicopter, with the call sign 'F4J40', took off for the last time and departed for Scotland.

Chapter Three

The Accident Investigation

The UK Air Accidents Investigation Branch (AAIB) is responsible for the investigation of civil aircraft accidents and serious incidents within the UK. It has its origins in the Accidents Investigation Branch (AIB) of the Royal Flying Corps, which was established in 1915. After being attached to various ministries, the Branch came under the supervision of the Department of Transport (DoT) in 1983 and acquired its present title in 1987. In 1994 it was still part of the DoT, but today it is part of the Department *for* Transport (Df T).

The inspector sent to investigate this accident was Anthony Cable (50). He is a Senior Inspector of Air Accidents Engineering with a BSc (Hons) degree in aeronautical engineering from London University. He had begun his career with the Boeing Aircraft Corporation, the very company who had manufactured the Chinook. Later, he worked for British Aerospace in Weybridge before transferring to the AAIB in 1976. Cable had investigated air accidents all over the world, some forty or so major ones and some 200 less serious ones. About one third of the accidents had been to helicopters. He held a private pilot's licence for both fixed-wing aircraft and helicopters and was qualified to fly a Bell 206, a 5-seater helicopter. Evidently, he was well qualified to investigate this accident. However, he made it clear to the FAI that he was not an expert on anything; he described himself as *'a total generalist'*. An aircraft is such a complex machine with so many specialized components, that an accident investigator could not possibly be an expert on any of them. He had to rely on expert advice on each system or component and draw general conclusions.

The AAIB does not have a statutory duty to investigate military air accidents, but they are usually consulted and asked to assist, as they were in this case.

At the request of the RAF Inspectorate of Flight Safety[53], Cable travelled to the site of the crash the day after the accident and remained there until the site was cleared on 14 June. He was assisted by Sergeant Technicians Tighe and Carter from RAF Odiham. About 8 June, two investigators from Boeing arrived on the site to conduct their own investigation. Parts of the primary navigation unit were removed directly to the manufacturer (Racal Avionics Ltd[54]) for data extraction and analysis.[55] This was supervised by Cable's colleague Rex Parkinson, who made a separate report on it to the Board. The remainder of the wreckage was removed, first to RAF Machrihanish and then onwards to the Defence Research Agency at Farnborough, where it was laid out for detailed examination; it was analysed there between June and December 1994. Extensive assistance with the investigation was provided by the manufacturers of various components, especially by Boeing Helicopters, and by engineering staff from RAF Odiham. The engines were strip-examined by the manufacturer (Textron Lycoming) at their plant in Connecticut, USA.

The site evidence

From his site investigation, Cable was able to determine that, after striking a rocky outcrop, the aircraft had travelled a considerable distance clear of the ground and climbing, while continuing to break up. Eventually it landing inverted and broke into two major pieces. He conducted a detailed and lengthy examination of the crash site in an attempt to establish both the initial impact parameters and in order to assist in assessment of the behaviour of various systems and the break-up sequence. The initial impact point was approximately 42nm from Aldergrove on a bearing of 20 degrees true (27 degrees magnetic). It was at a height of 810ft (247m) above sea level and 515m east of the lighthouse. Parts of the wreckage reached a height of 900ft (274m), near the peak of Beinn na Lice ('Mountain of the Ledge';

1,404ft/428m), one of the highest mountains in this area of South Kintyre. Cable was told by the Board that the aircraft's 'all-up weight' at the time of the accident was 17,100kg. They also told him that the wind at the impact point was 30kt (15.4m/s) from 170 degrees true.

From the ambient pressure of 998mb and the surface temperature of 9 degrees C, he was able to calculate that the density altitude at 247m geopotential[56] was 123m. He also found that the sea-level dewpoint temperature was also 9 degrees C (i.e. the air was saturated). Examining marks made by the aircraft as it crashed, especially those made by the landing gear, Cable was able to deduce something about its attitude at the time; he concluded that it had less than 10 degrees yaw[57], banked[58] 5–10 degrees left and pitched 30 degrees up at the front. He could also determine that the aircraft had been travelling at well over 100kt (184kph) ground speed and climbing at about 20 degrees to the horizontal. Cable concluded that it had been travelling on a track of 025 degrees magnetic or 012 degrees true.[59] Much of the wreckage had been damaged by fire, some of it completely destroyed. Little was left of the sponson structure and nothing of the fuel cells. However, there was no evidence of explosive damage or that any damage had occurred prior to impact.

Instruments

Despite considerable disruption to the flight deck, the instruments were mostly intact except for the maintenance panel. These were strip-examined and, where the condition allowed and facilities were available, they were functionally tested at an instrument-servicing bay at RAF Odiham. Because of the impact, the readings on the instruments could not be relied on (to varying degrees). Attitude indicators all provided indications of left roll and substantial nose-up pitch (consistent with the conclusion from the site inspection). The heading cards both showed a heading of 045-046 degrees (magnetic) and the course (track) selectors showed 028 degrees (left) and 035 degrees (right). A fault was detected in the radar altimeter, making it unreliable, but it was not thought that this had any bearing on the accident.

Transmission instruments indicated normal operations, including normal engine operations. The Ground Speed and Drift Indicator (GSDI)[60] was jammed at 147kt (270kph), a speed corroborated by the attitude of one of the longitudinal cyclic trim indicators (it was fully extended as for a speed of 150–160kt (276–294kph). Both vertical speed indicators were relatively undamaged: one showed a climb-rate of 4,000fpm (20m/s); the other showed 3,500fpm (18m/s). Each pilot had a separate radar altimeter, which he could set to warn of ground proximity directly below the aircraft. Cable found that the left altimeter was set to warn at 850ft (259m) and that the right one was set at 69ft (21m). Both of these had visible and audible warnings and the latter could sound to either or both pilots, but it could not be determined whether or not these were switched on. There was an indication that the left system might have been off at the time of impact, but Cable could not rule out the possibility that this may have been due to power loss before final impact. No conclusion could be drawn about the right system. The Aerial Direction Finding Control Unit, usually used for locating radio beacons, was set to 252kHz, the frequency for Atlantic 252, a commercial radio station.

Background noise

It is sometimes possible to detect deterioration of mechanical systems in the background to radio transmissions by examining the frequency spectrum of the background noise. In the case of Chinook BV234 G-BWFC that crashed in the North Sea on 6 November 1986 with forty-five fatalities (Air Accident Report 2/88), Cockpit Voice Recorder (CVR) analysis had, within forty-eight hours of impact, pinpointed the component whose failure caused the loss of the aircraft. It had also produced data on the progression of the failure. Consequently, Mr P.F. Sheppard, Assistant Principal Inspector of Air Accidents of the AAIB Recorder Section, examined recordings of radio transmissions from the Chinook using a Hewlett-Packard signal analyser. This did not indicate any mechanical malfunction.

Engines and FADEC

Examination of the two jet engines showed that both were running at high speed with turbines hot at the time of impact. There were no signs of pre-impact failure or malfunction that could have affected the operation of either engine. As a Mk2, the aircraft was fitted with a digital engine control system (Full Authority Digital Engine Control, FADEC for short). This consisted of a Digital Electronic Control Unit (DECU) for each engine connected to a Hydro Mechanical Assembly (HMA) mounted on each engine and interconnected to the other DECU. The purpose was to ensure that the engines operated at maximum efficiency at all times and provided all the power necessary, sharing it between each engine. The interconnection meant that each DECU could, if necessary, control both engines and had a record of the performance of both engines. Each DECU had a non-volatile memory, i.e. a memory that remains intact even when power is cut off.

Although one DECU was destroyed, the other remained partially functional, with deficiencies that were consistent with the effects of impact damage. Its memory showed that the operating programme and constants had not altered since delivery, that no excessive parameters or faults had been detected over its life, which included duty on another Chinook for the previous seventeen days, and that no faults had been detected on the last flight. This indicated that the engines had operated relatively normally and with uninterrupted power supplies until the crash. Examination of the HMAs indicated matched power demands for both engines and that they were operating at less than maximum power (70 per cent torque[61]) at the time of the crash. Cable concluded that either this indicated a last-minute dynamic manoeuvre that relieved the load on the engines, or it resulted from the engines continuing to operate, but without load, after the initial impact. It could not be determined whether or not emergency power had been called for.

Flight controls

Although the possibility of a control system jam could not be eliminated absolutely, examination of the flight controls showed no evidence of pre-impact failure or malfunction. Cable noted that, during a recent service, a bracket had been found detached from the thrust/yaw control pallet (it had been re-attached). After the crash, it was again found to be detached, but so had most of the similar inserts. Cable could not eliminate the possibility of pre-impact detachment of any of the pallet components. Nevertheless, detachment in the crash was to be expected. Detachment would have caused a change in the feel of the control channel and possibly a loss of some automatic functions in the channel. There might have been a jam or a control restriction resulting in an inability to achieve full travel in one or more of the control channels. However, Cable thought such a detachment inconsistent with the evidence provided by the disposition of the wreckage and the way the aircraft had crashed. He noted that the earwitnesses reported no change in the sound of the aircraft and that the navigation equipment recorded no flight control problems.

Indications were found of controls positioned at approximately 25 degrees aft stick (pitch), 23 per cent left stick (roll), 77 per cent left yaw and full collective thrust. Cable could not say whether these were the pilot's chosen positions or whether they resulted from the crash.

All hydraulic and electro-mechanical actuators were identified and found to remain functional, except for the aft swivelling Upper Boost Actuator, the No. 2 DASH Actuator and the aft Longitudinal Cyclic Trim Actuator. These were strip- examined, but no evidence of pre-impact anomaly was found. At the point of power and/or signal loss, the DASH had been 23 per cent extended, and both Longitudinal Cyclic Trim Actuators had been virtually fully extended. This was consistent with a sharp pull-up manoeuvre at high speed at the time of impact.

Meaningful information could not be obtained from the No. 2 Automatic Flight Control System computer because of fire damage. The No. 1 computer passed Built-in Test Equipment checks. DASH and Longitudinal Cyclic Trim Actuator settings indicated normal Automatic Flight Control System operation (the AFCS provided long-term airspeed stabilization and helped maintain equilibrium in flight).

Strip examination of the Lower Control Actuator systems showed no anomalies except for considerable wear on the boost actuator piston rods of both systems of the pitch ILCA, a large quantity of very small metallic particles in residual fluid in parts of the boost actuator for both pitch and thrust and four fine metal slivers up to 5mm long on one of the servo screens of the yaw ILCA boost actuator. There were no indications that these particles and slivers had contributed to the accident.

The Boeing simulation

The settings of the flight controls indicated that a dynamic manoeuvre was in progress at the time of the crash. To assess the consistency of the settings and to define the possible manoeuvre, Boeing attempted to reproduce the manoeuvre necessary to produce the initial impact conditions derived from Cable's investigation. The response of the aircraft to a series of postulated control inputs was predicted by mathematical modelling simulating the Chinook's behaviour from a range of initial steady flight conditions. For each case, a predicted time history of flight path, airspeed, attitude and DASH and LCTA extension conditions resulting from combinations of large collective thrust and aft cyclic stick control input was produced and assessed for a simultaneous match of the parameters with the initial impact conditions. In some cases, control inputs were modulated during the manoeuvre. This showed that close simultaneous matching of the predicted conditions with the criteria was possible in only a few cases, and was very difficult or impossible in all cases with an initial airspeed of 135kt (248kph) and below, and/or an initial climb rate of 500fpm (2.54m/s) and below. However, a close match was found where initial conditions combined an airspeed of 150kt, a climb rate of 1,000fpm (5m/s) and large collective and aft cyclic control inputs. The best correlation was one where the manoeuvre was commenced 2.9 seconds before impact. The parameters assumed in the modelling included an aircraft weight (mass) of 37,700lb (17,100kg), density altitude of 420ft (128m) and a 24kt (12.2m/s) tailwind component.[62] At impact in the simulation, the aircraft was pitched nose-up 31 degrees, rolled (banked) 5 degrees left and with 1 degree left yaw. Its flight path was rising 20 degrees, it was climbing at 4,670fpm (23m/s) and it had slowed to an airspeed of 135kt. All this indicated that, just about three seconds before impact, the handling pilot pulled the nose of the helicopter up, attempted to turn to port and increased the climb rate. Cable accepted that this conclusion was close to what he predicted from the analysis of the wreckage. The Boeing simulation also confirmed that, some minutes prior to the accident and the dynamic manoeuvre, the helicopter had been in a moderate climb. This was already clear from the fact that it crashed at about twice the height it had maintained earlier in the flight.

Navigation

The Chinook's navigation system was provided by an RNS 252 SuperTANS[63] navigation computer manufactured by Racal Avionics Ltd. It was recovered from the wreckage of the flight deck, slightly scorched but with little apparent impact damage. It was found switched off, but subsequent examination showed that it had been operating up until impact. Racal produced a detailed report on what their examination showed, but this report has not been published. Cable himself only saw the report a few days before giving evidence to the FAI, and only parts of the report were read out there.

The SuperTANS is an area navigation system which provides navigation information from two independent sources, one based on a Trimble global positioning system (GPS) using satellites, and the other maintained by a Doppler velocity sensor used with the aircraft compass heading. Its memory was battery-backed and the content of the memory was extracted for analysis.[64]

Analysis revealed that the SuperTANS, and the navigation sensors with which it interfaces, had performed perfectly at the time of loss of power. The accuracy of the Doppler position also indicated that all had worked equally well throughout the flight.

The pilots had performed the correct initialization procedures, and had made use of the navigation facilities. Power had been lost at 16:59 UT at a position recorded by the GPS as 55° 18.61' north and 5° 47.80' west. The Doppler system recorded a slightly different position, 330 metres to the east. There was no alert at the time power was lost. A pressure setting (QNH) of 998 millibars had been entered. This parameter was used to calculate altitude above Mean Sea Level by the SuperTANS. The altitude was recorded as 665ft (202m) plus or minus 50ft (15m) at power-down. The altitude had been 468ft (142m), plus or minus 50ft, approximately fifteen to eighteen seconds earlier. There was no rate of climb information within the SuperTANS but these data can be used to deduce a rate of climb of between 660 and 780fpm (3.3–4m/s), much lower than the rate assumed in the Boeing simulation. The memory showed that the crew had used the system to select a new waypoint (B at Corran) 0.95nm (1.7km) before the initial impact point. Consequently, the SuperTANS had commanded a steer left to turn 10–15 degrees towards the new waypoint on a track of 025 degrees M.[65] However, the SuperTANS showed that the rate of change of heading was very close to zero, turning slightly right. At power-down, the SuperTANS recorded a pitch-up angle of 17.3 degrees (close to the flight angle). It also showed a roll (bank) left of 10.1 degrees, but this was interpreted as a 'synthetic roll' calculated from the change of heading required to turn towards waypoint B. It was concluded that, due to transport delays within the system, the SuperTANS records came from a time about 0.5–1 second before power-down.

The SuperTANS recorded the last 'switch-on' time as just after 16:06 UT. It also recorded various data about the aircraft's heading, track and speed, but there is doubt that these are correct. It recorded a magnetic compass heading (the direction in which the pilot needs to point the aircraft in order to maintain his track) as 42.2 degrees, which, allowing for a magnetic deviation[66] of 7.8 degrees west, corresponded to a true heading of 34.4 degrees. It also recorded a track of between 23 degrees and 27 degrees true. The airspeed was recorded as 127.6kt (234.7kph), 94 per cent of that assumed in the Boeing simulation. The GPS system recorded a ground speed of 150kt, again 94 per cent of that assumed in the

Boeing simulation. The system noted a wind of 30kt blowing from 170 degrees and calculated a west drift of eight or eleven degrees due to this wind.

The SuperTANS recorded all the waypoints entered by Tapper. It showed that the coordinates for waypoint A were 55° 18.5' north and 5° 48.0' west. This turned out to be a position some 280m south-east of the lighthouse.

Conclusions of the AAIB investigation

Cable noted that the absence of either an Accident Data Recorder and/or a Cockpit Voice Recorder considerably hindered the technical investigation. Either might have indicated the cause of the accident. As it was, his technical investigation failed to reveal any mechanical cause. He found nothing seriously wrong with any of the parts of the aircraft that remained. His recommendations included: the fitting of CVRs and ADRs; frequent downloading of data from the DECU memories; improvements to the radar altimeters; ways to verify the attachment integrity of the flight control pallet inserts; monitoring of the Lower Control Actuator wear and debris system; and a requirement that both the DASH and LCT actuators be tested under load during acceptance testing.

Cable submitted his sixty-page report to the Board in January 1995, but it was not made public until the House of Lords Select Committee did so on 10 August 2001, publishing most of it with most of the Board's report (see the next chapter) in November 2001. Cable read out parts of his report and the Racal report in the FAI in 1996.

Chapter Four

The RAF Inquiry

Following the accident, and as required by RAF regulations, the then Air Officer Commanding Headquarters No. 1 Group, Air Vice-Marshal John Day[67], ordered the convening of a Board of Inquiry. The appointed president was Wing Commander Andrew Pulford[68] (35) from HQ Directorate General Land Warfare at Upavon in Wiltshire. He was a qualified helicopter pilot with about 4,000 hours flying experience, half of it in Chinook Mk1s. This was his first Board of Inquiry. The other members were Squadron Leader E.J.W. Gilday from RAF Odiham (aircrew) and Squadron Leader P.L. Cole from HQ 1 Group (engineer). In attendance as required, besides the AAIB investigators, were Squadron Leader S.P. Jarmain[69] from the RAF's Inspectorate of Flight Safety, Major M. Chambers from HQNI (Lisburn), and Corporals C. Jones and N. Sagar from RAF Odiham. They all assembled at RAF Benson in Oxfordshire, the HQ of No. 1 Group, the day after the crash.

The Board's terms of reference were as follows:

a) Investigate the circumstances of the accident to Chinook HC2 ZD576 at Mull of Kintyre on 2 June 1994;

b) Determine the cause or causes of the accident and examine related factors:

c) Ascertain degree of injury suffered by persons both service and civilian;

d) Ascertain if the service personnel were on duty;

e) Ascertain if all relevant orders and instructions were complied with;

f) Ascertain if aircrew escape and survival facilities were fully utilized and functioning correctly;

g) Ascertain extent of damage to aircraft, public property and civilian property;

h) Assess any human failings;

i) Investigate the loss of all classified material carried on or in the aircraft at the time of the accident;

j) Make appropriate recommendations.

The Board heard evidence from twenty-two witnesses, eighteen of them RAF personnel, and saw statements taken from witnesses by Strathclyde Police and the RUC.

The Board became aware of almost everything mentioned in previous chapters and noted it in its report. It noted that Tapper was the captain, occupying the left-hand pilot's seat with Cook, whom it described as the 'co-pilot', in the right-hand seat. It assumed that Cook was the handling pilot (the usual arrangement). Among its incidental conclusions were the following:

- the flight was properly authorized, except that MALM Forbes did not hold a current aircrew medical category;

- the flight was adequately briefed, except that Tapper did not outbrief the 230 Squadron Duty Authorization Officer;

- the crew were competent to undertake the flight;

- the aircraft was serviceable to undertake the flight;

- the weather was suitable for the flight, but would have required flight in accordance with IFR near the Mull of Kintyre.

Apart from assistance from the AAIB, the Board also received assistance from:

The RAF Institute of Pathology and Tropical Medicine (IPTM);

The RAF School of Aviation Medicine (SAM);

The Aircraft Recovery and Transportation Flight (AR&TF);

The Meteorological Office;

Air Traffic Control;

The Defence Research Agency[70] (DRA) at both Farnborough and Bedford;

The Aircraft and Armament Experimental Establishment (A&AEE).

The Board also consulted the manufacturers, not only of the aircraft (Boeing) but also of its various components and made use of British International Helicopter's Chinook simulator at Farnborough. AR&TF provided a detailed survey of the crash site and the aircraft's most likely overland flight path. This provided information for the computer simulation of the terrain.

Contributory factors

The Board considered many factors that might have contributed to the accident: the crew's mental and physical state; their currency[71]; human factors; operational procedures; birdstrike; mid-air collision; hostile action; structural failure; technical failure; loose article/control restriction; electromagnetic interference; crew incapacitation; spatial disorientation; visual illusion; task factors; weather; navigation error; IF climb procedures; altimeter procedures and crew distraction. Their report discusses each of these factors in detail and they are summarized below.

The Board concluded that many factors had no bearing on the accident. It dismissed the crew's mental and physical state, their currency, birdstrike, mid-air collision, hostile action, structural failure, loose article/control restriction, electromagnetic interference, crew incapacitation, task factors, and navigation error. It noted that the crew may not have eaten properly beforehand and that they were probably stimulated by 'the more interesting sortie to Scotland'. It established that three of the crew had taken breakfast, but it was unable to establish that Flight Lieutenant Tapper had done so.

This left several factors that it thought might have contributed

45

to the accident. It was advised by the IAM principal psychologist (Chappelow) that impairment of a pilot's performance was possible because of mutual acquiescence, particularly in rapidly deteriorating circumstances. There was evidence that, although experienced and respected, both pilots were quiet and relaxed in their manner, lacking assertiveness in a crew environment. Although the other two experienced crew would not have tolerated any extended uncertainty in the conduct of the sortie, even a small delay in making a decision could have had serious consequences. Consequently, the Board concluded that it could not eliminate human factors.

Naturally, the Board considered operational procedures in detail, three aspects in particular. It noted some confusion over whether or not a self-authorizing captain was required to outbrief a Duty Authorizing Officer, but accepted that Tapper had attempted to comply with outbrief procedure. Even though he had not complied with procedures, it was concluded that a face-to-face outbrief would have made little difference. Consequently, this was dismissed as a factor. On the question of crew duty time, it was noted that the evidence was contradictory on whether or not Tapper intended to stay overnight in Scotland and that, whatever he did, the crew would have exceeded the 8-hours' limit and required the authorization of SRAFONI. It concluded that, if Tapper had intended returning that day to Aldergrove, he might have felt under pressure to complete the sortie as quickly as possible and that this may have been a contributory factor in the accident. The Board noted the problem of icing clearance vis-à-vis safety altitudes and how this precluded a flight in IMC over the Highlands to Inverness. Nevertheless, it noted that it would have been possible for the aircraft to have pulled up to safety altitude over the Mull of Kintyre and flown by IFR to Prestwick or Glasgow airports. However it was concluded that Tapper had 'mentally dismissed' this option and that his unwillingness to convert to IFR may have contributed to the accident.

The Board also considered technical failure in detail. It noted the very comprehensive and detailed AAIB report and its conclusion that there was no evidence of a major technical fault. Even so, it could not rule out the possibility that a minor technical malfunction could have distracted the crew. The report mentioned in particular an abnormal utility hydraulic temperature.[72] It also considered various aspects of the aircraft's technical history, including the GPS system, engine malfunctions, the collective flying control, maintenance work in the previous twenty-four hours and the general performance of the Mk2 Chinook in RAF service. It noted that all reported faults had been attended to and parts replaced where necessary. Although it could not exclude pre-impact detachment of the collective balance spring bracket, it was considered most unlikely. Noting Tapper's report of the GPS system tracking seven satellites but seeing only five, the Board concluded that this was not a fault in the system. While it noted that there was no evidence of the technical malfunctions and air incidents that other Chinook Mk2s had suffered, it could not discount the possibility that something similar had occurred. However, overall, the Board ruled out technical failure.

Because the flight path indicated that the controls were functioning at impact, the Board ruled out a loose article or control restriction. It discounted the idea that the crew were incapacitated, not only because there was no evidence of drugs or alcohol in their bodies, but also because Tapper made a routine call to Scottish Military only a few minutes before the crash.

The Board was concerned about spatial disorientation. In the conditions of poor visibility, there may have been a 'goldfish bowl' effect, where pilots lose their orientation. In that case, they would have had to rely increasingly on their instruments. Even though both pilots were experienced in flying by instruments and there was no evidence of spatial disorientation, the Board concluded that it might have been a contributory factor. There was similarly concern about visual illusion.[73] The Board attempted to simulate the visual conditions from the flight deck using computer-generated terrain displays, flight video and photographs. The results were inconclusive, but the factor could not be discounted.

The Board noted that, although the weather forecast for most of the route was favourable to VFR flight, part of it was forecast to be less so. Over coastal areas, it was predicted that there would be an occasional risk of less favourable but acceptable conditions and an isolated risk of conditions that would preclude VFR flight.

Such deteriorations were to be expected in the area of the Mull of Kintyre with a thirty per cent probability of weather below VFR limits forecast for Machrihanish. The Board accepted that this did not prevent an attempt at a VFR flight, but that it did demand a suitable bad weather contingency plan. This could have been a VFR diversion around the bad weather, a VFR return to Aldergrove, or a pre-planned climb and conversion to IFR flight. Since the accident occurred in low cloud with very poor visibility, the Board concluded that weather was a contributory factor.

Although the Board concluded that the waypoints had been programmed 'with no gross errors and to a sufficient accuracy for the planned VFR flight', it did note that the coordinates for waypoint A, to which the aircraft was heading at the time of the crash, placed it 280m from the true position of the Mull of Kintyre lighthouse. It concluded that this was due to plotting the position from a 1/500,000-scale chart (i.e. too small a scale).

The Board noted that there were no formal procedures within the Support Helicopter Force for conducting an IF abort from low level or for climbing from low-level flight under VFR to flight under IFR, and that these flight profiles are not taught or generally practised. However, it was noted that similar procedures *are* practised by Special Forces crews during NVG[74] training. Because the aircraft was apparently climbing at the time of the accident, the Board concluded that this was a factor to be considered. It did not comment on the failure of the crew to flare the aircraft to safety altitude.

The Board made detailed comment on altimeter procedures, but was concerned only with the radar altimeters (RadAlts) and the fact that, while the right hand one was set to 69ft, the left hand one was set to 850ft. It regarded this as contradictory and concluded that the left-hand RadAlt audio warning would have been muted and so could have given no warning of proximity to the ground. The right-hand RadAlt would have given warning only at 69ft. Consequently, it considered these settings a contributory factor.

Crew distraction was considered from three aspects: distraction by radio communications, passengers or a technical problem. The Board dismissed any distraction by a passenger but was concerned that the VHF/AM radio was found tuned to

128.875MHz, not the frequency of any known ground or air-to-air source. It concluded that this setting was the result either of the radio being retuned at the time of the accident or of it being disturbed during the crash. The VHF/FM radio was found switched off. Nevertheless, the Board could not rule out the possibility of some distraction because of a frequency change or an attempt to use the VHF/FM radio. Because the crew were relatively inexperienced with this Chinook and there was poor guidance by the Flight Reference Cards, the Board took the view that even a minor technical malfunction could have distracted the pilots and that this could be a factor.

Both A&AEE and DRA Farnborough gave evidence on the possibility of electromagnetic interference, the former on any interference with the GPS system from ground or airborne transmitters and the latter on any from the transmitter adjacent to the lighthouse. The Trimble TNL8000 GPS was found to be immune to most interference, but sensitive to the frequencies used by Hutchinson Telecom's 'Orange' and Mercury's 'One-to-One' cellphone systems. At the time, the latter was not available beyond the Outer London area, but the former was available in the Glasgow area. The field strength of the transmitter at the lighthouse was found to be insufficient to affect any of the aircraft's systems. Nor could any interference have come from three transmitters on Torr Mor, a 1,358ft (414m) mountain beside The Gap.

A&AEE also examined the possibility of portable telephones interfering with either the AFCS or RadAlt systems. No disturbance was apparent. Nor could portable computer equipment have upset either the AFCS system or the FADEC.

Reconstruction of the flight

In attempting to reconstruct the events immediately prior to the crash, the Board concluded that the low-level flight over Northern Ireland was *'for tactical reasons'*, and that, over the sea, the aircraft is likely to have climbed to about 1,000ft, but no higher. Then, because it was seen flying lower than that over the trawlers in the North Channel, it was assumed that the aircraft

49

had descended to 200–400ft. This was about three minutes after its unanswered call to ScATCC (Mil).

From the SuperTANS data, the Board calculated the position at which the change in waypoint was made. The Board assumed that, from that point, the aircraft continued on a straight-line track to the impact point. This was based on the data from the Doppler that showed that there had been very little change in the heading throughout the flight. It also took into account that the earwitnesses did not report sounds indicating aircraft manoeuvres. The Board had confidence in the SuperTANS altitude calculation of 468ft, but not in that of 665ft, and noted the Boeing simulation showing a cyclic flare. It concluded that this covered only the last four seconds of the flight and involved a height gain of 145ft (44.2m). Earlier the Board had arranged for an investigation of Chinook flare performance by DRA Bedford. Although this was not modelled on a Chinook, it was later found to correlate well with the Boeing analysis. The Board concluded that it was most likely that, while coasting in at the Mull of Kintyre, the aircraft was established in a steady climb with airspeed of about 150kt and that, at approximately four seconds before impact, it was flared to an attitude of 30 degrees nose-up.

The Board was confident that the flight had proceeded as planned at least until the call to ScATCC (Mil). It calculated that this call, four minutes before impact, was made roughly midway across the North Channel. It did not know the purpose of the call, but from the calm tone and absence of any emergency prefix, it was concluded that the aircraft was not in any difficulty at that point. The Board noted that, by selecting the next waypoint, the crew lost position information relating to the Mull of Kintyre. Consequently, the Board attempted to establish the conditions that would have prompted the crew to make this change. It accepted that, while it was unnecessary for the aircraft to fly over the lighthouse, the crew would have needed to establish visual contact with it if they were to follow the coastline north. However, this was impossible due to its being in fog, as was the Mull above it. The Board stated that, close to the Mull, there was broken cloud at about 200ft with 500 metres visibility below. This, it concluded, should have caused the crew to reduce height and speed well below those at impact in an attempt to see the lighthouse. The Board concluded that, in the event, it was most unlikely that the crew saw either the lighthouse or the Mull. It was thought possible that, due to a visual illusion, the crew misidentified their position with reference to the Mull. However, because it could not envisage circumstances where this would be so compelling for the crew not to have reduced speed, mis-identification of the waypoint or the Mull was thought unlikely. This did not explain why the next waypoint had been selected, but it concluded that the crew 'had consciously dispensed' with navigation information relative to the Mull and it noted that the selection of the Corran waypoint indicated an intention to proceed according to plan. According to the Board, if the crew had decided not to attempt a landfall in the vicinity of the light-house, they had two alternatives: either turn away from land and attempt a VFR route to Corran parallel to the intended track, or climb to safety attitude over the Mull on track, accepting a change to IMC if necessary and hoping to revert to VMC before reaching Corran. It noted that there was no evidence of the first option; the aircraft had continued on track. Although the impact evidence indicated an element of left bank, it was concluded that this was either the result of a late awareness of a collision or the start of the 'small 14 degree' turn required for the heading to Corran. The evidence of a climb before impact tended to support the idea that the crew had chosen the second option. However the rate of climb and the airspeed at impact were not thought consistent with an emergency IF abort. It was concluded that the crew had lost all external visual reference and that any alert from the RadAlts was too late. In trying to explain why the crew had not chosen a rate of climb that would have allowed them to clear the Mull, the Board appears to have assumed that the crew were responding to their 'changing circumstances'. It concluded that a suitable rate of climb might have been discussed but not implemented. The alternative was that the crew selected an 'inappropriate' rate of climb. Discounting a major navigational error, the Board believed that 'inordinate reliance' may have been placed on the accuracy of the GPS system and that the crew may have believed that they were further west than they were. This, and the imminent change of track away from the Mull, may have led the crew to believe that a 'cruise climb' (the type of climb chosen) was adequate

51

separation. The Board stated that, because the degree of vibration discouraged cruise flight above 135kt in the Mk1 Chinook, with which the crew were more familiar, they were 'unfamiliar' with operating comfortably at high airspeeds in the Mk2 (it had less vibration). It concluded that the high ground speed and closure rate with the Mull allowed only a small power margin available for climbing and that the consequent rate of climb would have been low (500–1,000fpm). It thought that the crew may not have been aware of the low rate of climb they had achieved due to the amount of power being taken to achieve the high airspeed. It also thought that the crew might have been reluctant to reduce speed to complete the sortie quickly and reduce the amount of time they exceeded the crew duty limits. Out of three possible causes of the accident (suitable rate of climb determined but not flown, no decision, and inappropriate rate of climb selected), the Board opted for the last. It added that there were several contributory factors (already noted above).

Orders and instructions

The Board concluded that all relevant orders and instructions had been obeyed, except that Tapper did not outbrief the Duty Authorizing Officer, that the latter did not ensure that Tapper outbriefed through him, that no maintenance work-order log entry was raised for the engine PTIT fault, that the PTIT gauges were transposed without raising a maintenance work-order, that Tapper did not raise a maintenance work-order for the (alleged) SuperTANS/GPS fault, that tests on the latter were conducted without raising a maintenance work-order, and that MALM Forbes' periodical medical examination was overdue.

Human failings

The Board concluded that the failures by the supervisory and engineering personnel to comply with regulations were not factors in the accident. Nor did it think that it was unreasonable for Tapper to decide to conduct the sortie that day. It noted several contradictions but, overall, it found that the facts did not allow it to make an objective assessment of any human failings in respect of Tapper. It was also unable to determine his preparations for encountering bad weather. Even so, it concluded that he may have *'mentally dismissed'* the possibility of flight in IMC. Its main concern was why Tapper, as the navigator, selected an inappropriate rate of climb over the Mull of Kintyre. It concluded that, when the decision to climb was made, Tapper might have thought he was further from the Mull than was in fact the case. Although it could find no evidence that Tapper had approached and prepared the flight in anything other than a thorough and professional manner, and it thought it incorrect to criticize him for human failings, it thought it likely that he made an 'Error of Judgement'[75] in the attempted climb over the Mull of Kintyre. It found no human failings with respect to Cook.

Recommendations and observations

Except for some that dealt with minor administrative and technical matters, the principal recommendations were that all RAF Chinook aircraft should be fitted with both cockpit voice recorders (CVRs) and accident data recorders (ADRs) at the earliest opportunity. It noted that a similar recommendation was made by the Boards of Inquiry into two previous Chinook accidents. It also recommended that formal IF climb procedures should be developed for the RAF Support Helicopter Force (SHF).

Among nine observations made were that the Flight Reference Cards were confusing and that outbriefing procedures provided ambiguous information.

The Board signed its report on 3 February 1995.

Remarks by senior officers

The Board's report consists of five parts: part 1, its composition and terms of reference; part 2, its main report (summarized above); parts 3–5, 'remarks' by several senior RAF officers. These officers, although not part of the Board itself, could uphold or change the Board's conclusions.

Part 3 recorded the views of two station commanders. The first was RAF Aldergrove's station commander, Group Captain Wedge (SRAFONI). He was impressed by the meticulous and detailed examination of events produced by the Board but thought that the exact train of events could never be determined absolutely. He agreed that, while not ideal, it was reasonable for Tapper's crew to undertake the Inverness sortie. He stated that, because of the extended daylight in June at their latitude, it was routine for crews to take advantage of it to 'preserve' if possible the 'day-on day-off' crew rota. Acknowledging that Tapper had properly applied for and obtained a crew duty time extension, he did not think it useful to speculate on Tapper's further intentions on arriving in Inverness. He explained that outbriefing anomalies had since been removed, but not because of the accident, and he thought that Tapper had made an effort to make details of his planning available to the Duty Authorizing Officer. He explained that the majority of Chinook ground crew were now on Aldergrove's posted strength and not attached from RAF Odiham. These 'remarks' were dated 2 March 1995.

The second station commander was Group Captain P.A. Crawford[76], Officer Commanding RAF Odiham, the Chinook's home base. He also complimented the Board on its thorough and detailed investigation. However, he and other *'senior Chinook operators'* found it difficult to accept their conclusion that, faced with the expected deteriorating weather, the crew consciously elected to climb using a speed and power combination *'un-recognisable as a Chinook technique'*. This would go against all the crew's instincts and training and was the antithesis of the professionalism and careful planning that had been undertaken. He pointed out that no crew would trust a GPS position close to a potentially dangerous obstruction unless they had the oppor-tunity to cross-check with another aid and that they would not be concerned about *'niceties of a few hundred metres'*. He did not think that undue reliance on the GPS would make them accept a cruise climb. Nor did he accept the Board's idea that the crew, unfamiliar with the Mk2, were seduced into accepting a higher speed causing them to miscalculate the gradient of the climb. He declared that not even 'the most junior crew' would have selected a cruise climb technique that close to the Mull, 'whatever the cruise speed'. He also disagreed with the notion that the decision-making process was complex, and thus vulnerable to distraction. The choice, he declared, was relatively simple and ingrained into the crews during training, especially into Special Forces crews. They could slow down, and if necessary stop, turn away, and if necessary turn back, or climb at full power to safety altitude. Crawford proposed an alternative view of what happened. In his opinion, the crew saw the coast and decided to continue in VFR to the west of the Mull, changing the waypoint as they did so. He noted yachtsman Holbrook's report of seeing the lighthouse and cloud covering the Mull and also his estimate that there was 'structured' (layered) 80 per cent cloud above the helicopter, which was flying at 200–400ft. Crawford concluded that, if the crew had intended to abort and climb over the Mull, they would not have selected the next waypoint. Apart from removing information about the high ground, because of the icing limitation, they would not have been able to climb to safety altitude on track for Corran in the hope of reverting to low-level VFR. For a climb over the Mull, they would have needed to retain data about waypoint A (the lighthouse). According to Crawford, selection of waypoint B indicated an intention to follow the western coast of Kintyre and regain the planned track as soon as possible. Nevertheless, he was unable to explain why the aircraft then crashed where it did. He suggested that the crew might have become disorientated, that there may have been an unregistered technical malfunction, or that some human factors were involved. He noted in particular that spurious engine failure captions, lasting about seven or eight seconds, were an increasingly frequent occurrence at the time. This would have required an urgent and very careful check of engine instruments and the Flight Reference Cards. Crawford pointed out that, fundamentally, the accident was caused by the crew flying the aircraft *into the ground*. The reason for this was less clear. He thought that little was to be gained by speculating on the actions that led to the last few seconds of flight. He was also convinced that there was no major technical failure that would have implications for the Chinook fleet. He agreed with the idea of introducing formal procedures for transition from VFR to IFR, including IF abort, but did not accept that training in the SHF was lacking. He stated that Cook carried out such a transition during an exercise on 20 May 1994. Regarding human failings, he concluded with regret that, because the captain had an overriding duty to ensure the safety of the aircraft, its crew and the passengers, Tapper failed in his duty. These 'remarks' were dated 3 March 1995.

The AOC's remarks

Part 4 of the Report consists of 'remarks' by Air Vice-Marshal John Day, then AOC No. 1 Group, who had ordered the convening of the Board. He noted that, in direct contravention of the rules for flight, the aircraft had crashed while flying at high speed well below safety altitude in cloud. In his opinion, until that altitude had been achieved, the aircraft should not have continued to approach the Mull of Kintyre. He thought that, having been warned of low cloud around the Mull, the crew should have taken great care as they approached it. He agreed that, if VFR could still be maintained, they could have slowed down, turned away or turned back. Otherwise, they should have climbed at maximum power to safety altitude while turning away, which they should have done anyway if they entered IMC inadvertently. He conceded that the crews preferred to fly VFR where possible and that the icing limitation may have reinforced this preference. Nevertheless, around the Mull, the icing level was above the safety altitude, which the crew had calculated correctly. He noted suggestions that the crew may have been distracted, but he could see no reason why the crew could not have maintained safe flight. He rejected Group Captain Crawford's view that the actions of the crew were not the direct cause of the crash[77] and he rejected the idea that Tapper made an *error of judgement*'. However, he agreed that Tapper, as captain, failed in his duty; failing to exercise appropriate care and judgement. Aware of the forecast of poor weather and the actual bad weather around the Mull, Tapper allowed the aircraft to proceed at both high speed and low level directly towards the Mull, notwithstanding the obvious dangers. Tapper also broke the flight rules. This led Day to conclude that Tapper was negligent to a gross degree. Nor did he exonerate Cook. Day accepted that Cook was engaged primarily with flying the aircraft and that he may not have been fully aware of all aspects of the situation. Nevertheless, as an experienced Chinook captain, he should have recognized the dangerous environment into which they were flying. Therefore, Day also concluded that he too was negligent to a gross degree. Like everyone else, Day could not understand why two *'trusted, experienced and skilled pilots'* should have flown a serviceable aircraft into cloud, covering high ground, and he was so concerned that he instituted a review of training and supervisory procedures. This revealed no deficiencies that had a bearing on the accident. He accepted the Board's recommendations. His 'remarks' were dated and signed 20 March 1995.

The C.-in-C.'s remarks

Part 5 of the Report consists of 'remarks' by Strike Command's then C.-in-C., Air Chief Marshal Sir William Wratten.[78] He noted that, while there was an inevitable degree of speculation about the details, there was no evidence of anything that would have given the crew no option but to continue towards high ground at speed and at low level. He concluded therefore, that the accident was avoidable by the various methods described by the AOC (Day). He pointed out that the pilots would have known that hitting the ground without intending or expecting to carries the lowest likelihood of survival and that it must be avoided at all costs. This was the crew's pre-eminent responsibility and he could see no hint of any reason why they did not avoid this risk. All the evidence, he concluded, pointed to their having ignored one of the most basic tenets of airmanship i.e. to never attempt to fly visually below safety altitude unless the weather conditions are unambiguously under VFR. He agreed with the AOC's summary and that the actions of the pilots amounted to gross negligence. His 'remarks' were dated 3 April 1995.[79]

Annexes

The original report contained twenty-six annexes (A to Z), and another twenty or so with twin letter prefixes. The following is a list of annexes, the contents of which have been identified, sometimes only provisionally.

A A map of the Mull of Kintyre showing actual and planned track (part of Annexe S).*

B A map of the locality of the lighthouse.

C Details of the aircrew of the Chinook.

G RAF regulations?

H Aircrew course reports.

I The JATOC tasking sheet for the aircraft on 2 June 1994.

J The meteorological forecast.

K Extracts from F700 (the Chinook's service history record), including the low-flying booking form?; also Annexe AK?

L A transcript of radio communications with Aldergrove ground control.

M A transcript of radio communications with 81 SU.

O A transcript of the radio communication with Scottish Military.

P The meteorological aftercast[80] (see below).

Q The AAIB report.

T RAF School of Aviation Medicine report.

U Report on damage to aircraft?

V A report from a psychologist on possible crew behaviour prior to the accident.

W Mull of Kintyre terrain cross-section along estimated final track to initial impact point and most probable final flight path profile.[81]*

X   The Boeing simulation of the flight profile.

Y   The Racal report on the SuperTANS.

AB   DRA Farnborough Electronic Interference Report.

AC   DRA Bedford flight path simulation.

AD   A&AEE Boscombe Down Electromagnetic Interference Reports.

AI   An extract from the CA Release in relation to the Mk2.

AJ   Stills from the radar recordings at ScATCC.

AK   Extracts from Form 700.

AQ   A map of the Mull of Kintyre marked with tracks and various locations.*

Part 6 of the Report, which consists of the evidence given by the witnesses, is restricted but was available to the families of the deceased. Annexes T, X and Y are also restricted. Although Annexe P, the Meteorological Office's aftercast, has not been published, a summary can be reconstructed from the evidence given in the FAI, as follows:

Weather at and above the crash site at 17:00 UT

Visibility in hill fog and drizzle[82] 10 to 100 metres; below main cloud base 100 to 2,000 metres (2,000 metres to 10 kilometres at sea level). The stratus cloud base would have been variable and diffuse, between 200 and 800 feet (243.8m) AMSL. Tops of stratus perhaps 1,500 to 2,000 feet (457.2–609.6m). Moderate orographic turbulence below 1,500 feet over and to the north of the Mull of Kintyre, otherwise little turbulence. Surface wind, 170 degrees true, 20 knots, gusts to 30 knots; at 1,000 feet, 170 degrees, 20 knots. Temperature and dew point: 9 degrees C from

*Published by the House of Lords Select Committee.

59

surface to 2,000 feet; 8 degrees C at 3,000 feet; no icing below 7,000 feet (2,133.6m) and the 4 degrees C level at 5,000 feet (1524m).

Publication

Normally such a report would remain classified, protected by Section 2 of the Official Secrets Act. However, under the Open Government Charter introduced by Prime Minister John Major, copies were made available to the families of the deceased. Consequently, it was the first RAF accident report to be seen outside the MOD (so far it is the only one). Parts of it first became public when they were read out in the FAI, but the full report was not released until the House of Lords Select Committee published it with most of the AAIB Report and some of the evidence presented to them in November 2001. Even then, side notes referring to annexes were omitted and only a few of the annexes were included. The MOD issued a brief Accident Summary (see Appendix One) and the RAF Inspectorate of Flight Safety issued a longer report for circulation within the RAF.[83]

Chapter Five

The Fatal Accident Inquiry

If the accident had occurred in England or Wales, a coroner[84] would have held an inquest, in which a jury, guided by the coroner, would have been asked to state how, when and where the deceased died. In this case, a jury may well have brought a verdict of accidental death. However, considering the strange verdict given on the deaths of the people killed in the Selby train crash, it might have been 'unlawful killing' of the passengers (by the crew). In any case, there is unlikely to have been any detailed investigation of the cause of the accident.

Things are different in Scotland. Scottish law[85] requires that, where any sudden or accidental death occurs, a Fatal Accident Inquiry (FAI) must be held into the circumstances of the death on the grounds that it was sudden, suspicious or unexplained, or has occurred in circumstances such as to give rise to serious public concern. In particular, the FAI must determine where and when the deaths took place, the cause of the deaths and the accident, any reasonable precautions that could have prevented the deaths, any defects in 'any system of working' which contributed to the accident, and any other relevant facts. Consequently, an FAI would be expected to examine the accident in far greater detail than an inquest. Those who rejected the RAF's verdict hoped that evidence would emerge in an FAI that would undermine it.

The procurator fiscal[86] for the district where the death or deaths occurred must investigate the circumstances and apply to a sheriff for the holding of an FAI into the circumstances. The sheriff involved must be one whose sheriffdom is most closely connected with the circumstances of the death. Where it appears that more than one death has occurred as a result of the same accident, the procurator fiscal's application may relate to all such deaths. On receipt of an application, the sheriff must make an order fixing the time and place for the holding of an FAI, which must be held as soon as possible in a courthouse or other premises which appear suitable.

The procurator fiscal

In this case, the deaths occurred in the Sheriff Court district of Campbeltown in Argyll, where the fiscal was Iain Henderson, based at the Sheriff Court in Campbeltown. In June 2002, after he had retired, Henderson claimed that the MOD had tried to prevent the holding of an FAI by withholding the AAIB's report for eighteen months. Furthermore, he suspected that the MOD did not want an FAI held at all. He claimed that the report was ready in late 1994 and that he could not hold an FAI without this technical report. The report was made available to him in June 1995, but he was informed that it could not be used as evidence in an FAI without the MOD's clearance. However, after he asked the Crown Office[87] to take up the matter at ministerial level, in September 1995 he received what he described as 'a grudging letter' telling him that he could lodge the report. He claimed that this delay had made it almost impossible for the families of the deceased to prepare a case for judicial review within the stipulated three-month period following the RAF's verdict. However, the MOD declared that it believed that it had cooperated fully with the sheriff, but it made no mention of cooperating with the fiscal.

The Paisley FAI

Because the Sheriff Court in Campbeltown was too small for the FAI and inconvenient for witnesses and parties generally, it was decided to hold it in Paisley Sheriff Court, within the same sheriff-dom as Campbeltown (North Strathclyde). Paisley is a large burgh eleven kilometres west of Glasgow, easily accessible by major road and rail routes and close to Glasgow Airport. The FAI was set to begin on Monday, 8 January 1996, and expected to last four weeks. On Tuesday, 23 January, in the third week, the sheriff wondered how long it was going to last. In fact, it was completed in the four weeks, meeting on eighteen working days and finishing on Friday, 2 February. Such was the public interest in the FAI, that not only was it closely followed and reported in the press, but also the sheriff received many letters from the public (they have not been published). He was careful to point out that his final ruling (his 'determination') would be based on the evidence he heard and not on these letters.

The FAI was attended by many relatives of the deceased, by the press and a few other interested parties. The shorthand writers, Thomas Brisbane, David Healy and Alison Jenkins, working in rotation, kept a mostly accurate record of all the evidence and made this available to the lawyers daily. The eventual transcript runs to over half a million words.

The lawyers

The sheriff appointed was Sir Stephen Young, Bt[88] (49), the Sheriff of North Strathclyde at Greenock. An FAI is conducted like any other court case in Scotland, with counsel (in Scotland they are called 'advocates') wearing their wigs and robes as they address the sheriff and questioning and/or cross-questioning witnesses, although sheriffs themselves also do so. The principal evidence is led by a counsel representing the Crown and is usually the fiscal, or a depute. In important cases, it may be led by Scotland's Lord Advocate, the head of the system of public prosecution, or by his or her assistant, the Solicitor General. More usually, as in this case, it is led by someone deputizing for the Lord Advocate (an 'Advocate Depute').

In the FAI, the Advocate Depute was John Logan Mitchell QC (49), although the fiscal, Iain Henderson, was present in the court. Throughout the FAI, Mitchell was referred to as '(The) Advocate Depute', not by his name. The MOD was represented by R. Alistair Dunlop QC, LLB, with Mr S. A. Bennett, Advocate. Also in attendance was a 'Mr Morgan', apparently representing the MOD[89]; although he was listed as a Crown witness, he never gave evidence. The Boeing Helicopter Co. was represented by

Michael S. Jones QC, LLB (48). He is a former fighter pilot and an expert on aviation law who had participated in several FAIs into aircraft accidents, some involving helicopters. The relatives of Flight Lieutenant Tapper were represented by Aidan M. O'Neill QC, LLB (Hons), LLM (Hons), LLM. The relatives of Flight Lieutenant Cook were represented by Peter Black Watson BA, LLB, SSC, a Solicitor-Advocate and partner in Levy and McRae and their consultant Len Murray, a well-known Glasgow solicitor. The relatives of the remainder of the deceased were represented by Colin Malcolm Campbell, QC (43), now Dean of the Faculty of Advocates.

On 18 December 1995, a preliminary (procedural) hearing opened in Paisley Sheriff Court. This was to discuss who was to be represented and the order of the cross-examination before the case opened on 8 January. Mr O'Neill stated that he would be testing the evidence for the claim that the pilots were responsible for the crash. He also took the opportunity to point to malfunctions of the aircraft only a few weeks earlier. These were listed in a letter from Colonel Hodgkiss of Boscombe Down to the Scottish Office (the UK Government department that administered Scottish affairs before the establishment of a Scottish Parliament and the Scottish Executive). Hodgkiss had alleged that tests on Mk2 Chinooks had been suspended after an engine 'flame-out' and five computer malfunctions. O'Neill called on the MOD to provide more information aout these incidents and those involved. John Mitchell countered that background evidence about previous faults was not directly relevant in the hearing. The Court also heard from the advocates representing the MOD, 'the relatives of the deceased' and Boeing.

The hearing considered appointing an assessor to help the sheriff understand the technical issues involved. A motion to this effect had been proposed by the counsel for the pilots' families. However, they were unable to state at what point such an assessor would be necessary or what technical matters were likely to be in dispute. Considering that, and the Advocate Depute's opinion that an assessor was unnecessary (the material to be placed before the Court would not be so 'incomprehensible'), the sheriff refused the motion. He may have had in mind the fact that, as an experienced yachtsman, he was familiar with navigation and map reading and could expect to cope with much of the technical evidence. After hearing that the MOD had refused to fund legal representation for the pilots' widows to clear their husbands' names, the hearing was adjourned.

Although a sheriff normally does not know what evidence is going to be presented to an FAI, in this case Sheriff Young did see a copy of the Board's report before the inquiry began. However, he admitted that he understood very little of it at the time. He had to draw his conclusions from the evidence presented in the FAI. The Racal report on the SuperTANS navigation computer was only made available at the start of the FAI, as one of a set of 'productions' by Peter Watson (each counsel had his own list of 'productions'). Andrew Fairfield, a former RAF pilot, was allowed to sit with Peter Watson and Len Murray.

The witnesses

These six advocates and the sheriff questioned thirty-eight witnesses over the eighteen days of the Inquiry.[90] All the witnesses gave evidence standing in the witness box. Twenty of the witnesses were RAF officers, some very senior (one was SRAFONI himself) and one was the president of the Board (Pulford). There was one Royal Navy officer, and five officers from Strathclyde Police. Of the civilian witnesses, four were forensic pathologists giving evidence on how the deceased died (one was Professor Venezis), one was a journalist, two were the lighthouse keepers, one was a civilian air traffic controller, one was a housewife, one a sailor, one a tourist and one the AAIB inspector.

Some of the witnesses took a long time to complete their evidence. Tony Cable of the AAIB was in the witness box for over three consecutive days and Wing Commander Pulford gave evidence on four separate days. Thirty-six of the witnesses were called by the Crown and two were called on behalf of the Tapper family. Although they appeared in uniform (which indicated their rank), most of the RAF officers were allowed to conceal their rank and unit at the time by handing the sheriff a paper showing this information. Sheriff Young asked the press not to report the names of any of the RAF witnesses. In his Determination, the sheriff referred to these witnesses by letters of the alphabet. However, during the FAI the advocates often referred to a witness's rank in questions to other witnesses and the witnesses themselves often did so. Since then, the ranks of all the military witnesses have been made public. Although an FAI is not adversarial, i.e. there is no basic dispute to be resolved, it is obvious that not all the counsel had the same agenda or purpose. The counsel for the MOD was at pains to defend the actions of the RAF and the counsel for Boeing defended the integrity and safety of the aircraft. Naturally, they were opposed by counsel for the families of the pilots, who tried to defend them. This conflict emerged clearly when witnesses for the relatives of Flight Lieutenant Tapper gave evidence (see below). Some of the counsel clearly regarded some of the witnesses as hostile and did their best to undermine their evidence. Counsel for the remainder of the deceased took a more balanced position, but tended to blame the pilots.

The evidence from witnesses was heard in a particular order. First the evidence for the Crown led by John Mitchell; that took fourteen days. It was followed by evidence for the relatives of Flight Lieutenant Tapper, until the sixteenth day, when evidence was led, briefly, for the MOD. The final two days were taken up with closing submissions by the advocates, starting with John Mitchell. All the advocates made such submissions. Squadron Leader Morgan arranged for Sheriff Young to inspect a Chinook helicopter and be given a forty-minute flight in the aircraft at Glasgow Airport on Saturday, 27 January 1996.

The turning point

Much of the evidence covered ground already discussed in previous chapters; in fact, its transcript is the source of much of that material. However, some new details did emerge. An important one is the location of the turning point, sometimes called waypoint A, near which the aircraft crashed. Because the crew had been following a track determined by Tapper's location of the waypoint, its exact location is relevant. Since he had been involved in planning the sortie and the route, Flight Lieutenant Kingston gave evidence about the location of waypoint A at the lighthouse, the obvious feature for the first turn. He distinguished between a *'turning point'*, the point at which the aircraft was expected to turn, and the waypoint coordinates entered into the SuperTANS navigation computer. The lighthouse, he explained, was *'the reference point'*, but there was no need for the aircraft to fly over it. The evidence was that he and Flight Lieutenant Trapp planned the turning point to be a little west of the lighthouse, over the sea. This was later confirmed by evidence from Trapp, who told Michael Jones for Boeing the same thing: that the turning point was *'just to the west of the Mull of Kintyre . . . to prevent having to cross land'*.

Evidence for the pilots

The evidence for the relatives of Flight Lieutenant Tapper, led by Aidan O'Neill, was given by Flight Lieutenants Carl Scott (37) and Ian MacFarlane[91] (32), both Chinook pilots. They both knew Tapper and Cook well and supported the hypothesis that the crew had been unable to change track away from the Mull because of some major systems malfunction. MacFarlane had been appointed as visiting officer to the Tapper family, representing the RAF. Neither had given evidence to the Board.

Scott was given a hard time under cross-examination by Alistair Dunlop, who demonstrated Scott's relative ignorance of much of the evidence and, in particular, details of the route and the weather. In cross-examination by Dunlop, MacFarlane claimed that the waypoint change to Corran was inconsistent with a pre-planned sortie into IFR and that it was even inconsistent with the speculation that the crew were attempting to continue the sortie after a low-level abort. He said:

> . . . to be selecting Corran as the next waypoint, at that point it was postulated they would continue to fly up the next leg of their route to Corran in the hope of gaining a visual sight of the ground and letting back down to low level again. It just doesn't accord with our teaching at all.

Nor did he think that the crew had intended to fly up into cloud in the hope that a break in it would allow them to come back down:

> *You may well do that. You could spend a long, long time looking for a hole. It is not for no reason these holes are known as 'suckers gaps'. You just do not go up unless you can get back down. It would be just as simple for the crew in terms of physical button presses to contact Prestwick [or] Glasgow as a diversion criteria [sic]. Even if the temperature calculation was ignored and we assume they could reach safety altitude in the region of the Mull of Kintyre they most certainly, my belief would have been they most certainly could not have done that for the remainder of that leg which required them to fly somewhere in the region of 5,800ft, and that would have involved a climb from 2,800ft up to 5,800ft, and based on the temperature calculations of the day that would not have been within the IFR clearance of the aircraft.*

MacFarlane disagreed with the Board's conclusion that the cause was the selection of an inappropriate rate of climb. He thought that *'unlikely in the extreme'* and preferred the idea that a control jam (loss of pitch and roll control) forced the crew to continue towards the Mull while trying to climb to clear it; that *'they were flown by the aircraft effectively into the Mull of Kintyre'*, only clearing the jam at the last moment. However, he did not think that a specious 'Engine Fail' caption coming on had any possible relevance to the accident.

MacFarlane was questioned at length by Dunlop about his alternative explanation (it had not been mentioned before in the FAI). He was also asked about his motivation (was it because he was a close friend of Tapper?) and his qualifications (he was not an engineer). After he had agreed that all the control channels were separate and designed to be very secure, it was pointed out to him that the expected rate of failure of a single channel was not more than once in a million flying hours. He was also informed that the probability of a failure of two channels simultaneously was one in 1,000 billion flying hours. He did not dispute these estimates and also accepted that the probability of both pitch and roll channels jamming simultaneously and then un-jamming simultaneously was *'one in a million billion billion flying hours'*. This is because his scenario required there to be two loose articles causing an obstruction, one in each of the two control channels. It turned out that MacFarlane was unaware that Boeing had, from December 1994, discounted the probability of a loose article jamming the flight controls and had withdrawn a previous requirement for visual checks. Questioned further about his motivation and why he had not volunteered his scenario to the Board, he explained that it was partly because of a widespread feeling of injustice throughout the RAF and partly an attempt to explain the accident. When it was pointed out that he had described his scenario as *'probable'*, he retracted that view and described it instead as *'possible'*.

MacFarlane was also cross-examined by John Mitchell, firstly about the aircraft's speed, getting him to agree that the flight to Inverness may have taken only one hour twenty minutes. While this could just have been accomplished within the daily seven-hour limit, a return journey would have meant exceeding that limit and even exceeding the eight hours already authorized. MacFarlane considered that Tapper had sought neither authority for an extension to ten hours nor authority to keep the aircraft overnight in Inverness because *'he might have been otherwise distracted in his pre-flight preparations'*. Nevertheless, he had to agree that there was no overriding reason for the crew to exceed their crew hours. He implied that Tapper was relaxed about the options, including keeping the aircraft in Inverness, because he knew that there was no tasking scheduled for the Chinook until the following afternoon.

Mitchell then asked MacFarlane about the waypoint change, where, according to the latter, the controls jammed. Because he had suggested that the climb was a response to the proposed control jam, he was asked why, if the cruise climb had begun before this event (he refused to concede that this would not fit his scenario), the aircraft was climbing at all. He suggested that the crew may have been climbing over seagulls surrounding a fleet of fishing boats, or they may have been adjusting their altitude to get them out of a turbulence layer. On the question of the control jam, he had to agree that the odds against it happening at all were *'astronomical'* and that he had never heard of such a thing happening to any Chinook. He also had to agree that proposing that the control channels freed themselves almost simultaneously only about two and a half seconds before impact made his scenario even more unlikely. He was reluctant to agree that the more likely reason for the final flare was sight of the ground. He would only agree that it was a more acceptable hypothesis because it was more likely, i.e. that the odds against it were lower.

Questioned by Sheriff Young, MacFarlane admitted that he had never heard of a simultaneous failure of two flight control channels, although this related only to RAF experience. In further questioning, MacFarlane agreed with the sheriff that Tapper could not have imagined that a rate of climb of only 1,000fpm would be sufficient to reach safety altitude by the time they reached waypoint A, only 0.81nm away. Nor could Tapper have been misled about the rate of climb.

No evidence was led for the relatives of Flight Lieutenant Cook, for the remainder of the deceased, or for Boeing.

Re-examination

The emergence of MacFarlane's alternative hypothesis led the Court to recall Wing Commander Pulford, to get his view of it. Questioned by Alistair Dunlop for the MOD, he was first asked about the rate of climb. He explained that use of the Chinook simulator at Farnborough had shown that the climb rate of 1,000fpm was achievable without the use of emergency power, but that the application of the latter could boost the climb rate to 1,250fpm. Because there was a device on the aircraft to indicate if emergency power had been applied for more than five seconds and, if so, for how long (it was an aid for service engineers), and because this had not been tripped, it was known that emergency power had not been applied for longer than that period. This did not rule out the application of emergency power in the final three seconds. He stated that the postulated control jam would not have prevented the application of full engine power, enabling the aircraft to clear the Mull. Of course, this

70

meant that, if there had been an emergency twenty seconds or so before impact, the pilots had not applied full engine power to try to clear the Mull. This cast doubt on MacFarlane's hypothesis. The Board had examined the possibility of control jams and had concluded that it was very unlikely. The jamming of more than one at once was even less likely. Not only was there no evidence of such jams, the controls were evidently free in the final seconds and, because they were flight critical, they were subject to very careful monitoring. In addition, he pointed out that Boeing had made the upper and lower actuators *'jam resistant'*. Pulford did not believe that the controls jammed and certainly not that they freed just before impact. He was sure that the final flare was the result of the crew realizing their proximity to the ground. Necessarily this implied that the crew had not known this before that point and so could not have known their true position. He believed that, at the time of the waypoint change, a decision had already been made to do something other than to turn left and fly visually. He thought that, having changed the waypoint and having lost information with regard to the waypoint, they changed their plan and decided to climb over the Mull. However, the crew failed to appreciate that their high speed required a higher power setting to give a rate of climb sufficient to clear the Mull. He added that, because of the slight errors in track, the crew might also have thought that the Mull was further to their right than it actually was.

Michael Jones for Boeing asked Pulford about the use of the yaw control (MacFarlane's hypothesis did not suggest any jamming of this device). He got Pulford to agree that continued application of left yaw, although it would have caused great discomfort to the aircraft's occupants, would have resulted in a change of track to port, albeit slowly. It was obvious to the Court that there had been no change of track (to port) and therefore that this manoeuvre had not been attempted. It was not known whether or not such an input would have enabled the Chinook to clear the Mull; Pulford explained that it had not been tested on the simulator.

Summing up for the Crown

On Thursday, 1 February 1996, the seventeenth day, the Court began to hear the closing submissions from the various parties, starting with that for the Crown.

In his submission, John Mitchell reviewed the result of the AAIB investigation, which found no serious mechanical faults. He noted in particular the evidence from the Boeing simulation that, in the last few seconds of the flight, the pilot had attempted to climb and slow the aircraft. He also noted the slight error in the location of waypoint A (280m SE of the lighthouse). He concluded that this error, combined with a slight error in the SuperTANS itself, may have led the crew to believe that they were further west than they were. The final flare in particular indicated that the crew did not expect to be where they were, raising the central question of how they came to be in that position. Mitchell also concluded that all the evidence from the eye- and earwitnesses, and that from the radio transmissions, indicated that the flight was normal with no problems. However, he expressed concern that the flight-time limitation had put some pressure or *'incentive'* on the crew to complete the sortie as quickly as possible and that this might have some bearing on the cause of the accident and explain Tapper's failure to outbrief.

Mitchell also questioned the decision to fly all the passengers in one aircraft and suggested that this also might have some bearing on the accident. During the FAI, he had expressed *'some difficulty'* in understanding why it had been decided to fly twenty-five mixed civilian and military personnel to Inverness at low level and he had asked Squadron Leader Stangroom to help him. Stangroom had agreed that a low-level sortie was *'more risky'* than a medium-level one; Mitchell observed that it was not clear who had decided this. He reminded the Court that he had asked Stangroom: *'Is it not extraordinary that in that situation that was the decision that was taken, to fly that low-level flight with all of these passengers on board?'* Stangroom had denied that it was *'extraordinary'* and had suggested that the passengers would have been familiar with low-level flights. He had also declared that the flight had been at low level *'to maximise the training value of the crew of a flight over that distance'*. Mitchell observed that in fact it had not been a *'training flight'*.

Dealing with the weather conditions, Mitchell reminded the Court that he had, somewhat incredulously, asked Wing Commander Pulford: *'So we have a situation —correct me if I am wrong —where one has an inherently dangerous low-level sortie over unfamiliar terrain, with passengers who are exposed to the risks of that, and there is an incentive on the crew in the circumstances to fly as quickly as possible. Would you agree with all of that?'* Pulford had agreed, but with some rather incomprehensible qualifications. Mitchell was asking the Court to determine that it been a mistake to fly these passengers in the prevailing conditions.

Finally, Mitchell came to the problem of finding the cause of the accident. Discounting any fault with the aircraft, he listed four questions that needed to be answered. The first was why the crew failed to steer toward waypoint B after selecting it (he noted a suggestion that they had decided to overfly the Mull). The second was why the aircraft had been climbing at about 1,000fpm before the accident and he noted that this was inconsistent with maintaining VFR. The third arose from the final flare, which indicated, not only that the crew had control of the aircraft, but also that they were surprised by the appearance of the Mull in front of them. It raised the question of why they should have been surprised. He regarded this as the most meaningful question: *'why did they fly into cloud which essentially everybody indicates was there'*. His final question was about the speed of the aircraft: why was it flying at or about cruising speed in such poor conditions? He dismissed MacFarlane's hypothesis as unsustainable and noted that an ADR and/or CVR might have helped in explaining the accident.

Sheriff Young tackled Mitchell about Group Captain Crawford's rejection of the Board's explanation and compared it with MacFarlane's rejection. Both were certain that the crew had not selected an *'inappropriate rate of climb'*. The sheriff pointed out that, even if the Court rejected MacFarlane's hypothesis, there was still Crawford's *'alternative view'*, recorded in the Board's report. Sheriff Young was concerned and regretted that Crawford had not given evidence. Mitchell was reluctant to address the matter, suggesting that, because Crawford had not given evidence, it was not a matter before the court. He did his best to dissuade the sheriff from further interest in the matter suggesting that it was *'a dangerous track to assume that that evidence would have remained the same had it been cross-examined from other parties'* and that it was a *'trap'*. He also thought it wrong to examine any view that was highly critical of the flying of this aircraft *'because that has not been focussed and has not been made the subject of cross-examination from parties representing the crew'*.

Summing up for the Tapper relatives

The next submission was from Aidan O'Neill on behalf of the relatives of Flight Lieutenant Tapper. He had written his submission, with copies available to the sheriff and the shorthand writers, although he had not circulated copies to the other advocates. He briefly touched on the matter of Sheriff Young's concern about alternative views expressed in documents but not put into evidence. Because the Court had not heard from their authors, he agreed that the views could not be relied upon as evidence. However, he thought that they could be regarded as a source of relevant views on such evidence as had been heard.

O'Neill emphasized how much evidence was lacking and consequently how tempting it was to speculate on what happened. He was sure that this could never be known, but that substituting one missing piece for another could produce very different conclusions. He argued that, because it was not known what the missing pieces were, it was not possible to determine whether one explanation was more or less true than another. He even discounted the application of Occam's razor[92] on the grounds that, because of coincidences, the scenario it produced *'need not be true'*. It was his contention that there were too many missing pieces of evidence to allow the Court to be satisfied that the cause of the accident had been established. He drew attention to the Board's acceptance that the crew might have decided upon a suitable rate of climb to safely overfly the Mull of Kintyre but, due to any of several factors, had not executed it. He linked this to evidence that a control jam, which could have left no evidence, might have prevented the aircraft from either turning away from the Mull or executing a suitable rate of climb to avoid the high ground.[93] He pointed to the paradox that the evidence on which the Board relied for their conclusion (steady flight straight into the land mass of the Mull of Kintyre, when a turn to port was expected) was the same evidence that was seen as justifying the claim that there was a control jam. He argued that if the crew could have turned or climbed then they would have done so and claimed that there was absolutely no factual basis for accusing the crew, and in particular Flight Lieutenant Tapper, of any failure in their duty to fly the aircraft safely and with due care and attention. He pointed to Tapper's good reputation and his thorough and professional preparation for the sortie and claimed that there was no foundation for the accusation of gross negligence. He suggested that the pilots had been made *'convenient scapegoats for an Establishment seeking to avoid detailed public scrutiny into its own activities'* and called for the Court to reject the allegation of negligence. Sheriff Young was doubtful; he thought that he should leave the matter open on the grounds that the accusation of negligence was a consequence of the accident and not part of it. O'Neill disagreed but had to leave the matter with the sheriff.

He concluded by submitting that the Court should determine the facts of the deaths on the day in question due to impact of the aircraft with the land mass of the Mull of Kintyre but that there was insufficient evidence properly to determine what caused the crash. It followed that it was not possible to say what precautions might have prevented the accident or what defects in any system of working might have contributed to the accident. Like John Mitchell, he noted how the lack of an ADR and/or a CVR hampered investigations and he pointed to the continued failure of the MOD to install such devices despite previous recommendations to do so. He emphasized that, if the Court were not satisfied that the cause or causes of the accident had been established by the available evidence, then there should be no finding on this point as to the cause of the accident.

Sheriff Young intervened to secure O'Neill's agreement that, because the law required the Court to apply rules of evidence *'as near as possible to those applicable in an ordinary civil cause brought before a sheriff sitting alone'*, the standard of proof to be applied was proof upon the balance of probabilities. Sheriff Young was not aware of any other standard and declared that, if there were, he had *'gone badly wrong over the years in applying any other standard'*. Reluctantly, O'Neill had to agree.

In his desire to introduce uncertainty, O'Neill continued, somewhat tediously and repetitively (he quoted at length from the transcript of the proceedings), to list the factors which he alleged *'significantly limited'* the evidence presented. These were the lack of eyewitnesses, the limited evidence from the earwitnesses and the fact that the Court heard from only three, the loss of much of the aircraft in the fire and the lack of an ADR or CVR. He noted evidence that the latter often indicated a cause for an accident which otherwise would be blamed on the pilots. He also noted that Pulford had admitted that the Board's conclusion was *'the most probable'* one, not the definitive one and that the Board had not found the crew negligent. He submitted that the evidence before the Court was insufficient to allow the sheriff to be satisfied that the cause of the accident had been established.

Again, he was interrupted by Sheriff Young, who wanted his view on how he could reach a conclusion when he had not heard from the dead pilots due to the lack of a CVR. O'Neill was at pains to deter the sheriff from reaching a conclusion on the balance of probabilities, even though that was what the Board did and even though (contradictorily) he urged the sheriff to do the same. He claimed that the sheriff could not fill in the missing pieces and build a picture of what probably happened because, in his opinion, there were many possible causes of the accident.

Undeterred, O'Neill continued with his list of limiting factors, most of which he had already mentioned. He added comment that, although the crew's system of working appeared to be defective, there was no evidence about the speed of the aircraft prior to impact (he was conscious of allegations that the crew were in a hurry and that this contributed to the accident). He was interrupted by the sheriff to point out that the speed could be calculated (see below). O'Neill attempted to show that the crew had no reason to hurry and that the evidence of Special Forces pilots Scott and MacFarlane should be preferred to that of Squadron Leader Stangroom. He claimed that it was not feasible for the crew to have flown a 400-mile (640km) round trip in 140 minutes and that Tapper in particular would never have compromised the safety of the passengers and aircraft by attempting to do so. In his opinion, the suggestion of a breach of crew duty time was a *'red herring'* that should be disregarded. Sheriff Young wondered if this was a matter, like Group Captain Crawford's 'alternative view', which he was not entitled to consider. Strangely, O'Neill addressed what he described as the suggestion that flying at *'low-level VFR'* compromised the safety of the passengers. Confusing the two matters, he quoted Pulford in defence of the decision to fly both low level and VFR and cited the icing limitation, claiming, in justification, that Stangroom was unaware of it. Commenting on the conclusion of the Board, O'Neill pointed out that it rested on several assumptions, none of which was supported by any of the evidence presented to the FAI. Indeed, he claimed that they were inconsistent with much of the evidence, e.g. the yachtsman's report that he could see the lighthouse and the fact that the crew had instruments which could tell them their ground speed and rate of climb. He claimed that the experienced crew would have ensured that they were at safety altitude well before they approached land. In defence of the accusation that the selection of waypoint B was inconsistent with a properly planned sortie or entry into IFR, he pointed to the fact that, with a surface temperature of 9 degrees C, the crew would expect to reach the icing ceiling at 2,500ft (762m) and that Tapper in particular, because of the advice he had received from Odiham, was unlikely to break the icing clearance. This led to the alternative scenario presented by Flight Lieutenant MacFarlane, which had the advantage that it took into account the likely actions of the crew and was at least consonant with the reports of potential control jams on other Chinooks, which he reviewed. O'Neill claimed that both scenarios, that of the Board and the alternative, were consistent with the evidence heard in the FAI, but Sheriff Young challenged that. The sheriff referred to Pulford's evidence that no emergency engine power had been demanded, at least for no more than five seconds. O'Neill

77

responded that the evidence was consistent (with the alternative hypothesis) on the basis that emergency power had been supplied for a number of periods of less than five seconds.

O'Neill referred to the 'remarks' made on the Board's report by senior RAF officers, and claimed that the air marshals had misread the Board's conclusion as a *'finding of fact'*, on which they based their accusation of *'gross negligence'* against the pilots. He pointed out that this accusation was subsequently publicised by the MOD as the result of an *'exhaustive inquiry'*. He regarded this as an *'unsubstantiated speculation'*, which should be rejected by the Court. He also called for rejection of any suggestion that the crew were pressured into flying at high speed and low level, compromising the safety of the passengers. He ended by telling the sheriff that the calculated speed of the aircraft between the control zone boundary and the crash site was 150kt (276km/h) ground speed, 128kt airspeed (235.5km/h). He then left the Court and took no further part in the proceedings.

Summing up for the Cook relatives

Peter Watson summed up on behalf of the relatives of Flight Lieutenant Cook. He made it clear from the outset that his clients' interest was in clearing Cook of any blame in the accident. He was sure that Sheriff Young had to proceed on a balance of probabilities and quoted an authority[94] in support. However, he also referred to several legal authorities who indicated that the more serious the allegation, the less easy it is to say that it is established on a balance of probabilities. In other words, the weight of evidence required to tip the scales may vary with the gravity of the allegation to be proved. Although, as an example, he claimed that a party alleging fraudulent conduct will generally require to adduce weightier evidence than a party alleging negligent conduct (as in this case), he nevertheless claimed that any allegation that Cook acted in such a way by act or omission to cause the accident was a serious allegation that would require the sheriff to give great consideration to the question of the weight of evidence. He referred to an authority that regarded the latter as depending on the Court's impression not only of the credibility and reliability of each material witness, but also of the coherence of the evidence as a whole. He asked the sheriff to consider how the evidence in this case lacked *'coherence'*.

Watson referred to a number of *'special factors'* relating to the evidence and began with the Board's report. He pointed out that, while it was very helpful, because it proceeded on speculation—an approach he thought the FAI could not follow—and was not a public inquiry, it could not usurp the function of the FAI. In particular, he considered that Group Captain Crawford's view was not available as evidence; all it offered was evidence that many different views could be entertained and that there was no certain conclusion. Nevertheless, Watson took the opportunity to quote the Board's conclusion that there were no human failings with respect to Cook. He pointed out that nothing heard in evidence had undermined this conclusion. He also pointed out that Cook, like the rest of the crew, relied on one source for navigation—the captain (Tapper). Watson could not understand why any reasonable criticism could be made of Cook.

Watson then turned to the matter of expert witnesses, declaring that, if their evidence was based on speculation, it should not form the basis of any determination. He contrasted the, perhaps quite proper, speculation by the Board with the absence of speculation by the AAIB. Like O'Neill, he pointed to evidence that the use of CVRs had often cleared pilots of blame which otherwise might have been attributed to them and argued that the MOD was wrong to invite speculation about the cause when their failure to fit such equipment left so much unknown. He also argued that it was wrong to dismiss some possible causes simply because there was an absence of evidence as the result of a decision not to fit recording devices. He quoted authority for the view that inherently improbable evidence should not be rejected on that basis alone. He thought that there was nothing *'particularly wrong'* with the flight plan, although Cook's involvement was unclear. He regarded the question of whether or not the sortie began as a training flight a *'red herring'*. The matter of the flight hours was confusing and unclear; he could not tell what had been planned, but suggested that Tapper may have forgotten to take the Form 700 with him. He suggested that the sheriff could draw no conclusion on the matter. Watson then returned to the matter of navigation, emphasizing how Cook and the other crew members were unable to assess their position over the sea and that only the captain could have known the position of the aircraft. He referred to the yachtsman's evidence that the lighthouse was visible and extended that into a discussion of the weather around the Mull and whether or not the aircraft was in fog. He argued that, although the evidence was that there was dense fog around the lighthouse, it could not be assumed that this was widespread. He concluded that the aircraft had in fact approached the Mull in *'acceptable weather'*, as predicted and contemplated by Tapper in his discussion with Stangroom. In passing, he cast doubt on David Murchie's evidence by noting how he had claimed to hear the aircraft approaching for two minutes. He thought the speed of the aircraft made the latter estimate *'unlikely'*. It was also curious that Murchie had not heard a final flare of the engines. Sheriff Young intervened to express the view that, considering Murchie's location behind the lighthouse building, this was not surprising. Watson attempted to cast doubt on the flare theory by observing that the emergency power flags had not been triggered, but the sheriff reminded him that there had, apparently, not been time for that to happen. Watson alleged that this matter was something that *'is not picked up'*. He concluded that the Mull was visible to the crew at the waypoint change and that they did not inadvertently enter cloud. If they did, or there was a change of plan, it was the captain's choice and decision. He observed that only two main theories had emerged to explain the accident: the Board's *'inappropriate rate of climb'* and a technical malfunction. He regarded the former as a navigation error; if the aircraft had been in the position that the navigator thought, then the plan was *'all right'*. Sheriff Young intervened to suggest that the plan would not have been *'right'* if they had missed the ground by only 10 to 30ft. Watson pointed out that, whether it was a track error or a rate of climb error, it was a navigational matter, for which the captain was responsible. Regarding MacFarlane's scenario, he stressed that it was *'only one theory'* based on several variables, including the Boeing simulation, about which, he alleged, little was known (Sheriff Young questioned that). He thought the question of debonding (detaching) was a matter of serviceability rather than manufacture and noted that little was known of the servicing on the day in question. It led him to recommend that the sheriff find that the pre-impact serviceability of the aircraft could not be verified, contrary to the AAIB's conclusion (*sic*). In short, a control jam could not be dismissed. He urged the Court to follow the Board in concluding that it was impossible to find a definite cause for the accident and, most importantly, that Flight Lieutenant Cook played no part in it.

Summing up for the MOD

Alistair Dunlop then summed up for the MOD. From the outset, he repeated the MOD's explanation for the accident (the selection of an inappropriate rate of climb over the Mull of Kintyre, which was insufficient to secure adequate terrain clearance on the track being flown). On the matter of procedures, he agreed with John Mitchell that the annexes of the Board were not available for consideration because they had not been introduced into evidence. He also agreed that the standard of proof required was on the balance of probabilities and that this should be determined on the evidence before the Court. He rejected the sheriff's concern that he could not balance probabilities because he had not heard from the pilots. Dunlop addressed the matter of negligence raised by O'Neill and expressed surprise that the latter had done so; in his opinion, the matter was *'wholly irrelevant'* and had not been mentioned in evidence. He invited the sheriff to disregard O'Neill's comments, declaring that it was not the function of the FAI to make a finding of negligence, or even absence of negligence. He claimed that the facts established might or might not give rise to such an inference, but in another place. He himself would not be apportioning responsibility among the crew, either individually or collectively. He observed that, on the basis that no one knew what had happened on the flight deck, Peter Watson had urged the sheriff not to speculate and yet had asked him to exonerate Cook, a finding of fact based on speculation. He also criticized O'Neill for claiming that Pulford was not *'definite'* and that the Board's explanation was *'simply the most probable of a number of probable causes'*; he described this as

81

'*misrepresentation of . . . Pulford's evidence*', which was to the effect that the selection of an inappropriate rate of climb was the probable cause of the accident. He urged the sheriff to note the distinction, and that the Board had come to a definite conclusion.

Dunlop then listed what he thought should be found as facts: the serviceability and airworthiness of the aircraft, albeit subject to weight and icing limitations; the crew briefing with adequate weather data for a VFR flight; the known details of the flight plan left by Tapper; the data entered into the navigation computer and the take-off with no evident abnormalities; the normal radio communications, with no emergency calls; the low-level flight to the coast and across the sea at steady speed; the poor weather around the Mull of Kintyre; the change of waypoint and the subsequent slow climb when a steep climb was necessary and possible; the evidence of an attempt to avoid collision with the ground and the fact that impact occurred, with devastating consequences. Dunlop emphasized that, at all material times, the aircraft was airworthy and fully serviceable with no technical failures relevant to the accident and, in particular, no failures prior to impact. He observed that the primary responsibility of the crew was the safe operation of the aircraft and repeated the Board's explanation for the accident (implying that the crew made an error).

Dunlop was at pains to comment on a brief reference made by John Mitchell in his submission to suspension of the Chinook Mk2's CA Release. The suspension, he insisted, related to testing and did not undermine the CA Release then in force. He also commented on discussion in earlier submissions about speculation; there could be no dispute about some matters, although they were often complicated and best left to experts. He cited the Boeing simulation; Peter Watson had questioned it in his submission, but he had he not questioned Tony Cable about it when he had the opportunity. He urged the sheriff to proceed on the basis that the simulation was '*essentially unchallenged and undisputed*' and that it provided otherwise unavailable data on the pre-impact characteristics of the flight. It was accepted by both Tony Cable and Wing Commander Pulford and was consistent with an independent study by DRA Bedford.

Dunlop made many confusing references to the speed of the

aircraft, often apparently confusing airspeed with ground speed. He appeared to claim that the evidence indicated that, before the cyclic flare, the aircraft had been travelling at 150kt airspeed (174kt ground speed) and that the flare reduced the speed to 135kt airspeed (159kt ground speed). He alleged that the loss of another 10kt on impact was consistent with the Ground Speed and Drift Indicator reading 147kt ground speed after impact. This original speed was also corroborated by the time taken by the aircraft to cover the distance from Aldergrove to the Mull and from the ground speed of 150kt recorded in the Racal report. This speed was also corroborated by the wreckage trail and the setting of the longitudinal cyclic trim actuator. Dunlop suggested that these five separate indicators, that the airspeed was 150kt before the cyclic flare, entitled the sheriff to conclude that this was the speed at which the aircraft had been travelling. The sheriff should also note the evidence given about the flight profile, particularly that of the final few seconds.

Sheriff Young intervened to question the assumption that the aircraft was travelling at 150kt airspeed in the final fifteen to thirty seconds and how it came to accelerate (from 150kt ground speed to 174kt) over the last minute. He calculated that the average ground speed must have been 152kt (128kt airspeed if the tail wind was 24kt). Dunlop claimed that that this was *'entirely consistent with overflying the Mull'* and repeated that the speed at the waypoint change was *'in the order of 150kt'* (airspeed).

Dunlop claimed that it must have been obvious to the crew that they were flying towards steeply rising ground, although he did this by referring to photographs of the Mull. Dunlop pointed to the final cyclic flare, which emerged from the Boeing simulation, as the most important clue to what happened. It indicated that the crew only became aware of their danger in the last 2.9 seconds. In turn, this led to the commonsense conclusion (it was Pulford's conclusion) that, up until that moment, the crew had not appreciated that they were so close to the Mull. Moreover, it indicated visibility of about 350 metres, consistent with reports about the fog on the Mull (*sic*). The only other explanation for the cyclic flare was MacFarlane's, which, contrary to his claims, did not fit all the facts, nor did it present a probable scenario.

83

Dunlop reminded the Court of Pulford's evidence that, with the collective alone, power could be increased in an emergency to push the rate of climb up to 1,250fpm or more. However, there was no evidence that this had been attempted. Nor was it likely that loose articles jammed the flight controls.

At this point, Sheriff Young intervened to compare the claim that jamming of the controls was extremely unlikely to the *'proud boast of the designer of the Titanic . . . that it would not sink'*[95]. He added, *'look what happened'*. Dunlop cleverly and appropriately responded that it was perhaps an example of pilot error.

Dunlop proceeded to stress the improbability of MacFarlane's hypothesis, which he described as *'flying in the face of fact'*. It required the coincidence that the jam should occur at the waypoint change, that it occurred in two separate flight control channels simultaneously, and that they should free themselves just before impact. He reminded the Court that, while MacFarlane had initially described the Board's hypothesis as *'unlikely in the extreme'*, his own had started as *'probable'*, later changing to *'possible'* and finally to *'very unlikely'* and unheard of. In the end, MacFarlane had admitted that the Board's scenario was more probable than his. While the possibility of a control jam could not be excluded, Cable's view was that, on *'the balance of probability'*, the pallet spring had detached in the crash. In short, MacFarlane's explanation was *'very ill-thought out'* and did not stand up to any kind of scrutiny. There was also reason to believe that MacFarlane's close relationship with the Tapper family obscured his objectivity.

Dunlop returned to the matter of the cyclic flare and how it indicated that the crew had not appreciated their ground closure rate until the very last moment. Nothing in the evidence offered any satisfactory contradiction to that conclusion, which was entirely consistent with the Board's explanation. Furthermore, there was evidence that excluded alternative causes: the engines, the DECU and FADEC were all working; there was no rotor overspeed; there was no electrical failure and the AFCS was functioning. He disputed O'Neill's claim that, because it had been destroyed by fire, it was not known what was happening in No. 1 DECU; No. 2 DECU had been receiving a signal from No. 1, showing that the latter had been functioning. He suggested that the cyclic flare should be taken as a *'clearly established fact'*.

Dunlop then addressed the claim that it was inconceivable that two experienced pilots would make an error that was obvious to them. It was like someone appearing before the court on a charge of reckless driving and being defended on the grounds that the accused is a competent and experienced driver who could not have been driving recklessly. He suggested that this defence would not find much favour with the sheriff. Sheriff Young intervened to point out that the difference here is that the pilots are not able to defend themselves. Ignoring that, Dunlop questioned the approach that assumed that the pilots could not do something dangerous and referred to Pulford's acceptance that they could and his explanation for the accident. The fact of experience and competence was not sufficient justification for ignoring all the other factors in the case, to set it up as of such importance that one is prepared to disregard the irresistible inference that one can draw from these other factors. As an example that Tapper was not perfect, Dunlop singled out his miscalculation of one of the safety altitudes; it was unrealistic to put him *'on a pedestal'* or to believe that he never strayed from the rulebook or did *'everything absolutely right'*. The matter of the crew duty times, which he reviewed, demonstrated that Tapper self-authorized the flight in the knowledge that he could not get to Inverness and back within the permitted eight hours.

Dunlop reminded the sheriff of Pulford's explanation i.e. that the crew had no visual contact with the Mull and decided to abort VFR with a transit to IFR. Almost all the pilots who had given evidence agreed that, in deteriorating conditions there were three options: 1) to continue VFR, slow down and descend to retain visual contact; 2) if in IMC inadvertently, slow down, climb at maximum power (3,000fpm) to safety altitude and turn away from known obstacles; 3) if entering IMC deliberately, slow down, climb at maximum power to safety altitude and either turn away from known obstacles or satisfy oneself that one has the necessary ground clearance to remain on track. MacFarlane claimed that, at the waypoint change, the crew could see the lighthouse, or at least the Mull. However, the aircraft's speed and height were inconsistent with that view.

While Dunlop was reviewing the weather conditions and

referring to the aftercast, Sheriff Young intervened to ask how anyone knew what the conditions were like at the time on the Mull. Dunlop understandably pointed out that such a question should have been put during the FAI; the aftercast formed part of the evidence (Annexe P to the Board's report). He could not help the sheriff without giving evidence himself. Dunlop stressed that the evidence indicated, not only that the crew were engaged in an IMC abort, but also that the weather conditions permitted them to do so. This left the matter of why the crew had selected an inappropriate rate of climb. This had been dealt with by Pulford in his evidence: the crew had a mindset that the Mull was more to their starboard than it was, they were seduced by their high ground speed, and the high power required for the high speed reduced the margin needed to climb.

Sheriff Young was sceptical that the aircraft could have been travelling at a higher speed than *'they were accustomed to'* throughout the flight, believing that this would have led to them arriving *'two minutes early'*. Dunlop pointed out that all that mattered was that they had approached the Mull at this high speed (150kt airspeed) and that, because of this, the rate of climb was inappropriate.

Sheriff Young expressed difficulty in understanding how the crew could possibly think that the Mull was to their right; they had plotted a track that aimed straight for it. Dunlop declared that what mattered, was that it was the high ground that lay to their right. If they thought they were on track to overfly the light-house, they would have believed that high ground lay to the east. The sheriff was unconvinced and referred to the requirement to reach safety altitude as quickly as possible to clear the high ground. Somewhat exasperated, Dunlop tried to explain that an IFR abort was determined by the meteorological conditions, not the terrain; it could occur anywhere.

At the end of his summation, Dunlop claimed that the evidence to the FAI had *'confused many issues'* and taken them down *'many blind alleys'*. He blamed O'Neill for most of these and noted that the latter had not sought to mention them in his summation. Dunlop referred to the claim that flying at low level was a cause of the crash and the suggestion that the fact that it was carrying passengers was a factor (he dismissed both).

However, he did think that flying at low level and high speed in the prevailing conditions might be a causative factor. It was not a low-level flight; it was a VFR flight that happened to be at low level. He dismissed any suggestion that the training element was a factor.

Summing up for the remainder of the deceased

Colin Campbell's summing up on behalf of the remainder of the deceased consisted of four main points: training, duty hours, the cause of the accident, and recommendations.

Campbell reviewed all the evidence that showed that the outward flight had been planned at low level to provide the crew with low-level flying practice over unfamiliar territory, practice that they rarely obtained due to the cost involved in dedicated training flights. He thought that Mitchell had been justified in asking Stangroom somewhat incredulously whether it *'really'* was his position that *'training considerations were relevant as to the level at which this journey was to be flown'*. Campbell noted that there was no evidence that either the passengers or the Board were aware of this factor. There was also a conflict of evidence as to whether or not the Board was informed of the matter (Stangroom said they were and Pulford said they were not). Nor was the FAI in general aware of this element before Stangroom's evidence; it had come as a considerable shock to the families of the deceased. Flight Lieutenants Kingston and Trapp were not asked about it. Campbell did not suggest that the flight could not have been conducted safely at low level; he wondered whether or not the training aspect directly influenced the conduct of the crew as they approached the Mull and poor weather. Did they persist with this training when they should have followed IFR procedure? In any case, it was the decision to fly at low level which put them at low rather than medium level as they approached the Mull.

Sheriff Young intervened to suggest that it was the cloud that kept the aircraft at low level. Campbell demurred and stressed the decision to fly at low level; there was no evidence of low cloud until the Mull was reached. There was legitimate concern that passenger flights were used by the RAF to train pilots. The concern was greater in this case because of the large number of security personnel involved. If the aircraft had approached the Mull at a greater height and the planned climb had started from a higher level, the implications were clear.

Campbell then turned to the matter of duty hours. The picture which emerged was that Tapper authorized the sortie knowing that the return journey as scheduled could not be completed within the authorized flying hours for that day (eight hours), despite an understanding with Stangroom that it could. In addition, Tapper knew that Stangroom considered a further extension neither appropriate nor justified. The sheriff interrupted to point out that he had only one side of the conversation (not Tapper's) and asked if he was to 'take [it] as gospel truth'. Campbell responded by asking if there was any reason to disbelieve Stangroom. The sheriff admitted that there was not, but continued to worry that he had 'not heard the other side of the story, if there is another side'.

Campbell took the opportunity to put his view on the probable cause of the accident and comment on the approach taken by O'Neill. It had been held that there were too many missing pieces of the jigsaw to enable a view to be taken. He pointed out that, while an FAI necessarily lacks evidence from those most closely involved (because they are dead), this can never be sufficient in itself to preclude a determination on the issues. He agreed with Dunlop that the only question which arose, having regard to the evidence, was whether or not the Court was satisfied that a determination could be made 'on the balance of probability'. If the evidence pointed to a 'probable cause', the lack of evidence from the pilot or from a CVR should not prevent an approximate determination being reached. The public interest required this. A determination could be made that it was pilot error, but made in the absence of evidence from the pilots. Sheriff Young intervened to conclude that the Court (he meant himself) had to be careful about drawing a particular conclusion 'on a balance of probabilities bearing in mind the absence of all this evidence'. He stated that, in a previous case, he had found that a dead skipper (of a boat) had been drunk; nevertheless, he was cautious. Campbell disagreed and claimed that the position was no different from that of most civil cases, where a conclusion is reached *'on a balance of probabilities'*. He claimed that it was the sheriff's duty to find pilot error if that is what the evidence indicated, although he understood the desire to avoid such a conclusion. There could be no presumption against any such finding, or burden to be rebutted, or onus of proof. The absence of some evidence was not a reason for not balancing or weighing the evidence that was led. The Court could express dissatisfaction with the evidence but it could not use the absence of some evidence to disregard properly led evidence and so avoid a determination.

Campbell resumed his discussion of crew hours, repeating his assertion that the Court should accept Stangroom's account of the conversation with Tapper. He noted that Tapper had been keen to fly the sortie, that no outbriefing occurred and, that if it had, the problem with duty hours would probably have been revealed. Because Tapper had not taken the Form 700 and had not booked accommodation, it was known that he intended to return to Belfast (*sic*) that day; he had told Stangroom this. It was also known that there was a passenger booked on the return journey that day. Campbell declared that, contrary to some claims, the evidence from Scott and MacFarlane did not contradict Stangroom's. Scott had explained that a telephone call seeking an extension of duty hours was necessary where a flight had been delayed unexpectedly. In this case, Tapper had known beforehand that he would exceed his duty hours. MacFarlane's evidence was also that Tapper should have sought an extension and that he must have been distracted not to do so. Campbell saw MacFarlane as trying to put the matter in the best possible light for Tapper. Yet the lack of proper authorization must have put the crew under some pressure to complete the sortie as quickly as possible, something apparently agreed with Stangroom and accepted by Pulford. Campbell noted several hints that Special Forces crews were a law unto themselves.

Sheriff Young interrupted again to suggest that that 152kt *'over the ground'* (sic) was *'not particularly fast'*. Ignoring that, Campbell claimed that the evidence demonstrated that Tapper's conduct could not be regarded as *'careful, competent and professional'*. Campbell thought that four witnesses had offered views on the circumstances of the accident: Pulford, Scott, MacFarlane and someone he called 'Mr Noble' (he may have meant 'Cable'). He considered that Pulford and 'Noble' were better placed to offer expert independent and authoritative opinions. Scott had made little preparation and showed no detailed consideration of the relevant facts and circumstances. He wondered whether MacFarlane's friendship with Tapper and his sense of injustice influenced his thinking and led to the claim that pilot error was inconceivable.

Sheriff Young intervened again to say that he understood why he should ignore MacFarlane's evidence, but he wondered whether he should ignore the view of Group Captain Crawford, who also disagreed with the Board's conclusion and yet was not friendly with the Tapper family. Campbell objected that he was not inviting the Court to *'ignore'* MacFarlane's evidence, just to weigh its value. He also pointed out that Crawford's view was not evidence before the FAI and so could not be considered; if it were considered, then all of it should be noted, especially the last two sentences (these refer to Tapper's responsibility as captain and claimed that he had failed in his duty). Campbell commented that published views were not relevant evidence.

Campbell went on to point out that the Board reached what it regarded as the *'most probable cause'* of the accident (pilot error) after very careful consideration, scrutiny and deliberation. Furthermore, Pulford gave powerful and convincing reasons for rejecting MacFarlane's explanation; he noted that counsel for the Tapper family (O'Neill) had not sought to contradict Pulford's evidence in cross-examination. All who were asked had agreed that the minimum precaution to be expected when approaching poor weather was a reduction in speed. Campbell claimed that the most cogent piece of evidence to emerge from the Board's report and the FAI was the final manoeuvre carried out in the last three seconds before impact. It was difficult to avoid the conclusion that, at that point, the crew were mistaken about their true position. Sensitive to the fact that this conclusion was at odds with the testimonials relating to the crew, Campbell reminded the Court of what he described as *'one of the most relevant comments in the whole of the Inquiry'*, viz. a statement by Pulford in evidence that *'if experience and capability prevented accidents we would have less* [sic] *accidents'*. Campbell interpreted this to imply that even the most capable pilots make mistakes.

Campbell noted the contradiction that, although O'Neill argued that the Court could not determine the cause of the accident because much evidence was missing, this had not prevented him arguing that the Court should find that the pilots were not negligent. He thought that Watson had echoed the same contradiction. However, because the accusation of negligence came from RAF officers who had not given evidence, the Court could not reject the accusation, or even deal with it. A finding regarding negligence was a matter for another forum altogether and O'Neill was in error in introducing the comments.

As to what precautions could have prevented the accident, on the Board's explanation, the aircraft should have slowed down and/or turned away from the high ground. The accident may well have been avoided if the aircraft had flown at a higher level, at least during that part of the route.

Summing up for Boeing

Michael Jones began by commenting on the standard of proof required, warning that a reluctance to come to a conclusion because of the absence of the views of the dead crew would elevate the standard of proof above the balance of probabilities and towards *'beyond reasonable doubt'* and nearly to *'certainty'*. He reminded the sheriff that he was required to deal with the evidence to the normal civil standard. Jones also commented on the matter of crew duty hours and the authorization of an extension of those hours, a topic of recent exchanges in the Court. He pointed out that the evidence was that requests for any extension to duty hours had to be made through the chain of command. Tapper had indeed consulted Stangroom about an extension and he could not later have telephoned SRAFONI.

Jones pointed out that there had been no evidence that anything about the design or manufacture of the aircraft caused or contributed to the accident. Consequently, he dealt with matters that had to be determined by the Court, especially the cause or causes of the accident. He noted nine findings of fact, as follows: the crew planned to fly on a track of 027 degrees (magnetic) *'so as to take the aircraft just to the west of the Mull of Kintyre lighthouse, and over the sea'*; they planned to fly VFR; over the sea they had to rely on the SuperTANS for their distance from the lighthouse and their position relative to the planned track; near the Mull the weather precluded continued VFR flight; the crew elected to make an IFR climb to safety height of 2,800ft, keeping the option of regaining VFR to the north and climbing at a rate of between 550 and 1,250fpm; at that time they selected waypoint B but the aircraft was not tracking *'to the west of the lighthouse'* as had been planned, but was flying towards the impact point; at the last moment, the crew realized their position and attempted a flare; had the aircraft been on the planned track *'to a point west of the lighthouse, or even to the lighthouse itself'*, it would not have crashed; if it had flared earlier, it would not have crashed. Jones claimed that the *'undisputed cause'* of the accident was that, at least from the moment of waypoint change, the aircraft was to the right of the intended track. The flight plan, he claimed, was to fly to a point over the sea just to the west of the lighthouse.

Jones noted that Watson had described the problem as a navigational one (an error in track or rate of climb). He thought that helpful and proceeded to explain his understanding that it was a track error. He pointed to evidence that, although the lighthouse was chosen as a reference point, it had not been planned to fly over it, rather to fly west of it. He noted that the weather forecast requested covered the whole route to Inverness and back from 17:30 to 22:00 and that it showed the cloud base expected at Machrihanish to be 200ft (60m). The crew must have noted this in particular and would have known that, in that area, conditions were marginal, with a thirty per cent probability of conditions below those required for VFR flight. Pulford had stated that, below 140kt airspeed, VFR flight in a Chinook was permitted clear of land and within sight of land or sea and with a minimum cloud base of 250ft (76.2m). Above 140kt, it required a minimum cloud base of 500ft with 5km visibility, 1.5km horizontally clear of cloud and 1km vertically clear of cloud. Therefore, the crew would have been aware that VFR flight in the Mull of Kintyre area might be precluded and the indication is that they did abandon VFR as they approached the Mull. All options involved climbing first to safety height with no danger of infringing the icing limitation at that point; they could have calculated that the 4 degree isotherm lay at 2,900ft (883.9m). The evidence was that, at the point of waypoint change, the crew could not see the Mull and were unable to tell whether they were to left or right of track or how far they were from the waypoint. This was only contradicted by the variable and unreliable evidence of the yachtsman. Everyone agreed that, if the crew had been able to see the Mull and realized their position, they would have reduced speed and turned away from the land. The selection of waypoint B was consistent with the options available to them: the option to continue toward Corran in the hope of regaining VFR flight. Inaccuracies in the (navigation) system led them to believe that the Mull was to their right, not directly ahead.

Sheriff Young intervened to ask why they did not turn back after the navigation system told them that waypoint A was on a bearing of 18 degrees true and that the lighthouse was to their right (*sic*). Puzzled, Jones pointed out that his submission was that, while the crew thought they were headed towards the lighthouse, they were headed towards Beinn na Lice. The sheriff declared his intention to read the reports again.

Jones again declared that the crew must have thought that they were headed for the lighthouse, if not for a point to the west of the lighthouse as intended by Flight Lieutenant Trapp, on a track which would take them clear of land.

Sheriff Young intervened again to suggest that, even if the aircraft had flown slightly to the west of the lighthouse, it would still have flown over land slightly further on and '*run into the next hill*'. Jones denied that the evidence showed that, but left the matter hanging to continue his summation. He wanted to draw attention to the fact that, after entering IMC, there was always a transition period where the aircraft had not yet reached safety altitude. The evidence was that this transition was not only acceptable, but was being undertaken by the crew from somewhere south of the Mull. That the crew thought that the climb they selected would enable them to clear safely to the west of the Mull or overfly its western extremity was demonstrated by two facts: emergency power had not been selected and the final flare showed their sudden appreciation of their position. Jones was at pains to point out that evidence of a final flare came, not from the Boeing model, as alleged several times in the FAI, but from Cable's examination of the site and the wreckage. Based on initial parameters supplied by Cable, Boeing had been asked to model a flight in which this flare occurred. In the event, the model was able to corroborate Cable's findings.

Jones acknowledged that there were only two possible explanations for this final flare: either the crew were unaware of their true position and only realized it in the last few seconds, or they were aware of their position but were somehow unable to prevent the aircraft from flying toward Beinn na Lice. The first alternative was accepted by Pulford, a highly experienced officer who had conducted a lengthy investigation into the matter and who was the only witness to express a view on the most probable cause of the accident. His views deserved the greatest respect. While he was reluctant to accept that such a competent and experience crew could have made an error of judgement, Pulford acknowledged that crews did make mistakes and he could not avoid the conclusion that, in this case, aircrew error was the most probable explanation. This conclusion contrasted with MacFarlane's lack of objectivity, which clouded his judgement and impaired his ability to assess the evidence dispassionately. In any case, there was no evidence for any alternative to Pulford's explanation. MacFarlane had had to admit that an intermittent double control jam was *very highly unlikely* and unprecedented, that a simultaneous *double un-jam* made his theory even more improbable and that the Board's theory was more probable. MacFarlane postulated that the crew flew towards Beinn na Lice, at first able to see it but unable to climb away from it or above it because of a double control jam. They raised the collective to maximum to achieve the maximum rate of ascent, then, just 2.9 seconds before impact, the controls freed. Jones claimed that, not only was this theory inconsistent with the evidence, it was improbable and he invited the Court to find that it was negated by the evidence. Cable had found no flight control problems and the Board had specifically excluded them. Use of the Boeing simulator had found that the application of emergency power could achieve a rate of

94

climb much greater than 1,250fpm (6.35m/s), sufficient to have avoided a collision with the ground and it is known that emergency power was not applied during the cruise climb, when, according to MacFarlane, the controls were jammed. Jones claimed that there had been no evidence as to where the system had jammed, or what had jammed it, and the late flare demonstrated that, at that critical moment, the controls were responding to control inputs.

Jones pointed out that MacFarlane's hypothesis depended on the assumption that, at the point of waypoint change and travelling at 150kt airspeed, the crew could see the Mull. Yet the crew required forward visibility of 5km to continue flying VFR. If the Mull had been in view up to that point, they would surely have corrected their track to head for *'their planned turning point to the west of the lighthouse'*. That they did not do so is confirmation that they were unable to see the land ahead. Jones also pointed out that, if the aircraft had been, as the crew thought, flying towards the lighthouse, they would not have crashed; with their rate of climb, they would have cleared the lighthouse by about 400ft (122m).

That completed the FAI. Sheriff Young thanked everyone: the counsel and their assistants, the Press for not reporting the names of certain witnesses, the shorthand writers for their work, the Sheriff Clerk and her colleagues and the Court officers. He assured the families of the deceased that, despite all the detail considered, the fact that twenty-nine people had lost their lives was never far from his mind. He expressed his sympathy and respects to the families and hoped that the proceedings had been of some help to them.

Determination

After the Inquiry, the sheriff, as required by law, wrote a 'determination', a statement which must address the questions the FAI was held to answer (as listed at the beginning of this chapter). The sheriff principal[96] gave Sheriff Young leave of absence to write the determination, which he thought would take six to eight weeks. It was published in Paisley just under seven weeks later, on 21 March 1996. A sheriff's determination is not admissible in evidence and cannot be used in any subsequent judicial proceedings.

The Determination, originally available from Paisley Sheriff Court but later published by the House of Lords Select Committee (but without sidenotes), consists of fifty specific findings of fact, most of them uncontroversial (see Appendix Three), followed by ten notes. In determination 22, the sheriff concluded that the aircraft's airspeed before the final flare was 150kt (174kt ground speed). In determination 26, he concluded that, after the flare but before initial impact, the ground speed had been 150kt (in effect that the aircraft had slowed by 24kt in only three seconds). In determination 30, he listed the names of the dead and the cause of death in each case.

Note I was a brief summary of the various parties involved and the events.

Note II dealt with the legal framework: Sheriff Young claimed that a sheriff is often put in the invidious position of having to find that a deceased person was responsible, not only for his (*sic*) own death, but the deaths of others. He noted that this '*situation . . . could have arisen in the present case*', especially since the MOD's submission was that the accident resulted from pilot error. Clearly, this situation *did* arise in this case. Equally clearly, he did not wish to blame anyone or associate himself with the MOD's accusation. Instead, recognizing that it was unusual, he quoted from Colin Campbell's closing submission and his own interventions during it (see pp 87ff). Campbell's view was that the sheriff could not avoid determining the cause of the accident just because some evidence was not available, e.g. from the pilots. Sheriff Young accepted that this was the correct approach (but see below).

In Note III, he declared that he did not doubt the honesty of any of the witnesses. Nevertheless, impressed as he was by Pulford's evidence (he called him 'H'), he claimed that there were '*cogent reasons*' for believing that his evidence '*should not be accepted*'. On the other hand, he saw no reason to doubt the evidence of Flight Lieutenant Scott ('J') and was '*favourably*

96

impressed' by Flight Lieutenant MacFarlane ('K'), on some of whose evidence he did not hesitate to rely. At this point, he made it clear that he had tried to *'illustrate'* his reasons for rejecting the Board's conclusion. His reasons followed in subsequent Notes, where, unfortunately, instead of paraphrasing the evidence of witnesses, he let them *'speak for themselves'* by quoting from the record.

In Note IV (1), after quoting at length all the praise that had been heaped on Tapper, the sheriff commented on the evidence that he was not a *'paragon of virtue'* and cited the failure to raise a maintenance work order, the error in calculating one of the safety altitudes, and a possible breach of the visibility requirements for VFR flight in excess of 140kt on the first leg. The sheriff accepted the view that either these were trivial breaches or that it was unclear whether or not they were breaches at all. However, he devoted more space to discussion of the matter of Tapper's failure to obtain authorization either for an extension of crew time or to keep the aircraft in Scotland overnight. There was also the matter of whether or not the crew felt under pressure to complete the sortie as quickly as possible. It had been suggested that Tapper's conduct in this regard could not be categorized as *'careful, competent and professional'*. The sheriff concluded that Tapper could not have thought that he could complete the sortie to and back from Inverness in the two hours twenty minutes left of the eight hours permitted by Wing Commander Stangroom ('G'). He noted Stangroom's evidence that authorization to keep the aircraft in Scotland overnight was *'required* before departure [from SRAFONI]' (his italics). However, the sheriff thought Stangroom mistaken on this matter and relied instead on Pulford's evidence, that permission was required, not from SRAFONI but from JATOC. He appeared to exonerate Tapper by concluding that there were circumstances in which it would have been permissible to seek authorization for an extension of flying hours or for an aircraft to be kept out of Northern Ireland after a sortie had been commenced. Commenting on Stangroom's evidence that the latter would have felt a *'loss of trust'* in Tapper if he had called from Inverness asking for authority to keep the aircraft out of Northern Ireland and that Tapper would have faced disciplinary action, the sheriff preferred the evidence of

Scott and MacFarlane that this was nothing remarkable. He again appeared to exonerate Tapper by accepting MacFarlane's evidence that Tapper would have been very busy before the sortie and did not have time to meet Stangroom. Although he could not say what Tapper intended to do about the time limit, he did conclude that Tapper intended to return to Northern Ireland that evening. On the question of time pressure, he concluded that there was no evidence that the aircraft had been flown at excessive speed and that, even if it had been, this did not contribute to the accident.

In Note IV (2), the sheriff turned to the matter of the crew's working relationship, making it clear that he apportioned no blame to either MALM Forbes or Flight Sergeant Hardie. He then quoted extensively from the evidence of several RAF officers that the whole Special Forces crew worked very closely together as one unit. One could have concluded from this that if any one of the crew was to blame, then the whole crew was to blame (the MOD blamed only the pilots). However, he drew no conclusion.

Note IV (3) concerned the procedure to be adopted on entering IMC. He noted that it had been established that the pilots had trained for and practised aborts from low level in IMC. There was also evidence that, faced with cloud ahead, the crew had several options. However, having entered IMC, they needed to undertake a cyclic climb to safety altitude and turn away from any known obstruction. There was also evidence that a planned entry to IMC could lead to a slower climb over *several miles* and that this was *not inappropriate*. However, the sheriff noted that there was no evidence that such a climb was appropriate in the circumstances of this accident. Again, he reached no conclusion.

Note IV (4) dealt with preparation for the sortie, which the sheriff summarized without comment or conclusion.

Note V is headed 'THE FINAL FLIGHT OF ZD576' and consists of a summary of the known events, with some extracts from the FAI evidence. The sheriff commented in particular on the conflict in the yachtsman's evidence regarding whether or not he could see the lighthouse.[97] He declared that his evidence to the FAI should be preferred, albeit that Holbrook was referring to visibility at sea level. On the question of Holbrook's estimate of the aircraft's speed (60–80kt), he noted that this was about half the generally accepted speed. He was not convinced that Holbrook had made a mistake, but allowed that, if he had not, this raised the question of why the aircraft should have accelerated later. Holbrook was certainly mistaken about the wind speed and might also have mistaken the helicopter's speed. In the end, he decided that it was unnecessary to reach a conclusion.

Sheriff Young expressed great surprise at the claim by Murchie (the lighthouse keeper) that he had heard the aircraft approaching for two and a half minutes. He calculated that the aircraft would have travelled more than five nautical miles (9.2km) in that time.[98] He then alleged that the wind, blowing from 170 degrees (just east of south) at 30kt (15.3m/s), would have tended to carry the sound to the NNW, away from Murchie.[99] He concluded that only if the aircraft were travelling at the slower speed estimated by Holbrook did it come within Murchie's range of hearing. But then, it was 'odd' that Murchie did not hear the aircraft accelerate to the final impact speed. He also wondered why Murchie did not hear the sound of the final flare. While all this led him to doubt the reliability of Murchie's evidence, he thought it unnecessary to reach a conclusion 'on these matters'. Nevertheless, he questioned Murchie's evidence once more in the face of Ellacott's evidence that he had not heard the aircraft approach.

In Note VI, the sheriff dealt with the AAIB investigation and the Racal report, recording agreed data.

In Note VII, Sheriff Young discussed the cause of the accident. Referring to his earlier rejection of the Board's explanation, for reasons which he hoped would become apparent, he emphasized that it had not been established to his satisfaction that Wing Commander Pulford's opinion on the matter was well founded. In support, he rehearsed the relevant parts of Pulford's evidence, firstly the evidence on the route and the rate of climb chosen. Pulford had been referred to a map of the area showing various crucial positions and tracks. This showed, not just the assumed actual track of the aircraft, but also the track that the crew might have thought they were following (it led straight to the lighthouse). These tracks originate from the position where it was thought the leg transfer had been made, 'K' in the case of the actual track and 'L' in the case of the track the crew might have assumed. Sheriff Young declared that, in the course of his determination, it appeared to him that point 'L' had been wrongly located. He thought it should have been rather closer to the lighthouse and Rubha na Lice ('Point of the Ledge') at a point he labelled 'R' (see sketch map on p. 189) and he referred to a note he had issued a month earlier.

On 17 February 1996, Sheriff Young had issued a note about what he believed to be an error on the Board's Annexe AQ (the track and position map). The Racal report had noted that the SuperTANS had recorded the change to waypoint B at a position ('J') 0.85nm[100] (1.56km) from waypoint A, with the latter on a bearing from the aircraft of 018 degrees. On the basis that the crew thought they were actually headed for the lighthouse, the Annexe also showed a track to the lighthouse from a corresponding point marked 'L', the point the crew may have thought they were at when they made the waypoint transfer. Yet, Annexe AQ showed 'L' at a position where the track to the lighthouse was 022 degrees (the track which the aircraft took after the waypoint transfer). The sheriff suggested that the crew *'must have assumed that they were 0.81* [sic] *nautical miles from the true position of the lighthouse on a bearing of 018T'* and that, if a line were drawn south from the lighthouse on a bearing of 198 degrees (reciprocal of 018 degrees) a new point is reached, which he labelled 'R'. He could also have pointed out that the Annexe did not show a connection between 'J' and waypoint A, something the sheriff corrected on his version of the map. Sheriff Young then suggested that the track assumed by the crew would have corresponded to a line drawn through 'R' parallel to the track 'K-A' (the assumed track of the aircraft to the initial impact point on a track of 022 degrees). He noted that, if he were correct, then the extent to which the aircraft was further 'west' (he meant 'east') than the crew believed was reduced by about 120 metres. He was reluctant to place any reliance on what might be of only marginal significance without giving all the parties to the FAI the opportunity to comment on his calculations. He was also reluctant to reconvene the FAI simply for that purpose. Instead, he sent the note to all the parties and asked them to respond by 23 February 1996.

While the representatives of the remainder of the deceased were neutral on the matter, the Crown, the MOD and those representing the Tapper and Cook families all accepted the sheriff's correction. The sheriff described the response he received from the representatives for Boeing as *'not entirely clear'*, but ending with the observation that, if more was to be said about the implications of the proposed correction, then it appeared necessary to reconvene the FAI *'to lead evidence on the issue'*. Failing to see what further evidence could be led, because the data on which he was able to make the correction had been led in the FAI and because he was reluctant to reconvene the FAI, the sheriff decided to leave the issue *'to one side'* on the basis that it would make *'next to no difference'* to his eventual decision. He observed that, wherever 'L' should have been, the crew must have known that the aircraft was heading on a track that would take it to the southeast of the lighthouse. The SuperTANS would have shown the crew that they were to the right of the planned track to waypoint A.

Reviewing the evidence given by Wing Commander Pulford about the cause of the accident, the sheriff concluded that five questions needed to be answered (his italics):

(i)   *'Were the weather conditions encountered by ZD576 at the Mull of Kintyre such as to persuade the crew that they could no longer fly along their planned track to Corran at low level under VFR conditions?'* On balance, he thought not.

(ii)   *'On reaching the Mull of Kintyre would the crew have been satisfied in light of the aircraft's icing clearance that an ascent to the required safety altitude of 2,800 feet was feasible?'* The sheriff noted that, although the weather forecast had given a surface temperature of 12 degrees C, suggesting that the aircraft's ceiling due to the icing limitation would be around 4,000ft, the aftercast showed a surface temperature of only 9 degrees C, giving a ceiling of 2,500ft. He concluded that the crew would have had to act on the temperature they discovered en route and so take the latter limit, which was below the safety altitude for the first leg of the route. He then failed to answer his own question by noting that the climb indicated that the crew had decided that they could climb to safety altitude,

101

while at the same time he thought it reasonable to conclude that the crew would not have thought it feasible.

(iii) *'Is it likely that the crew would have had the mindset attributed to them by H [Pulford] to the effect that the Mull of Kintyre was to their right and not directly in front of them and hence to underestimate the imminence of their landfall?'* Considering all the information available to the crew and the fact they knew that they were approaching the Mull, he thought not.

(iv) *'Is it likely that the crew would have considered it appropriate to overfly the Mull of Kintyre at cruising speed?'* He noted evidence that this may have been planned and that it was feasible. However, he was sure that, had Tapper proposed it, the rest of the crew would have pointed out 'the obvious dangers'. In effect, he did not answer this question.

(v) *'On the assumption that the crew did decide to climb at cruising speed over the Mull of Kintyre how likely is it that they would have selected an inappropriate rate of climb to do so?'* He thought this 'very unlikely' and he could not accept the Board's conclusion about the cause of the accident. He also concluded that, although the crew may not have been able to see any part of the lighthouse buildings, they probably did see the coastline below it. He concluded that he did not know the cause of the accident. In answering this question, the sheriff drew the surprising conclusion that Tapper had altered his course (track) selector to indicate the new track to Corran (028 degrees[101]). Surprising, because there had been no evidence to this effect.

In Note VIII, the sheriff discussed training. He discounted Tapper's decision to practise low-level flight as a causative factor in the accident and declined to criticize him or Stangroom on that account.

In Note IX, the sheriff commented on the lack of both a CVR and an ADR and, in Note X, on miscellaneous matters. He did not think it appropriate to comment on the installation of a ground proximity warning radar system in RAF Chinook helicopters. He declined to reject the RAF's findings of negligence on the part of one or both pilots because it was not the FAI's function to make findings of negligence (or the absence of negligence) or to impute personal responsibility to any one or more individuals.[102] He explained why he had not appointed an assessor to assist him with the technical matters involved and commented on the fact that it was only on the ninth day that the normal operation of a helicopter was explained to the Court. Clearly, he felt that such evidence should have been introduced earlier, before evidence of the damage to the helicopter was led. He had also wanted clearer photographs of a complete Chinook Mk2 and its layout. He ended by noting how useful it had been to inspect a Chinook and fly in it around Glasgow Airport, regretting that bad weather had prevented him being flown to the site of the accident[103], or a similar site. He thanked the captain and crew of that aircraft.

Chapter Six

The *Computer Weekly* Investigation

In May 1999, the magazine *Computer Weekly* (CW) entered the debate by claiming that MPs had been misled over the significance of the role safety-critical software could have played in the accident. It claimed that it could prove that the Government's decision to blame the crash on pilot error was based on inconclusive evidence. It claimed that its *'three-month investigation'* showed how problems with the safety-critical software that controlled the helicopter's engines offered an alternative explanation for the cause of the accident. It also claimed that Dr John Reid, then the Minister for the Armed Forces, had made a 'series of misleading and inaccurate statements' to the previous year's special Defence Committee hearing (see Chapter Seven). Dr Reid had been asked about previous FADEC-related incidents and to detail the most serious FADEC failures that had occurred. Reid replied that, prior to this accident, five failure incidents had been reported, none of them relating to the software; they were all *'relatively trivial'*. CW claimed that Reid did not tell the Committee that a design flaw in the FADEC system had precipitated the near destruction of a Chinook in 1989 and that, at the time of the 1994 accident, the MOD was suing FADEC's contractor, Textron Lycoming (TL), largely on the basis of a design fault in the system (it also sued Boeing, who conducted the test). It seems that this was not known to the AAIB during their investigation of the accident. Reid had explained that the legal action against Boeing and TL was in respect of their testing procedures, not against the software itself. However, CW claimed that the case related mainly to flaws in the software design, that FADEC was not *'airworthy'*, that it failed to accommodate loss of inputs, that it failed under unexpected circumstances, that the software design was not *'adequately verified or documented'* and that it was *'defective'*. CW also claimed that the MOD had wrongly told the Committee that Boeing did not consider FADEC safety-critical. The MOD did not believe that it had misled the Committee.

Apart from claiming that a gross injustice had been done to the pilots and their families, CW questioned the regime under which safety-critical software is developed and suggested that we are all vulnerable to defects in the systems. It called on the Government to open a new investigation into the crash, not just to *'right the terrible wrong done to the pilots and their families'*, but to see if there are lessons to be learned from these particular software problems which could help prevent future software-related tragedies. CW published its 140-page report on the Internet and in print.[104] The investigation was mainly the work of CW's reporter Tony Collins.

CW noted that, in 1994, as a result of so many Mk1s being in workshops for modification, availability fell to 40.6 per cent (usually 68 per cent). This was why the RAF could not meet Tapper's request for a Mk1 to be on standby. In addition, his CO thought that agreeing to it would allow too many Chinooks to be in Northern Ireland.

In its account of what happened at RAF Aldergrove, CW drew on the experiences of Squadron Leader Prowse.[105] He took three pilots, including Tapper, for twenty-minute flights around Aldergrove to familiarize them with the Mk2. Prowse felt that Tapper was content with his abilities, but that he was not inclined to believe compliments on them. Prowse himself was content with Tapper's ability to operate the Mk2 and particularly noted that Tapper was familiar with the Flight Reference Cards.

FADEC

CW's report dealt at length with FADEC (Full Authority Digital Engine Control); the doomed helicopter was one of several Mk1 Chinooks that had been upgraded by Boeing to a Mk2, and among the upgrades was the installation of a complex and

105

innovative computer system to control the engines. This would sense the power needed by each engine and supply exactly the right amount of fuel to achieve it. The alleged advantages were greater reliability and economy with less maintenance—overall a cost saving to the MOD.

CW described the development and operation of FADEC. It consists of two main parts. One is the Digital Electronic Control Unit (DECU) for each engine; this is a computer which monitors electronic signals that indicate things like engine and rotor speed. It also receives electronic commands from the pilot and converts them into data that are transmitted to control the flow of fuel to the engines. The DECU also controls ignition and displays faults and information relating to the performance of the engine and FADEC itself. The second part of FADEC is a hydro-mechanical unit that receives signals from the DECU and, in response, pumps the correct amount of fuel to the engines. CW admitted that automatic control of the engines is desirable, making them more efficient and saving the pilot from actively monitoring their performance and making frequent adjustments to maintain optimum performance. It also reduces wear and tear on the engines and components, reduces maintenance costs, increases reliability and engine life, smoothes engine performance and fuel flow and reduces fuel consumption. In short, FADEC automatically ensures that the engines provide the power to meet the pilots' varying requirements. Such engine control systems have been used widely on military aircraft since the 1970s and entered general service in commercial aircraft from the early 1980s.

CW noted how, originally, the digital lane of FADEC was designed to have an analogue (mechanical) back-up. However, during development, this was changed to digital lanes in both primary and back-up mode. Development since then has seen a return to a mechanical back-up. CW was critical of the award of the contract to TL without either competition or public announcement and of the complicated relationship between the various contractors involved. It was also concerned about the lack of input from the RAF.

CW noted some problems that resulted; spurious warning signs (ENG FAIL) which nevertheless required the pilots to check that the engines had not failed. One of the engines on ZD576 was replaced six weeks before the crash because of a faulty torque meter. It seems that these problems gave the Chinook pilots some concern and CW made much of the fact that the AAIB was told neither about the law suit against TL nor about severe damage caused to a Chinook in 1989 by a FADEC fault. It also implied that there was something suspicious about asking TL to help in the investigation. CW also criticized the Boeing simulation; it claimed that it took no account of the speed of the engines or the rotors, or of the unusual position of the pilot's foot pedals, used to control yaw. While admitting that this could have been a result of the crash, it suggested that it could have been an attempt by Cook 'to save an aircraft in which the flying controls were not responding'.

CW challenged the claim by Dr Reid to the HOC Defence Committee that if one DECU was functioning normally, then so was the other. CW claimed that, while the two DECUs shared some information, they operated largely independently, one controlling each engine. It also challenged the MOD's claim that the evidence from the SuperTANS was that the 'aircraft kit was functioning properly'. The SuperTANS, it pointed out, did not monitor the engines. CW also observed that the RAF's version of FADEC was not the same as that installed in the US Army's Chinooks[106] and that the Assistant Director Helicopter Projects had questioned the validity of comparing tests that had been carried out on the US's FADEC-equipped engines with tests on the RAF ones. It alleged that the aircraft's assessor at A&AEE had expressed concern. It noted that, the day before the crash, the airworthiness assessors had suspended trial flights on the newly modified Chinook because they had not received satisfactory explanations from Boeing over a number of unexplained incidents, mostly involving FADEC. Trials pilots actually refused to fly a Mk2 from A&AEE's base at Boscombe Down to RAF Odiham. This suspension did not apply to operational pilots like Tapper and Cook. Only after modifications did trial flights resume in November 1994.

CW devoted considerable space to the problem of an un-controlled engine overspeed. It pointed out that, unlike cars, helicopters have no manual accelerator and that engine speed is largely an automatic process, whether or not FADEC is fitted. A

107

helicopter's rotors should revolve at the same speed no matter what the pilot is asking the aircraft to do. In a Chinook, this revolution speed is about 225rpm (3.75Hz), and is described as 100 per cent rotor speed. To accelerate or climb, the pilot would normally put the nose down and/or raise the pitch of the rotor blades via the collective lever. The fuel system should then automatically detect a deceleration of the rotors because of the demand for additional lift and instruct the engine to deliver the power required to keep the rotors turning at 100 per cent speed.

CW reported a case where a US Army Chinook, not fitted with FADEC and which had just taken off, suffered an overspeed up to 120 per cent, despite efforts by the pilot to bring it down. Eventually he had to shut down the engines and managed to land safely. No cause for the malfunction was found. CW observed that, because well written software is more reliable than hydro-mechanical units, FADEC should reduce or eliminate such overspeeds. Nevertheless, it also observed that, when things go wrong, the cause can be harder to find. It also described the problem of designing the software to cater for overspeeds while at the same time ensuring that the engines did not run down automatically. It claimed that there was a fundamental flaw in the software that could lead to the destruction of a Mk2 Chinook. On 20 January 1989, during a full ground test of an RAF Chinook fitted with FADEC, a rotor overspeed caused millions of pounds' worth of damage. This was at Boeing's Flight Test facility at Wilmington, Delaware, USA, and was the cause of the MOD's legal claims.

CW discussed the appearance of various fault codes in FADEC. Testing had thrown up several fault codes, resulting in the correction of the faults responsible. These codes were B2, indicating a possible failure of the backup reversionary mode; F3, indicating that a DECU had sensed differences in the sensor signals that registered the speed of the gas generators; and E5 (see discussion below). It claimed that three fault codes, A7 (*sic*), F3 and E5 were found recorded in one of the DECUs recovered from the wreckage of ZD576. CW was critical of a Government assurance that FADEC was not '*safety-critical*' because the aircraft could fly on one engine if necessary and that, even in the unlikely event of a double engine failure it could '*glide down to the ground in a controlled manner'*. CW claimed that, in 1987, Chandler Evans had described FADEC as a *'safety-critical system'*, pointing in particular to the danger of an *'unlimited runaway up* [overspeed] *or down* [run down] *condition'*, estimating the possibility as 1 in 10,000 million per flying hour, i.e. *'extremely remote'*. The January 1989 accident appeared to show that it was not *'extremely remote'*.

An E5 fault code indicated that a DECU had detected a difference of more than 5 per cent between two independent sensors telling FADEC the rotation speed of the engine to which the DECU was connected. This speed was coded as 'N2'. E5 also indicated that the DECU had ignored the signal from the sensor showing the lower speed and was reading only the higher signal. Unfortunately, the designers had overlooked the possibility that a DECU could lose the signal from *both* sensors. In that case, FADEC would assume that the engine had no engine speed and needed more fuel. The engine speed would continually increase. Apparently, this is what happened in the 1989 accident when a fail-safe cut-out also failed to operate. One sensor was deliberately disconnected (to simulate a failure) when, unknown to the operators, the other sensor was not being read. At least one engine raced away to such an extent that the aircraft attempted to take off. The pilot eventually stopped the overspeed by cutting the fuel supply when the rotors had reached 142 per cent normal speed. The stresses imposed on components and equipment were so severe that the aircraft had to be rebuilt and it was the cost of this rebuild that led to the suit against TL. Eventually the MOD received $500,000 compensation from Boeing and $3 million from TL.

CW pointed out that, during the overspeed, the torque meter for one engine had read about 70 per cent (a clear indication of a runaway), while the other had read zero. This, they claimed, was also the case in the Mull of Kintyre accident, although the AAIB had been unable to test the functioning of the torque meters and attributed the mismatch to the impact. CW was concerned that the investigators were not told of the 1989 accident or the significance of the E5 fault code. Because of the 1989 accident, FADEC was modified so that, if an E5 code indicated that one of the N2 sensors was latched out and the other sensor was for some reason lost, then FADEC would re-aquire the original sensor's signal. The MOD also required that, in the event of a serious failure, the system would freeze the fuel controls at a safe, constant level rather than allow an engine runaway.

CW was critical of the expert evidence about FADEC given to the FAI, describing Cable as *'not a helicopter specialist'* and as someone who did not have an *'exhaustive knowledge'* of FADEC. It also noted that he had declared ignorance of the meaning of the E5 code. CW declared that 'the most able FADEC adviser' would have been Malcolm Perks, formerly Head of Technology at Rolls Royce Aerospace Group and later Head of Engineering for Control Systems during the development of a FADEC system for large-engine aircraft such as the Airbus A330 and Boeing 777. At the time of the FAI, Perks was acting as the MOD's chosen FADEC expert in its case against TL. CW was concerned that Perks had not been asked to help the AAIB, not consulted by the Board nor called to give evidence to the FAI. Indeed, CW claimed that his very existence was not known to Sheriff Young, nor to the families of the pilots. CW also claimed that Robert Burke, a former squadron leader and the senior RAF Odiham test pilot, who was very knowledgeable about the DECUs and who had experienced two engine runaways on FADEC-equipped Chinooks, was ordered not to participate in *'the inquiry'* (Board). CW asked why the MOD was *'apparently going out of its way to reduce the odds against discovery of information about the real problems with FADEC'*. Apparently ignoring the modification described above, it claimed that the 1989 accident demonstrated that a faulty design of FADEC could endanger the aircraft and its occupants and that, prior to the 1994 crash, Chinooks were still prone to overspeeds and *'FADEC-related'* incidents. It suggested that details of the 1989 accident were kept from the investigators and the FAI so as to prevent people asking why the cream of Northern Ireland's intelligence community and a Special Forces aircrew lost their lives in a newly-modernized helicopter that was *'not demonstrably safe'* and that *'perhaps* [it] *should not have been allowed to fly at the time'*.

Because of uncertainty about the reliability of FADEC, the A&AEE studied it in detail and commissioned an independent report from EDS-Scicon, one of the world's largest military IT companies. A&AEE decided that the software should be rewritten in a verifiable form prior to recommending a CA Release.[107] However, the Chinook project director also considered that a Release could be issued subject to a temporary weight restriction. This was a precaution against the failure of one engine due to a FADEC malfunction; the restriction would mean that the aircraft was light enough to continue to fly on one engine. Permission was therefore given for the new FADEC-equipped Chinook (Mk2) to enter operational service in November 1993, but with the weight restriction mentioned in Chapter Two.

CW reported Burke's view of FADEC after test flying in December 1993. It seems that a large number of DECU faults were due to electrical power interrupts. At one point, these became so bad that the operational squadrons developed their own procedures to get around them. On several occasions, there was a problem with the Engine Control Levers: FADEC disabled them. Other problems included engines exceeding their normal temperature range and numerous cases of torque mismatches. So many DECUs were returned to TL for fault investigation that, at one time, aircraft were grounded for lack of DECUs. Burke also experienced rotor overspeeds, although not in the UK.[108] Burke explained that the effect of an overspeed when flying at low level is that the helicopter climbs, possibly entering cloud inadvertently. To slow the rotors, he would raise the collective, and, on one occasion, had it so high that it was *under my armpit*. CW wondered if this explained the crash of ZD576, *unexpectedly and inexplicably* flying into cloud. Was this the reason for the collective being found raised so high, or was it because the pilot was pulling up the nose to avoid a crash? CW claimed that some RAF pilots, including Cook, were increasingly anxious about the problems with the Mk2.

CW noted that an RAF database listed many faults with the Mk1s, mainly spurious *engine fail* signals. It also listed some faults with ZD576. On 21 April 1994, during a transition to hover, it seemed to have a torque mismatch of 40 per cent, although no engine warnings illuminated and it was not possible to determine which engine had been at fault. Nevertheless, one engine was replaced and the diagnosis was that there was a faulty torque meter. A check of the DECUs showed no fault codes. Five days later, it was reported that, with the Engine Control Levers in the flight idle position, there were no torque indications to either engine and No. 1 engine was *'running high'*. Two weeks later, on 10 May, a large spring became detached from the collective lever after bonding failed. This did not make the collective inoperable, just heavier. The assembly was replaced, but CW was concerned that the loose spring could have jammed the controls. CW went on to suggest that, because the AAIB could not exclude the possibility of a control system jam, the problem might have recurred on the last flight. They speculated that a control jam while the pilot was dealing with (say) a torque mismatch, temporary overspeed or an emergency signal, could have been sufficiently distracting to cause a fatal accident.

A week after the spring came loose, a pilot flying ZD576 noticed an engine power warning come on three times. In addition, the engine temperature rose above normal. Consequently, part of FADEC (a DECU?) was sent to the US for investigation and the engine was removed and rebuilt.[109] On 26 May, a week before the crash, various warnings appeared in the cockpit, including a *'master'* caption and No. 2 engine fail signal (for ten seconds). Because of these incidents, the aircraft was diverted to Luton Airport.

Because CW was convinced that there were faults in FADEC, it seized on any misinterpretation of the evidence relating to it. It noted how Air Chief Marshal Sir William Wratten, in a letter to *Aerospace International*[110], had stated that (at the time of the crash) the engines had been at *'high power settings'*. This was apparently consistent with the idea that the pilots had, in the last few seconds, attempted to climb at high power (CW wrongly thought that this derived from the Boeing simulation). However, CW pointed out that the AAIB had in fact found that both engines had been 'at similar ***intermediate*** power levels' (their bold italic). Furthermore, according to CW, the Boeing simulation indicated that the rotors were *under*speeding at 91 per cent (presumably before the crash). CW also thought that, with the collective lever at maximum, the engines should have been delivering high or maximum power. CW quoted Perks's opinion that, even if the engines had been running correctly, this did not mean that there was nothing wrong with FADEC. CW pointed out that Cable had

112

admitted that he did not have a full understanding of FADEC and did not know of the problems reported by the pilots in the weeks before the crash. It implied that this information was deliberately withheld from him and that its absence hindered his investigation. CW also implied that it was improper for the engine and DECU manufacturers to examine and report on the condition of their own equipment (they noted O'Neill's questions on this in the FAI).

CW was excited by the admission by Cable (in the FAI) that he did not know the significance of various DECU fault codes and quoted many statements he made about his ignorance. It questioned whether an aircraft newly fitted with *'safety-critical computer systems'* that had shown abnormalities should have been allowed to fly. It even wondered whether Cable's ignorance explained why the Boeing simulation was based on the assumption that the aircraft was fully under control.

CW noted that an E5 fault code was found in the surviving (No. 2) DECU from ZD576 and appeared to suggest (their text is unclear) that this, combined with the loss of the signal from the other DECU, could have resulted in an uncontrolled rotor over-speed (this is inconsistent with their concern elsewhere to show that the engines were not at maximum power at the time of the crash).

Accidents to RAF Chinooks

CW noted that Dr Reid had declared that, although Chinooks were in use by several countries, there had been only one accident prior to that on the Mull, and that was to a Mk1. It also noted that, shortly afterwards, the MOD had had to issue a correction: between 1984 and 1994, there had been nine serious accidents in the UK.[111] In five of them, the pilots had survived and were exonerated. Of the four remaining (fatal) accidents, three were attributed to pilot error and the fourth was 'not positively determined'. This last was in the Falklands, where there was evidence of a technical malfunction. The nose had dipped slightly, after which the aircraft fell to the ground nose first. The last words of the pilots were unintelligible. Subsequent

113

investigation found that there had been a failure of the cyclic trim actuator, but this was not thought to be serious enough to cause an accident on its own. However, a second problem was discovered in the Upper Boost Actuator; if the pilot had applied a rapid control input in response to an unidentified nose-down pitch, it was possible for the actuator to jam. This, together with failure of the cyclic trim actuator, could have produced the fatal trajectory. The subsequent RAF inquiry did not find against the manufacturer, maintenance specialists or any subcontractors, but also it could not completely discount a number of other causes, including crew incapacitation or psychological problems. CW claimed that, during their training, Chinook crews were given two different explanations. The official version was that of the RAF inquiry (as above); the unofficial version was that it was due to a technical malfunction and crews were given advice on how they should react to such an emergency in future.

Accidents to US Army Chinooks

CW noted that, of 460 Chinooks in use by the US Army, Army Reserves and National Guard, only twenty-five were fitted with FADEC, none exactly the same as the RAF's FADEC. It also noted that, between 1994 and 1998, there were 116 serious accidents involving US Chinooks. Some were fatal and one, in March 1996, details of which CW could not obtain, involved a FADEC-equipped Chinook. A US Army newsletter published in 1998 reported that the pilots of a Chinook were initially held responsible for its crash after it had passed from VMC to IMC. It had passed through its assigned heading when radar contact was lost. Subsequently, investigators found that seven Chinooks had experienced varying degrees of electrical power failure that could have affected all primary and stand-by instruments and the AFCS. Investigation concluded that the crew were making a turn when they had lost at least the primary flight instruments and the AFCS. Consequently, although the investigators could not say for certain what had caused the crash, the pilots were cleared. In April 1999, the US Army Safety Center in Alabama reported on a succession of *uncommanded manoeuvres or flight-control lockup in flight'* that had affected Chinooks. It noted that, at that time, computer simulation was not sophisticated enough to produce the exact manoeuvres of the aircraft concerned and so no absolute cause-and-effect relationship had been established.

CW related the experience of US pilot Bric Lewis when flying a Chinook three years after the crash.[112] They were at 1,100 to 1,500ft (335–457m) in cold but clear weather, flying at 130–135kt (239–248kph). Trying to correct a slight nose-down pitch, Lewis pulled back on the cyclic, one of the main controls between his knees. At about the same time, the helicopter started to yaw, which he attempted to correct with the pedals. Nevertheless, the yaw continued, making the aircraft uncontrollable. By the time co-pilot Pat Nield took the controls, the aircraft was on its side and the cyclic seemed to be stuck. Then the nose pitched up, but continued until the aircraft was on its back! Now falling toward the ground, the pilots struggled with the cyclic, which suddenly came free, but loose and ineffective. Fortunately, the right pedal and the cyclic began to respond and the aircraft flipped back the right way up, but now only 250ft (76.2m) above the ground. Moreover, the rotors were in overspeed and in danger of flying off. However, this gave the helicopter immediate lift, slowing its descent. Then it started to yaw again and the nose began to lift without command. Desperate to land before the aircraft inverted again, the pilots tried to use the collective (thrust lever), but it would not move. By now they were so near to the ground, fortunately flat, that they could use the cyclic to get the rear wheels on the ground and the helicopter stopped. The collective freed itself and was working correctly and only a pedal was stuck. As the engines ran down, there were three loud bangs as the rotor blades struck the fuselage and they feared for their lives again. Eventually the engines stopped and all went quiet.[113] CW did not report that the cause of this accident was never determined. There was certainly no evidence that a FADEC was involved. However, CW's point was that, if this Chinook had crashed there would have been no evidence of malfunction and the pilots would have been blamed. Consequently, because no evidence of malfunction was found in the Mull of Kintyre crash, it should not be assumed that nothing went wrong or that the pilots were responsible.

Dead pilots tell no tales

Admitting that pilots are the cause of most major (*sic*) crashes, CW pointed out that, while the manufacturers of the aircraft and its components, the certification authorities, the air traffic control centres and meteorologists can all defend themselves, dead pilots cannot. It claimed that some authorities might find it difficult to begin a fatal accident inquiry without a preconception that the likely outcome will implicitly impugn the competence and professional reputation of the pilots. Less than a day after the accident, Prime Minister John Major commented that it looked as if it was *'a straightforward accident in appalling weather'* (implying that it was caused by the weather). CW claimed that (unidentified) specialists *'can see that it is sometimes the pilots who are blamed because the alternative of an ambiguous conclusion is less attractive'*. Ambiguity might suggest or even point a finger at politically sensitive contributory factors such as serious technical malfunctions. After a fatal crash, these could raise difficult questions about legal liability, about why the aircraft was allowed to fly, about how it was certified and whether the crash was really the result of an oversight or incompetence by a governmental agency or authority. CW stated (strangely) that the AAIB had *'made no attempt to blame the pilots'* and pointed to their conclusion that, although no evidence of malfunction was found, the *'pre-impact serviceability of the aircraft could not be positively identified'*.

Low-temperature limitation

On the icing limitation, CW observed that Tapper would have been very conscious of both the weight and icing restrictions. It suggested that those who criticized him for flying too low as his Chinook approached the Mull of Kintyre may not have been aware of the *'facts surrounding the icing restriction'*. However, believing that Tapper was concerned about flying over the Mull up to safety altitude (2,800ft), CW thought that it was for this reason that he consulted Squadron Leader Milburn. CW also quoted a warning from the US Army Safety Center that helicopter

1. The memorial cairn with the lighthouse far below.

(Picture by author).

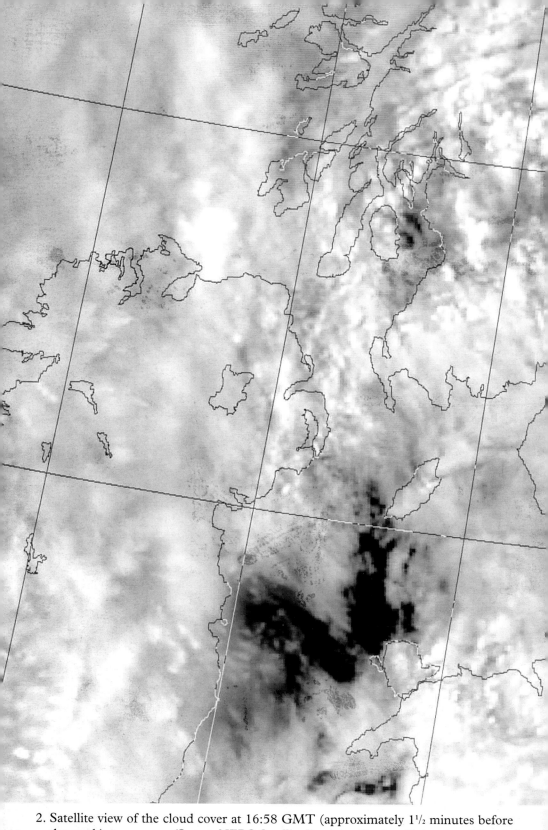

2. Satellite view of the cloud cover at 16:58 GMT (approximately 1½ minutes before the crash).   *(Source: NERC Satellite Receiving Station, University of Dundee).*

3. Some of the wreckage at the crash site. *(Source: PA Photos).*

4. An aerial view of the crash site. *(Source: PA Photos).*

5. Flight Lieutenant Jonathan Tapper.

6. Flight Lieutenant
Richard Cook and a
Chinook.

7. What the crew expected to see – the Mull of Kintyre lighthouse. *(Source: Hector Lamont)*.

8. The Mull of Kintyre lighthouse from the south (note the islands beneath the cliff).
   (Source: Royal Commission on the Ancient and Historical Monuments of Scotland).

9. The fog signal building at Rubha na Lice today. In 1994, the emitters were mounted
   through the walls of the building and there was no battery cabin.
   (Source: Hector Lamont).

10. The fog signal station at Rubha na Lice (indicated by arrow), with one of the islands below. (*Source: Paladin Invision © Channel Four Corporation. Taken from the documentary* The Last Flight of Zulu Delta 576).

11. The memorial garden at Thiepval Barracks. Plates showing each victim's name, rank and unit are attached to the inside of each post where it forms a cross with the rail. *(Source: British Forces Northern Ireland. Crown copyright).*

12. The inscribed stone at the memorial garden at Thiepval Barracks. The inscription reads: 'IN LOVING MEMORY OF THOSE WHO LOST THEIR LIVES / 2ND JUNE 1994 MULL OF KINTYRE / MAY THEY REST IN PEACE'. *(Source: British Forces Northern Ireland. Crown copyright).*

pilots should be aware that icing can occur in stratified clouds (stratus) at between 1,500 and 6,000ft (457–1828m).

Flight Reference Cards

CW observed that the Mk2 flight manual lacked any information on limitations and that the Flight Reference Cards were hardly complete; in fact, they were based primarily on the Chinook D Model, which is not fitted with FADEC. Squadron Leader David Morgan told the Board that the cards did not cover undemanded engine shutdowns, engine run-ups, spurious failure warnings or misleading or confusing cockpit indications. According to Morgan, what the cards *did* contain was confusing: '*A number of emergency drills, in particular electrical and hydraulic, were poorly laid out and required the crew to be familiar with the drill to avoid confusion. The shortfall in the Chinook HC2 Flight Reference Cards was discussed with the crews during their conversion courses.*' Cook himself had made notes on his Cards about whether or not an '*engine fail*' signal was likely to be genuine and Tapper expressed concern to his father about the Mk2, telling him that it would have to be checked out '*very carefully*'. Cook had also expressed concern to *his* father, telling him that the Mk2 was not '*ready*' and that he and the other pilots had not had enough time flying to cope with all the (spurious?) warning signals that appeared.

Boeing's flight simulation

CW described a computer simulation as one of the most potent and credible means of showing what happened in the last few seconds of a flight. However, it pointed out that few if any of the simulations carried out after large-scale crashes had pointed to a technical malfunction as the main cause. Some of the most notable (they gave some examples) pointed to pilot error, as in this case. However, CW persisted with the idea that it was Boeing's simulation that gave evidence of a flare in the last 2.9 seconds. CW appeared to suggest that the simulation should have allowed for the possibility that the pilots were distracted by warnings, spurious or genuine, as they approached the Mull. CW also appeared to suggest that the simulation should have incorporated data implying an engine or rotor overspeed. There can be a debate, it argued, about the data used and the emphasis given to those data. It claimed that computer experts and pilots were concerned that no account was taken of the possibility that the aircraft could have been out-of-control, weaving and undulating. While CW noted that the position of some of the controls was consistent with a last-second attempt to pull up, it persisted with the notion that this was belied by the fact that the engines were not at full power. It also thought that the position of the yaw pedal (77 per cent towards the stop) was inconsistent since this control is not (normally) used to turn the aircraft. It quoted Burke's view that the position of this pedal suggested that the aircraft might not have been under control and it criticized Boeing for leaving it out of the simulation. Although the MOD argued that massive yaw is employed by pilots to stop the aircraft as quickly as possible, using the fuselage as a brake, CW claimed that pilots know this to be effective only below 45kt (82.8kph) and that, to do so at 150kt would be suicidal. Several times CW referred to Burke's opinion that the crew of ZD576 were struggling with a problem, *'such as a temporary overspeed'* or a control jam, before the crash. CW argued, somewhat speciously, that there was no evidence to prove (*sic*) that the pilots were flying *'with a reckless disregard for their lives, and for all the lives on board, towards the fog on the Mull, in an aircraft which was otherwise behaving perfectly'*. It also argued that the fact that the engines were working at the point of impact did not mean that FADEC could not have been a factor in the accident (they implied an overspeed).

CW's explanation for the accident?

CW claimed that there was *'a clue in the wreckage of ZD576'* to what might have gone wrong. It referred to the discovery by the AAIB of contamination of the hydraulic fluid in one of the Lower Control Actuators by metal particles (see p. 39). It pointed out that, at the time, it was not known that the US Army suspected such contamination as being responsible for uncommanded control inputs in its Chinook aircraft. CW suggested that the crew of ZD576 might have been struggling to control yaw at a time when the aircraft may have been unresponsive to control inputs. It implied that this might have been due to the contamination discovered by the AAIB.

In short, CW condemned the air marshals for blaming the pilots when, in CW's opinion, the blame should have fallen on more senior officers who had put an unserviceable aircraft into service. The implication was that the crash was caused by some unknown control malfunction, either distracting the pilots or making the aircraft unsteerable, which left no convincing evidence of its brief existence in the wreckage. In particular, CW was obsessed with historical problems with FADEC, alleging that the RAF hid these problems and its case against Boeing and Textron Lycoming from both the Board and the FAI. The implication was that, had these problems been known to the investigators, their conclusion might have been different.

Chapter Seven

The House of Commons Debates and Inquiries

Because Parliament was in recess at the time of the accident, no announcement was made there. Nevertheless, Sir Patrick Mayhew[114], then the Secretary of State for Northern Ireland, immediately travelled to Northern Ireland to receive a report. He held a press conference the following day at Stormont Castle and was interviewed on radio and TV. Meanwhile, Jeremy Hanley, the Minister of State for the Armed Forces, visited the site of the crash and also held a press conference.

The Commons did not consider the matter until just over a year later. Asked by Bill Walker MP if he would make a statement on the Board's findings, the then Secretary of State for Defence, the Rt. Hon. Malcolm Rifkind QC, MP, gave a written answer on 15 June 1995. After expressing deep regret and condolences to the widows and families of those who died, he wrote:

> I have this afternoon placed in the Libraries of both Houses a summary[115] of findings of the inquiry into this tragic crash which claimed the lives of twenty-nine people. After an exhaustive inquiry into all the circumstances, the possibilities of major technical or structural failure, hostile action, or electro-magnetic interference with navigation equipment were eliminated as possible causes. On all the evidence, it was concluded that the cause of the accident was that the two pilots had wrongly continued to fly towards the Mull of Kintyre, below a safe altitude in unsuitable weather conditions. This constituted a failure in their duty and, regrettably, therefore, it was concluded that both pilots had been negligent.[116]

This verdict outraged the pilots' families, who refused to accept it and called for it to be withdrawn. They complained that the accusation of negligence was either unfair or unjustified, or both. Their cause was gradually taken up by members of both Houses of Parliament as they reacted to a growing popular movement that attracted considerable mass media interest and comment.

The Defence Committee

Following the later FAI and the Sheriff's Determination, the House of Commons standing Defence Committee took an interest in the matter. This Committee, which has considerable powers to make its work effective, is appointed to examine the expenditure, administration and policy of the MOD and associated public bodies. After the general election in May 1997, a new Committee consisting of eleven MPs[117] was appointed on 14 July. The Committee perceived a conflict between the verdicts of the RAF and the FAI. Perhaps not understanding that they were addressing different issues, the Committee wrote to the MOD on 31 July 1997 asking to be briefed on the accident; this took place on 25 November 1997. Subsequently and after some discussion, it was decided that it would be helpful to clarify some of the conflicting messages about the possible causes of the crash in a public forum. The Committee does not usually investigate individual incidents unless they raise wider questions. In this case, there was concern about the safety of the Chinook fleet. In its press notices about these hearings, the Committee made it clear that it sought neither to challenge nor to endorse the findings of previous inquiries into the crash. Nevertheless, it did establish that the MOD would be obliged to reopen its inquiry if new information appeared.

Following the briefing, the chairman of the Committee wrote to the Minister of State for the Armed Services on 5 December 1997, asking about the performance and reliability of Chinooks, the attribution of blame, training, FDRs[118] and the transportation of VIPs. These questions were answered by memorandum on 19 January 1998.[119] As a result, the Committee took evidence in public on 4 March 1998 from the Minister of State for the Armed

Forces (Dr John Reid MP), the Assistant Chief of the Air Staff (Air Vice-Marshal Tim Jenner) and the MOD's Assistant Director, Helicopter Projects 1, Procurement Executive (Colonel Barry Hodgkiss). Some members of the families of those who died and other interested parties attended the hearings.

AVM Jenner told the Committee that there had been only one previous Chinook accident (in Hanover). However, he had to add a note to the Minutes correcting this with a list in an annex. Over the previous fourteen years, there had been seven other accidents involving Chinook helicopters, all Mk1s (see p. 183 and Appendix One).[120] The overall accident rate was stable at about 0.2 per 10,000 flying hours.

On reliability, the Committee was told that, for complete aircraft, the contract with Boeing required that 'unscheduled maintenance events' should not exceed 520 per 1,000 flying hours over the first 3,000 flying hours, a mean time between failures (MTBF) of a little under two hours. In fact, there were only 367 such events per 1,000 flying hours (an MTBF of 2.7 hours), with which Dr Reid was satisfied.

Engine reliability was measured separately. The hydro-mechanical fuel system on Mk1 Chinooks had a MTBF of between 500 and 800 flying hours. Because a lower failure rate was expected with FADEC, its MTBF target was agreed at 5,500 hours after seven years.[121] However, at the end of the first year, the MTBF was only 380 hours. At the end of two years, when the MTBF was 1,415 hours, the software was modified, after which no further software failures occurred. After four and a half years, FADEC's MTBF had reached 3,180 hours. Although this meant that, at the projected flying rate, the warranty condition could not be met, it was expected that the target would be met in the long term.[122] The MTBF over the last two and a half years had been 5,730 hours and FADEC was operating ten times more reliably than the Mk1 fuel control system. Engine problems constituted less than 0.2 per cent of all faults and were only twenty-fifth on the MOD's numerical list of all faults.

The Committee was reassured to hear that the supplier was meeting the cost of repairs and additional spares where required under the contract and it expected the MOD to continue carefully monitoring FADEC's performance and to seek liquidated damages due at the end of the warranty period. The operation of the DECU's controlling the engines and what happened when one failed was explained to the Committee. The Wilmington incident and the subsequent claim against Boeing and Textron were also explained. The Committee was told that, over the four and a half years since the Mk2 was introduced into RAF service, crews had not raised any concerns about the FADEC systems or otherwise reported such concerns at flight safety meetings. Dr Reid told the Committee that the MOD was convinced that, at the time of the crash, the engines and the FADEC had been working properly. The Committee noted that, because one DECU box had been destroyed in the crash of ZD576, its performance could not be verified directly.

After being told about the weight limitation imposed on Mk2 Chinooks (it does not appear to have been told about the temperature limitation), the Committee wanted to know why, if FADEC had a back-up mode, a weight limit was needed at all. It was explained that Boscombe Down (DERA) had been unable to read and validate the software in the FADEC system because their tool for reading it was based on the static code analysis applied by BNFL[123] in testing nuclear systems. The US and Dutch armed forces, using methods based on standards which satisfy NASA and the US Federal Aviation Authority, were satisfied with the software. Because the MOD did not regard FADEC software as 'flight-safety critical' (defined as a failure of a component which would prevent the safe continued flight and landing of an aircraft), the manufacturer was not required to demonstrate that it had validated the design of the software. The Committee was later told that, after EDS-Scicon had identified anomalies, the Design Authority (AlliedSignal Engines) had agreed to upgrade the software at no cost to the MOD and pay $0.5 million towards the cost of re-documenting it. This work was executed by Hawker Siddeley Dynamics Engineering, supervised by TACS, a company approved by Boscombe Down. Some temporary procedural checks and operational restrictions were introduced.

The Committee asked about 'de-bonding' failures in the 'control closet' and problems with the navigation system. It was told that Boeing had assessed the risk to flight safety of 'de-bonding' as minimal and that there had not been a reported

123

incident where any component had completely separated from the flight control panel, jeopardizing flight safety. Only in one Mk2 had there been a navigation problem: difficulty in keeping the GPS system locked on satellites when flying low among hills. Analysis of the system in ZD576 showed that there was a good correlation between the GPS and other navigation systems on the aircraft.

On the attribution of blame, the Committee was told of the relevant RAF regulations that categorize it and how *'negligence'* differed from *'error of judgement'*. Dr Reid explained how, after hearing of the FAI result, which he described as a *'different finding'*, he had *'aggressively'* questioned those involved in the RAF's verdict. As a result, he had decided that it should stand. He explained that Boards of Inquiry had never been intended primarily to lay blame, but to learn lessons, anticipate potential problems and prevent further loss of life. He informed the Committee that, as a result of a review of Board procedures late the previous year, he had decided that Boards of Inquiry should no longer allocate blame or attribute negligence in reporting the causes of accidents. Blameworthiness would be considered through other channels.

On flight rules which allow pilots to fly only 50ft above the surface provided that they can see at least five kilometres ahead and require them to be at least 1,000ft above the highest ground on the planned route when in cloud[124], the Committee was told that training was being tightened up, especially regarding switching between VFR and IFR. This was welcomed.

The Committee was also told that, although investigation of the wreckage of ZD576 allowed the RAF to reject equipment failure, the MOD had decided to introduce an earlier proposed Health and Usage Monitoring System (HUMS) in all Chinooks. This would incorporate both a CVR and an ADR. Installation would start in December and be complete by the end of 2000.

The transporting of so many key personnel in one aircraft was defended by the MOD, although Dr Reid agreed that he would approach colleagues to see if the policy ought to be reappraised.

During the hearings, the Committee asked many questions which could only be answered later in correspondence from the MOD (comments of 24 April 1998 included above). Later in

March, the Committee travelled to Northern Ireland, where it visited a memorial to those who died in the crash. This is at Thiepval Barracks in Lisburn, but it is not open to the public (see plates 11 and 12).

The Committee concluded that there was no compelling evidence that the crash was caused by any fundamental flaws in the design of the Mk2 and it made no judgement on the cause of the accident. It thought that the Mk2 fleet was operating reasonably safely and reliably, although they wanted the eighteen-tonne weight limit anomaly resolved. It was concerned by the failure of Boscombe Down to give final approval to the FADEC software, but concluded that this was a management failure and that it raised no safety-critical questions. The Committee was surprised that, four and a half years after entry into service, the Mk2 fleet was still operating under an apparently unnecessary restriction and it expected the MOD to resolve the matter as soon as possible. It welcomed the decision not to require Boards of Inquiry to attribute blame and the proposal to install FDRs in Chinooks and other aircraft and recommended that families of deceased crew should be represented in the appropriate parts of Boards of Inquiry proceedings. It saw no evidence that RAF safety procedures subjected personnel to unnecessary risk, but recommended a reappraisal of the procedures for transporting key personnel. The Committee published its report on 13 May 1998.[125]

The Burke and Perks submissions

The same month, an all-party group of MPs[126] urged the then Secretary of State for Defence, George Robertson MP[127], to reconsider what they alleged was the RAF's *'miscarriage of justice'*. They presented what they described as *'new evidence'*. This consisted of statements by former Chinook test pilot (Squadron Leader) Robert Burke and FADEC expert Malcolm Perks which, combined, suggested the possibility of either a rotor runaway caused by a FADEC fault or a control-system jam following a disbonding of a control-system component. On 2 June, John Reid promised to review the 'evidence' carefully.

Burke, formerly based at RAF Odiham but then retired, had sat through the Defence Committee hearing on 4 March 1998 and was very critical of many of Dr Reid's answers to questions. He listed some of these in a six-page list attached to a letter he wrote to MP Robert Key on 10 May 1998. His letter outlined what he believed to be the cause of the crash in order of probability, viz: '*A control jam caused by a spring coming loose*'; '*A runaway up caused by FADEC*'; '*An uncommanded flying control movement (UFCM) other than a control jam*'; and '*The Board's solution*'. He also enclosed a reconstruction of what he described as '*a likely scenario during a runaway up of an engine on ZD576*'. Malcolm Perks had written his eleven-page note[128] from Leader Consulting Ltd. in Mississauga, Ontario, Canada. He wrote it following a meeting that Robert Key, Burke and he had had with Dr Reid on 18 March 1998.

On 22 September 1998, the new Minister of State for the Armed Forces, Doug Henderson MP, issued a statement regarding the material submitted by Robert Key. He claimed that there was no new evidence to suggest that technical problems played any part in the crash of ZD576. A thorough analysis of the theories of Burke and Perks showed that they offered no new insight into the tragic events of the accident. The MOD's nine-page technical appraisal was made available through the MOD's Press Office.

The appraisal dealt with the two postulated scenarios for the crash (a control jam caused by a spring coming loose or an engine runaway caused by FADEC) and Perks's comments on software design. On the possibility of a control jam, the MOD stated that records showed only one incident of debonding, and that was in ZD576 itself in May 1994. This was found to be due to the poor application and quality of the insert potting compound mix. Despite the fact that it was an isolated incident in some 45,000 flying hours on Chinooks, the security of the thrust balance spring mounting bracket on ZD576 was subsequently required to be inspected on every pre-flight servicing. It was last checked prior to the aircraft's departure for Scotland on the day of the crash, when no evidence of debonding was recorded. Since the accident, there had been three incidents of debonding, two occurring in flight. Although only one of these was detected by the pilot (he experienced a feeling of 'heaviness' in the controls), neither pilot had trouble in controlling the aircraft. The third incident was detected during a post-flight inspection. Because Boeing had concluded that the debond to ZD576 was an isolated event, pre-flight checks were abandoned. However, after further debondings, pre-flight checks were reintroduced and Boeing was asked to review the design of the control pallet. Although Boeing did modify the inserts, it pointed out that, in over 1 million flying hours on all types of Chinook, there had been no reported occurrences of all inserts failing and components becoming detached and jamming other flight controls. The company regarded this possibility as so remote that it could be assumed that *'occurrence may not be experienced'*.

Noting that the AAIB had declared that, given the level of damage, the possibility of a control jam could not be excluded, the MOD also noted that the AAIB had explained that such a jam would have caused appreciable distress to the components, damage that was not found. The MOD regarded MacFarlane's suggestion to the FAI of a simultaneous double failure (a jam) followed by a simultaneous double release (unjam) as so improbable that it could be ignored. Although it recognized that a component could come loose, it emphasized that the change in 'feel' should be detected by the pilot, who should then treat the event as a control malfunction and follow guidance in Flight Reference Cards. These required the pilot to establish level flight below 100kt and check that the aircraft's automatic flight control systems were functioning. Because this would not detect a debond, the pilot should then land as soon as possible. To jam, the control rods would need to be unable to resist loads of about 2,000lb (907kg[129]), an improbable occurrence.

The MOD also addressed Burke's suggestion of an uncommanded flying control movement other than a control jam. He had asserted that it could not be inferred from the as-found position of the 'rudder'[130] pedal (77 per cent of full travel), that this was likely to have been caused by a last-minute attempt to turn the aircraft. This was because, above walking pace, the 'rudder' has no turning effect. The MOD accepted that, at high speed, little or no yaw input is required to turn the Chinook. However, it pointed out that large yaw pedal inputs are made, with cyclic collective, during hover turns and when performing an operational technique at speeds up to 45kt called '*quick stops*'. This uses all the flying control inputs (cyclic, thrust and yaw) to turn the aircraft into a sideways position, using its large surface area as a brake. The MOD suggested that it was reasonable to suppose that, in extreme circumstances, any known and practised procedure was used in a final attempt to avoid impact with the Mull. This would explain the position of the 'rudder' pedal.

The MOD pointed out that there was no evidence to support Burke's suggestion of an engine runaway some fifteen seconds or less before impact, taking the aircraft uncontrollably into cloud, suffering acute vibration and yawing severely. On the contrary, there was evidence against it; examination of the engines showed normal operations with no sign of pre-impact failure or malfunction. Because the cockpit self-tuning absorbers automatically adjust their response frequency to accommodate changes in rotor speed so as to minimize vibration, heavy vibration was implausible. Both the Design Authority and DERA advised that that the absorbers would not go out of authority to the extent imagined by Burke. No loss of aircraft control has ever been reported during significant rotor speed excursions and the evidence from the witnesses on the Mull was not consistent with the approach of an uncontrollably yawing and vibrating helicopter.

On an engine runaway caused by the FADEC, the MOD admitted that Boscombe Down (BD), rather than individual pilots, had suspended flying the Mk2. However, it explained that, at the time, BD did not know that runaway incidents could be caused by electrical power interrupts, speed interrupts or switching to the reversionary channel. Trials flying resumed at BD once this had been explained. The MOD also admitted that there were well documented initial difficulties arising from the introduction of FADEC and it listed several. They all appeared to be due to one or other of the causes listed above and explained to BD. There was criticism of technicians for changing DECUs instead of following diagnostic procedures; some of the DECUs were damaged due to short-circuits. An incident in ZD576 on 17 May 1994, mentioned by Burke and attributed to the FADEC, was caused by a dirty compressor with an inadequate air-bleed setting. Safety was not compromised. It was true that the primary and reversionary channels were not fully independent, but only during normal engine shutdown, when the two channels act in parallel to ensure that the reversionary channel is regularly exercised.

On Perks's claims that the Chinook FADEC was both high risk and unique, and that Hawker Siddeley Dynamics Engineering produced software that was not of the quality that the MOD expected and which later turned out to be unverifiable, the MOD pointed out that the core of all FADEC systems for the T55 engine is 95 per cent common. It was not dissatisfied with the quality and the software was not unverifiable; although it was not amenable to the method of interrogation preferred by BD, it was capable of verification using other recognized and accepted methods. The MOD explained that the independent software consultants commissioned to review the HSDE product had only raised minor comments and points of clarification. It restated that, according to the internationally agreed definition, the Chinook FADEC was not 'safety critical' because a failure would not be catastrophic. It was pointed out that FADEC displays fault codes for diagnostic purposes and that the E5 fault code found in one of ZD576's DECUs did not have the meaning that Perks attributed to it. It was merely a nuisance code, indicating that there was a more than 5 per cent difference between the two engine speeds, with the lower latched out, and that that there had been a power interrupt. Consequently, the code had no relevance to the crash; this was why it had been discounted by the investigators. The MOD disputed Perks's claim that a power loss might have caused a loss of data. After a fault has registered for only 0.096 seconds, its code is sent to a non-volatile memory. The AAIB had noted the absence of fault codes on the last flight. The MOD also disputed Perks's claims that the records showed that ZD576 had many FADEC problems and that there were cockpit warnings of engine failure and partial engine run-downs and run-ups that were not recorded by fault codes. It disputed that the aircraft had suffered a flying control system failure twenty-five hours after its conversion to Mk2. The records showed no partial run-downs or run-ups, and no flying control system failure at twenty-five hours, or at any other time. The debonding incident (already discussed) occurred thirty-five hours after its last maintenance during the Mid-Life Update, but this did not constitute a flying control failure. The only recorded FADEC-related fault was the illumination of the Engine Fail caption for ten seconds on 26 May 1994, a known nuisance fault subsequently rectified by the Block 1 modification. In response to Perks's claim that several main features of the Boeing simulation differed fundamentally from the evidence in the wreckage, the MOD explained that the simulation defined the manoeuvres necessary to produce the initial impact conditions derived from the technical investigation, ignoring the rotor and engine indications, which were not thought 'highly positive'. Only criteria derived from positive evidence, i.e. items not disturbed on impact, were used in the simulation. Consequently, there was no accepted evidence that detracts from a coherent model of the accident. Moreover, information from the navigation system supported the simulation.

The Government response to the Defence Committee

On 21 October 1998, the Government responded to the House of Commons Defence Committee's Fourth Report (which they called 'Fourth Special Report').[131] It contained a copy of a memorandum from the MOD dated July 1998, a copy of a letter from the Minister of State for the Armed Forces dated October 1998 and a copy of a Draft Defence Council Instruction (DDCI).

In its memorandum, the MOD dealt first with the issue of monitoring the performance of FADEC and the warranty. It explained that the warranty period would not end until the equipment had operated for eighteen months in full compliance with the stipulated performance targets. Consequently, there could not be any component in breach of the warranty at the time the warranty expired. Secondly, it dealt with the eighteen-tonne weight limitation, the weight at which a Chinook can safely operate on one engine. It was imposed to recognize the unknown probability of failure of FADEC software. Because only 10 per cent of all Chinook sorties are carried out above the 18t limit, and because the limit was not absolute, the effect of the limitation had been modest. With experience, Service Deviations had been introduced progressively permitting flying to take place in excess of the limit and the MOD stipulated the conditions. The matter was under constant review and the MOD (PE) was working with experts to provide advice on the validation of software. Information was being collected to allow the appropriate amendment to the CA Release to be agreed. The memorandum also explained that Boards of Inquiry no longer concern themselves with blame and that the procedure for transferring between VFR and IFR had been formalized, briefed and practised at every stage of helicopter training, including on simulators. The installation of the HUMS was proceeding and would be complete by the end of 2000. Meanwhile there was little scope to develop common guidance for the transport of key personnel beyond that pertaining to the security of travel for the Royal Family. Nevertheless, the accompanying DDCI described the factors to be considered in transporting key personnel.

In his covering letter, the Minister explained that the necessary confidence to allow amendment to the CA Release (regarding the 18t limit) had been realized through the application of statistical analysis. Consequently, amendment AL8 had been made on 30 September (1998); it raised the weight limit (all-up mass) for the Mk2 to 24,500kg.

The Public Accounts Committee

In March 2000, the House of Commons Public Accounts Committee (PAC), in the process of reviewing the acceptance of military equipment off-contract and into service with the MOD, took evidence on the FADEC for Chinook Mk2 helicopters (see References). In particular, the PAC considered the procurement of the upgrade of the Chinooks from Mk1 to Mk2. After considering reports from the Comptroller and Auditor General of the National Audit Office (NAO) and HM Treasury, it heard evidence from a Permanent Under-Secretary of State (Kevin Tebbit[132]), the Chief of Defence Procurement (Sir Robert Walmsley), the Deputy Chief of Defence Staff (Vice-Admiral Sir Jeremy Blackham) and the Deputy Chief of Defence Logistics at the MOD (John Oughton). It also received memoranda on FADEC from Malcolm Perks and *Computer Weekly,* both of which were published with the PAC's reports.

From the transcript of the evidence, it is clear that several members of the Committee were determined to discuss the accident to ZD576 and imply that it was due to some fault with the FADEC software. Mr Tebbit regarded most of these questions as irrelevant to the discussion of the NAO Report or even to the general question of the procurement of computer-controlled equipment. Nevertheless, he referred several times to the RAF's conclusion and emphasized that the faults found in FADEC were neither serious nor did they have safety implications. There was the usual conflict between a civil servant trying to keep to the matter under discussion and determined to answer as truthfully and politely as possible, and MPs equally determined to get him sidetracked into admitting something incriminating. The Committee demanded so many answers to be made in subsequent notes, that the latter cover nine pages of the 45th Report.[133] In addition, the Committee asked many more questions in a letter it wrote to the MOD on 3 July 2000. The MOD answered these on 29 September, telling the PAC, inter alia, that there was no evidence that Chinook Mk2 crews had raised concern about it through normal channels and that it was not known who made the decision to use the Chinook for the sortie to Inverness.

The PAC found the Chinook Mk2 acceptance process to be flawed, especially in respect of the FADEC system. Consequently, it suggested that Boards of Inquiry procedures were also flawed and that they had failed in this case to meet the necessary standard of proof. Unlike the Defence Committee, the PAC stepped outside its remit and declared the verdict of the Board 'unsustainable' and recommended that it should be set aside. It accused the MOD of *'unwarrantable arrogance'* in standing by it, particularly after the inconclusive outcome of the FAI. The PAC thought that a FADEC fault or other technical malfunction was a real possibility as a cause of the crash and that it was impossible to prove negligence in this case. It even cast doubt on the integrity of the reviewing officers, describing them as *'also responsible for the operational management of the Chinook fleet and minimizing the disruption*

*to support helicopter capability caused by the problematic intro-
duction into service of the Mk2'.*

The PAC's views on the Chinook were published in their 44th
and 45th reports. There was no debate in the Commons on these
reports, although there were comments on them in a debate on
14 December 2000 about the PAC's 39th and 41st reports.

The Government responded to the PAC's 44th and 45th
reports in a Treasury Minute (Cm 5078) published on 16 March
2001. It claimed that the reports offered no new evidence that
would undermine the judgement of the Board and it rejected the
PAC's conclusions. It denied that FADEC software was poorly
written and explained why Boscombe Down experienced difficulty verifying it. It gave reasons why the Board had ruled out a
FADEC malfunction and summarized the evidence that led to a
finding of negligence. The response declined to prefer the FAI
verdict and insisted that the finding of negligence would not be
set aside without new evidence.

Debates in the Commons

There have only been three debates in the House of Commons on
the accident and the air marshal's verdict.

On 27 June 2000, independent MP Martin Bell succeeded in
getting the matter debated in an Adjournment Debate (held
in Westminster Hall). Several members aired the usual criticisms
of the MOD, all of which were rejected by the Parliamentary
Under-Secretary of State for Defence at the time (Dr Lewis
Moonie). He concluded that the findings of the air marshals were
correct and that there was negligence on the flight prior to the
aircraft entering cloud. There was no vote.

On 19 March 2002, following the report of the House of Lords
Select Committee (see next chapter), there was a two and a half-
hour Opposition Day debate on the matter, the motion being
sponsored by members from several parties, not just the Tories.
It claimed that the air marshals were not justified in their conclusion and called on the Government to exonerate the deceased
pilots. The Secretary of State for Defence (Geoff Hoon) refused
to accept the Select Committee's report and defended his decision.

However, he announced that he would seek a further simulation from Boeing. There was no vote.

The matter was debated again briefly on 22 July 2002, after Geoff Hoon made a statement responding to the House of Lords Select Committee's report (the Committee's work, its report and the Government's response is reviewed in the next chapter). During the debate, Mr Hoon criticized the Public Accounts Committee for inconsistency in accusing the air marshals of *unwarrantable arrogance* without calling them to give evidence.

Chapter Eight

The House of Lords Debates and Inquiry

The accident was first mentioned in the House of Lords on 28 January 1997, shortly after the screening of Channel Four's documentary. Lord Chalfont[134], a former military intelligence officer and Labour defence minister taking up the pilots' families' case, asked whether the Government was still satisfied with the verdict reached by the Board and he referred to the documentary, which cast doubt on it. Earl Howe replied for the Government, defending its position. He claimed that no new evidence had caused it to doubt the accuracy of its conclusion and that the documentary had made a number of unsubstantiated allegations.

On 22 May 1997, after a general (UK) election and a change of Government (from Conservative to Labour), Chalfont asked if the Government would review the findings of the Board (he outlined the case for revoking the accusations against the pilots). Chalfont probably hoped that Labour would be more sympathetic than the Tories had been. However, at the end of a one and a half-hour debate, Lord Gilbert[135], the newly appointed Minister of State for the MOD, replied defending the RAF's verdict. The official position had not changed.

On 2 June 1998, Chalfont tried again, this time asking if, in the light of the Commons Defence Committee's report, the Government proposed to review the findings of the Board. At the end of only a fifteen-minute debate, Lord Gilbert repeated the Government's view of the matter.

In January 1999, some members of the House of Lords, led by Chalfont, formed what they called 'The Mull of Kintyre Group', campaigning for the air marshals' verdict to be withdrawn. Later

135

that year, on 1 November, Chalfont raised the matter for the fourth time in the Lords and asked the Government whether the issues raised in *RAF Justice* (see Chapter Six) were serious enough to justify re-opening the Board, and he rehearsed the arguments for doing that. At the end of a debate of about one and a quarter hours, the new Minister of State for the MOD (Baroness Symons of Vernham Dean) replied, repeating the Government's arguments for upholding the RAF's verdict.

On 5 March 2001, shortly before the Government responded to the PAC, Chalfont moved that the Liaison Committee[136] should consider the appointment of a Select Committee to consider all the circumstances surrounding the crash. Because the Government did not oppose the motion, indeed it seemed to like the idea, it was agreed to without a division. Subsequently, after taking evidence, the Liaison Committee advised against Chalfont's proposal on the grounds that it would be impractical, take too long, and that the Committee would not be equipped for the undertaking. It also rejected the idea of a review limited to justification for the decision of the reviewing (RAF) officers. It would take a long time, put the Select Committee in a position to make a better judgement than experienced and senior professionals, and was unlikely to end the controversy. The Liaison Committee also thought that Select Committees are not equipped to replicate the function of the higher courts in addressing alleged miscarriages of justice.

On 30 April 2001, when the House of Lords was invited to accept the Liaison Committee's report, Lord Chalfont moved an amendment calling for rejection of the report and, instead, for the appointment of a Select Committee of five members to consider the justification for the finding of those reviewing the conclusions of the Board that both pilots were negligent. There was also a motion to establish an independent review of the conclusions of the Board. For the Government, Baroness Symons rejected the latter motion because she could see no reason why the Board's judgement should be exposed to review (this motion was not moved). However, if the Liaison Committee were to reconsider the question on the lines of Lord Chalfont's amendment, the Government would not resist it. After the House was told that the Liaison Committee was very unlikely to change its mind, a vote was taken and Chalfont's amendment was accepted by 132 votes to 106.

The Select Committee

The Committee was established on 2 July 2001, with the remit described in Chalfont's amendment. The members were Lords Bowness[137], Brennan[138], Hooson[139], Jauncey of Tullichettle[140] (Chairman) and Tombs[141]. It was required to report to the House of Lords by 31 January 2002.

Two days after a flight in a Chinook to the site of the crash on 25 September 2001, when the pilot replicated the track taken by ZD576, the Committee began taking evidence, with most of the questions coming from Lord Tombs, an engineer and an honorary Fellow of the Royal Aeronautical Society (RAeS), who visited RAF Odiham to inspect a Chinook on 22 October 2001. The hearings were held in Committee Room 3 in the Palace of Westminster.

Group Captain Pulford's evidence

Their first witness was Group Captain Pulford, the president of the Board. He explained that he was soon to take command of RAF Odiham. He was asked many questions about the Board report, starting with the flight plan. Pulford explained that, although it showed straight lines between waypoints, the first of which was the Mull of Kintyre lighthouse, it was conventional and normal to *'fly in the gap'*; in this case he would have expected the crew to fly *'to the left of the Mull up to the next waypoint'*, over the sea and fairly flat land. He was then asked about the psychologist's assessment of the pilots; Lord Tombs asked about his *'cavalier dismissal of technical failures and ready acceptance of a psychologist's report'*. Evidently annoyed by this accusation, Pulford repeated the words *'cavalier dismissal of technical'*, as if weighing them before proceeding to explain that the Board had accepted that what the psychologist suggested could have been a contributing factor. Questions then moved on to examination of the wreckage and the possibility that minor technical mal-functions could have distracted the pilots. Pulford admitted that the Board had not been able to dismiss that possibility but empha-sized that it was not a cause of the accident. Nor did he believe that a detached pallet would cause loss of control; it would merely change the 'feel' of the controls. In discussion of the tracks found on each pilot's Horizontal Course Selector (HCS), 028 on the left and 035 on the right (see p. 35), Pulford declared that he did not understand how the sheriff had concluded that Tapper had set his HCS to 028 for the new track (to the next waypoint). He was sure that it was set to show the track they were on (027), but 1 degree out. The Chairman thought he had seen evidence that a change of track of 14 degrees was required[142], but Pulford merely stated that he made it '7: *from 027 a left turn on to 020*'[143], but he had to agree that this conclusion was not in his report. He explained that it was normal for both HCSs to be slaved to the non-handling pilot's. Later he claimed that the fact that the aircraft was on a track 2 degrees to the right of the planned track was insignificant and the result of manoeuvring as it flew over Northern Ireland. Other questions concerned the Macdonald EMI report (see Appendix Four), the speed of the aircraft, and the DASH system.

The AAIB inspectors' evidence

Next, the Committee questioned Ken Smart, Tony Cable and Rex Parkinson of the AAIB. It was evident that, after seven years, Cable had difficulty recalling some details of the investigation. There was some debate about the altimeter readings and then a discussion of the DECU readings, including the E5 code. Although Cable had to admit that he had not known of the E5 fault when he wrote his report, he pointed out that the E5 found in the DECU was in its long-term memory, not in the record of the last flight (it seems that the Committee had not understood that). Other questions concerned a fractured tie-bolt and the possibility of a control jam caused by a detached pallet in the *'broom cupboard'*. In the published report of the hearings, Cable added a note to explain that the inserts discussed did not attach the pallets, but were captive nut inserts fixed to the pallets;

the relevant flight control components were fastened to the pallets by means of bolts screwed into the inserts as described in his report. Lacking this explanation, the Committee pursued the possibility of in-flight detachment; Lord Tombs claimed that there was 'a history of their becoming detached in normal flight'. After a short discussion about the debris found in the boost actuator hydraulic system, the Committee moved on to the matter of the Boeing simulation, which Cable thought matched well with the parameters he had supplied to Boeing.

In a subsequent letter to the Committee, Ken Smart, the Chief Inspector of Accidents, who said very little during the hearing, stated that the Committee might have gained a more complete picture of the technical investigation process if it had questioned Tony Cable together with the engineering member of the Board.

Sir John Day's evidence

The final witness that day was Air Chief Marshal Sir John Day, by then the Commander-in-Chief of Strike Command. Before being questioned, he made a presentation accompanied by thirty-five colour slides.[144] When it came to explaining the Boeing simulation, Sir John showed a graph reconstructing the last 4.4 seconds of the flight, during which the flare appeared to have occurred. He claimed that the crew had started to flare the aircraft four seconds before impact, but this included an allowance of one second for reaction time. Day stated that, to match the parameters provided by the AAIB, the aircraft had to have been climbing before the flare at a rate of about 1,000fpm. To reach safety altitude in the region of the Mull at that rate of cruise climb, it would need to have begun some 12 miles (19.2km) back in the North Channel. He put the 4 degree isotherm at a height of 3,500ft (1,066.8m). Day then carefully explained how he was required to assess any human failings in accordance with Air Publication 3207 (RAF Manual of Flight Safety). Because the crew possessed the necessary skill or knowledge for the position they were in, but failed to exercise due care, he had found that they were negligent to a gross degree, excluding three other degrees: disobedience, recklessness and minor

139

negligence. He emphasized that, as required by the rules, he had absolutely no doubt that the accident was caused by the actions of the two pilots. However, it was the most difficult decision he had ever had to make.

Challenged as to whether or not he had any doubt about a transient control problem, Day pointed out that even his fiercest critics conceded that there cannot have been such a problem at the point of waypoint change, something that required *'three presses of the button'*, and that, if there were such a problem, drastic action would have been taken. No such action was taken until four seconds before impact. The Committee asked about the crew's intention of flying over the Mull and whether or not changing track by 12 or 14 degrees at the waypoint change would have avoided a collision. Day thought that they would still have crashed, but was more interested in pointing out that the crew had *'grossly breached the rules of airmanship'*. Asked about alternative strategies, although he declared that he did not know whether or not they were in cloud when the waypoint was changed, Day speculated that they could not have seen the lighthouse at that time. If they had, they would not have continued as they did. Lord Tombs thought there were two difficulties with what he described as *'Sir John's hypothesis'*. It assumed that the crew were in command of the aircraft as it approached the Mull and it assumed that they were in cloud. Day denied hypothesizing, except where the Committee put scenarios to him, scenarios he rejected. Tombs proposed a loss of control at the point of waypoint change while still in sight of the lighthouse. Day pointed out that, even with a loss of control in both pitch and roll, the crew could have called for emergency power from the engines, the evidence for which was lacking[145] (Tombs appeared not to know of the Emergency Power Meter). They would also have put on maximum left 'rudder'. When it was pointed out that there was evidence of left 'rudder', Day contended that, if they had put a great deal of left *'rudder'* on twenty seconds before, the aircraft would still have crashed, but much more sideways than it did. Asked why two competent and highly trained pilots should do something *'suicidal'* (a term Day rejected), he pointed out that, after spending the morning on other flying duties, there was barely enough time left to complete the sortie without either staying overnight in Inverness or asking SRAFONI for permission to extend their duty that day to ten hours. Consequently, and evidently unwilling to accuse the crew of being in a hurry, he declared his belief that the crew were *'not keen to slow down their sortie in any way, either by slowing down to climb or by deviating off-track'*. He also believed that the crew did not know that they were 280m (*sic*) right of track and that they thought the high ground would pass down their right hand side. Nevertheless he thought that, even if they had been on track, they would still have crashed, but into Cnoc Moy. He thought that the crew took a calculated risk, *'just breaking the rules a bit and it would be okay'*. He attributed the 280m (he later rounded it to 300m) to the mis-plotting of waypoint A and slight in-accuracies in the GPS system. Answering a question about Board procedures, Day explained that, although he had directed that the station commanders at both Aldergrove and Odiham should comment on the report, to avoid them commenting on the *'same bit'* he had also told them *'which bits they should comment on'*. This was why their comments cover different areas. He also explained how, although the officers responsible for each part of the report could come to their own conclusion, the final con-clusion was that of the final officer (the 'reviewing officer'), in this case ACM Wratten. He could have disagreed with the opinions of junior officers. In his time as AOC 1 Group, he had handled fifteen Boards of Inquiry. In ten cases, he agreed with the Board President and the C.-in-C. agreed with him. In two cases, including this case, he increased the severity of the finding, the C.-in-C. agreeing. In three other cases, he reduced the severity from negligence down to error of judgement or from error of judgement down to no human failings. In two of the latter cases, the C.-in-C. agreed with him, but in one case he put the judge-ment back up. Day added that, since then, the system had changed, but not because of this case. Several other accidents, including Army accidents, had led to a change in the rules. He also explained that, in reaching a conclusion in this case, he had taken legal advice. Lord Brennan asked Day if there was *'absolutely no doubt'* that there was no technical malfunction that might have played a part in the accident or that no technical event distracted the pilots. Day could exclude neither of these

141

possibilities, but pointed out that no evidence of either had been found. Nor could he imagine that a minor emergency would have so distracted the pilots that they forgot they were about to hit a mountain. Asked by Brennan if he could explain why the pilots behaved as they did, Day repeated his conclusion that they were negligent and spoke of the *'incomprehensible'* things people do. Asked about the choice of the members of the Board, Day observed that the fact that they were not prepared to find negligence indicated that they were perhaps *'not the right people'*, although he later apologized and confirmed his belief that they were independent and objective. It was pointed out to him that, of the five officers concerned, plus Group Captain Crawford, there were several different judgements: not negligent, one officer negligent or both officers negligent. Did that not indicate that there was doubt? Day disagreed, pointing out that the proposal implied that, if any one of the seven involved (including the Odiham commander) decided that there was no negligence, then that would be the judgement (he meant any officer below the final officer). He had earlier explained that the system did not work on the basis of *'a majority verdict'*. The judgement was that of the final reviewing officer. The last question was from Lord Jauncey about the FAI where the sheriff, he claimed, *'could not say that there was negligence on the part of the pilots'*. Day pointed out that it was not part of the FAI to decide on negligence, but he did wonder why he had not been called to give evidence.

Sir William Wratten's evidence

The Committee met again the following day to question Air Chief Marshal Sir William Wratten, then retired from his post as C.-in-C. of Strike Command. He had reviewed the Board proceedings and agreed with the judgement of gross negligence. He took some ten minutes explaining the reasons for his conclusion, illustrating them with two colour slides, variants of one of the slides presented by Sir John Day. He emphasized how many witnesses on the Mull testified to the poor visibility and that none of them had seen the aircraft. He also claimed that the yachtsman

(Holbrook), when asked by the Board whether he could make out the physical features of the Mull from his position 2 miles (3.2km) south, answered 'No'. This meant that, because the weather around the lighthouse was unfit for flight at low level under VFR, flight in the area would have had to be under IFR. In such circumstances, the pilots had several safe options, but chose none of them. Sir William pointed out on his first slide where the pilots would have sighted land if they had the 1km minimum visibility required under VFR when flying less than 140kt (in fact he assumed a ground speed of 150–170kt). This point would have been reached some seven or eight seconds before the change of waypoint was made, a matter on which both pilots must have agreed. But he could see no justification for the crew to continue flying towards the cloud-covered Mull at cruising speed, nor justification for suggesting that they were discharging their duty of care. He briefly commented on the idea that, immediately after the waypoint change, something happened to deprive the pilots of control of the aircraft (throughout he referred to it as an *'aeroplane'*) until just before impact when they were able to *'fly a flare'*. He thought this hypothesis stretched the *'bounds of coincidence'* too far and noted that it lacked *'proof positive'*. Nor was there proof that the crew never saw land or the ground and did not realize that they were displaced to the right. He pointed out where the crew might have thought they were when the waypoint was changed and thought it feasible that they planned to turn eighteen seconds later when they were over the lighthouse, leaving the high ground on their right. This was more feasible than a loss of control, but whatever happened they would not have crashed if they had observed regulations. To demonstrate the immediacy of the problem facing the pilots, Sir William timed the last twenty seconds on his stopwatch from the point of waypoint change to impact, describing the salient events. He concluded that the crew had neither reason nor right to fly the aircraft even to the point of waypoint change. This was why he confirmed the judgement of the AOC.

Without thanking Sir William, Lord Jauncey immediately asked if the pilots (*sic*) would have cleared the ground if they had been on track for the lighthouse. Although he was unsure, Wratten thought it possible, but reminded the Chairman that the

143

aircraft was not on the planned route; mis-plotting of the light-house and slight errors in the computation of the TANS combined to put the lighthouse '280 [sic] *metres to the east*'. It was because of such inaccuracies that the flight rules existed. He was further questioned about where the pilots thought they were and when they planned to turn for waypoint B. He thought it reasonable to assume that they intended to turn when they thought they were over the lighthouse, but that did not mean that they could ignore VFR. Asked about the extent of the cloud, he explained that, even if the cloud extended just beyond the coast, the crew could not have seen where the land was underneath it; they would have been totally reliant on their TANS and on their inaccurate plot-ting. Later he agreed that it was possible that they saw the coastline underneath the cloud if the cloud was clearly defined. Lord Tombs challenged Sir William over the latter's claim that the yachtsman (Holbrook) could not distinguish the Mull when he saw the helicopter. He pointed to Holbrook's claim to have seen the wall of the lighthouse when much nearer to it. Wratten replied that this was an hour before he saw the Chinook. Tombs was not sure and explained that they were going to question Holbrook later. In relation to the prevailing weather, Lord Bowness referred to evidence that, after the accident, a Navy heli-copter landed at the helipad beside the lighthouse. Wratten explained that it was a Sea King helicopter that was able to land because it was equipped with radar. An MOD footnote to the Minutes of Evidence confirms this, stating that Sea King R177 landed forty-five minutes after the crash; an extract from the Sea King's log book entry is included in the Minutes. This reported visibility as varying between 3–4nm (5.5–7.4km) and a 'quarter nm' (463m) and that cloud and smoke prevented them landing at the crash site itself, where it was also drizzling. It also reported the wind from 160 degrees at 15kt becoming 330 degrees also at 15kt with 7/8ths layered stratus at 200ft (61m), 7/8ths strato-cumulus at 900ft (274m) and 8/8ths (solid) stratocumulus at 1,500ft (457m). The temperature was 9 degrees C.

Lord Jauncey returned to the possibility of a control jam, asking if the crew were negligent even if that occurred. Wratten assured the Committee that they were; the crew had brought about a crisis. They were not under time pressure (*sic*), there were

144

no surprises regarding weather and there were no operational reasons for them to lay any risk on themselves or their passengers. He agreed that what the crew did was astonishing, but he had seen very experienced and capable pilots do astonishing things that defy explanation. He had seen a report of a two-pilot aeroplane lacking either ADR or CVR where neither pilot survived and both were found negligent. Lord Bowness referred to evidence given to the Board (by Squadron Leader Morgan) about problems with FADEC and the lack of any guidance on these problems in the Flight Reference Cards (FRC) and he asked Wratten if it was normal to fly in peacetime with these questions unanswered. Wratten pointed out that the AAIB had concluded that there had been no pre-impact anomalies in the engines, which had been running matched at high-power settings. He alleged that no malfunction of the engines would have prevented the pilots turning the aircraft and that such malfunctions as there were occurred during ground tests where the engines were tested beyond the control limits that applied to flight. In the air, there were no so such departures. He had seen no reason to enquire further into the FADEC system. The weight limit in force at the time was not unusual, just a precaution against the loss of one engine. Lord Brennan wondered if Wratten was expecting pilots to be trained so as to overcome defects whenever and however they might arise. Sir William explained that all pilots are trained to deal with engine malfunctions and that a limitation on newly introduced aircraft was not unusual. Lord Hooson wanted to discuss the standard of proof required and how negligence relates to the judgement of the pilots. Were the pilots grossly negligent because they failed to make the right decision twenty seconds before the crash? Wratten explained that there was no need for a quick decision at that point; they were quite capable of making a decision then. Again, he claimed that the crew were under no pressure of time and that they could not have been surprised by the weather conditions. Pilots were not trained to have to make hasty decisions; they were trained to follow rules. The crew had no right to be anywhere near that point when they could not see the Mull because it was in cloud. Lords Jauncey and Hooson interjected to claim that there was no evidence of that but Wratten repeated his claim that the Mull was in cloud and referred to the ten witnesses on the Mull. The Chairman responded that they were at the lighthouse, on land. Lord Tombs pointed out that Sir William had previously agreed that the visibility at the point of waypoint change was not known; now he disagreed. He asked Wratten to suppose that, at the point of waypoint change, the pilots had identified the land and decided to change track. If they had maintained their altitude, or perhaps climbed slowly, and flown on the track to Corran, would that have been satisfactory in good visibility? Wratten wanted to know what *'good visibility'* meant and what height was being supposed. Tombs did not know; nor did Wratten. Wratten agreed that, if the weather off the coast had been clear, the pilots could have flown around provided they had 1,000m visibility. Tombs preferred the yachtsman's assessment of the weather and returned to the idea that something prevented the crew from making the *'way change'* (he meant change of track). Wratten pointed out that the aircraft was flying above the level of the lighthouse, to which Tombs responded that they were at sea, whereas the cloud was predominantly on the land. Wratten pointed out that, seven seconds after the waypoint change, they were over land. Tombs agreed, but asserted that they may have been off the coast and decided to keep left. Wratten asked to be allowed to pursue this *'extraordinary hypothesis'*. He declared that, if he was invited to board a helicopter whose pilot told him that he was going to try to fly around the Mull of Kintyre, where the lighthouse upwards was in fog and the visibility off the coast could be 1,000m, he would not get on board. Tombs objected that that was not the situation; there was no invitation back at Aldergrove. Sir William pointed out that he was responding to Lord Tombs's hypothesis. Tombs persisted by asking if it was *'respectable'* to have changed track at the point of waypoint change if they had seen the land further back. He explained that, on the demonstration flight in good visibility, when he had asked for the waypoint change to be made, it occurred five seconds after the 0.8 miles (*sic*) was called out by the navigator. As a result, they *'cleared the ground quite adequately'*. Although he acknowledged that the conditions were different, he did not think that cloud over the Mull lighthouse *'tells us very much in this particular hypothesis'*. Wratten did not agree. Tombs then asked about FADEC. Did Wratten know

146

about the frequent false captions of engine failure? Wratten explained that he was not close to the actual day-to-day running of Chinooks at the time. Nor was he aware of the debonded control pallets until he saw them mentioned in the Board's report. Tombs assumed that Wratten had read the Board report (*sic*) and referred to the number of previous problems with the pallets which, he alleged, could have produced a control jam. He was astonished that an experienced crew should continue to fly into land when they had selected a new waypoint and felt that the possibility that they were prevented from turning had to be considered. He also referred to *'the number of defects on the aircraft'*. Wratten referred to Sir John Day's description of the impact profile, but was interrupted as he tried to explain the options open to the crew if the collective were jammed. Tombs referred to the control jam reported in a US Chinook that only cleared when the aircraft was 250ft (76.2m) above the ground. Wratten had experienced such a jam. Tombs then queried the claim by Sir John Day that the two crewmen were in the rear of the Chinook, when there was other evidence that MALM Forbes was probably in the jump seat behind the pilots. Wratten was aware of this practice and acknowledged that the Board found it likely that one of the crew was in the front. Tombs's point was that this meant they were looking at three experienced men failing, not just two. Lord Bowness returned to the question of the Board's decision about the investigation of FADEC. Wratten referred him to the President of the Board. Lord Brennan wanted Wratten to confirm that he approached the inquiry into the disaster in two capacities: as an experienced RAF officer determining the facts and also determining what to do about disciplinary action. When Wratten agreed, Brennan asked if the paper Wratten wrote in 1995[146] was provoked by this disaster. Brennan read a passage in which Sir William urged stronger discipline and then asked him if, in this case, he had wanted to establish failures by the aircrew. Wratten hoped that he approached accidents from the same position. As a pilot himself, his personal instinct was to seek to absolve pilots from a finding of negligence, especially in the case of deceased aircrew. When he wrote the note to which Brennan referred, which was a personal note to five group commanders directly responsible to

147

him, Strike Command had experienced a number of avoidable accidents. There was also an inclination on some stations to avoid the formal disciplinary route. He had tried to bring consistency (the MOD added a footnote to the Minutes of Evidence explaining the background to Sir William's note). Lord Brennan continued by asking Wratten to look at one of Sir John Day's slides from the previous day; it illustrated a decision tree concerning consideration of human failings. Brennan asked where, in the process shown, provision was made for dealing with doubt. Wratten replied that it was for those undertaking the review to establish where there is doubt; an allowance was made for it. Negligence could not be found if there was doubt. Brennan was concerned because Wratten had been compelled to issue a statement (15 June 2000) following publicity about the judgement, and he read a paragraph from the statement (it concerned the responsibilities of command and the need to expose mistakes and faults). He asked Wratten if such responsibilities would allow him to conclude that this accident might have occurred for reasons that could not be identified. Wratten agreed that that was an option. Asked what he had meant by claiming that the responsibilities of command cannot be shirked, Wratten explained that commanders have a responsibility to reach a conclusion on human failings. There was a demand that they do so. He denied that, when he said that it was unacceptable for commanders to protest insufficient evidence, he was referring to the Board. It was a reference to someone like himself or Sir John Day. Brennan persisted by asking whether the three-man Board had not failed on their assessment because they found that there was insufficient evidence to satisfy the burden of proof. Wratten agreed that they did not reach the conclusion that he had reached. They did so because they did not interpret fundamental obvious errors as negligence. Having rightly concluded that flights near the Mull had to be under IFR, the Board ignored that conclusion and instead addressed the reason why the pilots selected an inappropriate rate of climb. Pulford actually defined negligence when he concluded that Tapper had the responsibility, the capability and the skill to have avoided the inappropriate rate of climb—he simply did not apply the word to it. Wratten declined to accuse the Board of paying inadequate attention, being incompetent or lacking in guts (Brennan's proffered alternatives). He and Day had not sent it back to the Board because it had been Pulford's first Board and this was the RAF's largest peacetime tragedy. They had not wanted to impose such a responsibility on a young wing commander; it was the responsibility of senior commanders.

The session ended with Lord Jauncey asking to see the slide of the waypoint change again and asking Sir William to point out where the crew would have thought they were at the waypoint change, which Wratten did. He was then asked if it was his view that the aircraft should not have been even where the crew thought it was. Wratten confirmed that that was his view and that it would not matter whether or not there had been a malfunction or jamming of controls because they had put themselves in a position they should not have been in. Had they not been there, then any other problems could have been dealt with. He agreed with the Chairman that it came down to negligence in being where they were in the prevailing weather conditions. The Committee should forget about any supervening circumstances that may have affected the flight once it got to those positions.

The pilots' fathers' evidence

The Committee then took evidence from the fathers of the pilots, John Cook and Michael Tapper. Cook is a former RAF pilot and commercial airline captain with over forty years' flying experience; among various aircraft, he had piloted Concorde. Michael Tapper is a former Royal Navy submarine officer.

In his comments on various matters, such as pulling emergency power (he thought that would have been disastrous) and the position of the collective lever, John Cook referred to the fact that four, not three, experienced crewmen were involved in the incident. However, he also admitted that pilots could make mistakes. He then told the Committee of the concern his son had expressed about the Mk2. Michael Tapper also told the Committee of his son's concerns, not only about the Mk2, but also about navigators substituting for pilots. His son was particularly concerned that the other crew based at

Aldergrove consisted of a Navy pilot (Kingston) who was not very experienced on Chinooks and a navigator (Trapp). In an emergency, the pilot could not rely on the navigator for much help. Michael Tapper commented on the weather conditions, expressing surprise that the Board had ignored the evidence of a witness on the Mull (Mr Crabtree) who reported that it was clear *'down by the lighthouse'* (a footnote to the Minutes of Evidence refers to an MOD memo reproduced in the report, which noted Mr Crabtree's statement that, because of the thicker mist[147] higher up, he never saw the helicopter). Mr Tapper also claimed that the Sea King pilots who arrived forty-five minutes after the crash *'could actually see'*. Later, John Cook referred the Committee to still pictures taken from a holidaymaker's video[148] shot at the Mull shortly before the crash. Apparently, these showed a clear horizon and rocks about 300–350yds (274–320m) away. Michael Tapper reported how a Chinook (ZA707 from 7 Squadron), on a flypast over his local church on 13 July 1995, found that its TANS was *'two miles out'*.[149] He explained that, as an expert on the Racal TANS equipment, his son had advised everyone on his flight not to rely on the TANS. He was sceptical that the pilots approached the Mull using TANS as their navigation system.

Both fathers subsequently wrote to the Committee; Michael Tapper just to send a document he had promised, John Cook questioning many aspects of the evidence offered by the air marshals. He doubted the reliability and judgement of the witnesses on the Mull; he was sure that his son would have turned left on seeing cloud over the Mull. He even claimed that there was no evidence that the waypoint had been changed and that the air marshals were protecting someone or something by blaming the pilots. He was unhappy with the Boeing simulation and suggested that it did not eliminate several catastrophic situations such as that which occurred with the US Chinook (piloted by Bric Lewis). He claimed that the air marshals had offered no explanations to why the aircraft had not turned left, why it had flown straight on or why it had increased in speed (*sic*). He was also critical of what he called Day's arrogance in being satisfied that inadequacies in supervision, training or flying standards did not contribute to the accident. His scenario was that, at the point when a left turn was

150

needed, his son found that left cyclic pitched the nose down with right yaw caused by a stuck upper boost actuator. Applying back cyclic for a flare, he found that this caused right roll and yaw. Up collective increased right roll, yaw and pitched the nose down. All this caused an increase in speed and a climb before the jam cleared and he was able to flare, but too late.

Sir John Day's response

As already mentioned, the Minutes of Evidence include various comments and footnotes by the MOD. Among these is a letter from the MOD dated 12 October 2001 attaching comments by Air Chief Marshal Sir John Day on the evidence presented by the pilots' fathers.

Sir John acknowledged that the weather near the Mull was a key aspect. Consequently, he reviewed all the available evidence from the witnesses on the Mull. All ten had reported dense fog with very poor visibility at the time of the crash. Day compared that with the yachtsman's (Holbrook's) evidence that visibility was good when the Chinook flew past him two miles south of the Mull. Even so, his evidence was not consistent. Day concluded that it was feasible that Holbrook had seen the cliffs below the lighthouse, perhaps even the lower part of the lighthouse. As the cloud base moved up and down during the day, it was even possible that he occasionally saw the entire lighthouse. Nevertheless, the evidence was that, at the time of the crash, visibility both at the lighthouse and higher up the mountain was only fifteen to twenty metres. Consequently, the pilots could not have seen the lighthouse as they approached from the south.

Day considered the possibility that the crew saw the cliffs at the minimum VFR range (1,000m). At a ground speed of 160kt (it might have been 175kt), they would have flown on for over 500m before making the waypoint change. Day concluded that, if they had seen the cliffs at 1,000m, no reasonable pilot would have continued straight on before intending to turn left along the line of the cliffs whilst remaining below the cloud base. To see the cliffs and then cruise climb on track over the mountains amounted to 'recklessness', a more severe degree of negligence

151

than *'gross negligence'*. He thought it more likely that they had begun a cruise climb before making the waypoint change and had abandoned VFR. He illustrated this with a flight profile constructed from the known data and the Boeing simulation (see p. 191). It shows the Chinook in a cruise climb of 1,000fpm from the waypoint change at 373ft (113.7m) to 665ft (202.6m), after which it flares to 810ft, when it crashed. It also assumes a ground speed of 160kt (135kt airspeed plus 25kt tailwind). Day pointed out that, even at the point of waypoint change, the aircraft was 50ft above the top of the lighthouse, which was known to be in fog (cloud), as was the mountain above the lighthouse. This conclusively showed that, whatever the precise weather conditions at the time of waypoint change, the pilots were grossly negligent at that point and that any temporary major malfunctions after that were irrelevant to the judgement.

However, Day also dealt with a temporary control restriction and a FADEC-induced engine runaway. Not only was there no evidence of a control restriction, it was not credible that, faced with such a situation, the pilots would not pull emergency power to maximize their rate of climb and apply maximum 'rudder' to yaw the aircraft away from rising ground. Because the emergency power flags had not been tripped, it was known that emergency power had not been pulled for more than five seconds (it was probably pulled in the flare). Also, because the aircraft crashed with very little side-slip, it was known that maximum left 'rudder' had not been applied before the flare. The position of the collective was consistent with an emergency flare just before impact. It followed that a temporary control restriction could not have contributed to the crash.

On FADEC, Day stated that, if one engine overspeeds, the other engine automatically runs down to compensate and that, if the runaway is not severe, the two engines remain unbalanced. If it is severe, the rotor head may accelerate to 115 per cent before the higher-powered engine is automatically tripped and decelerates to low power. As the rotor speed reduces to 100 per cent, the other engine accelerates in an attempt to keep the rotors at 100 per cent. If there had been such an overspeed, the two engines would have been found with unmatched power settings at impact. Since they were found with matched power settings, it followed that no runaway had occurred on this flight and could not have contributed to the accident.

Squadron Leader Morgan's evidence

The Select Committee met again on 15 and 16 October 2001. Their first witness on 15 October was Squadron Leader David Morgan who, in 1994, was the flight commander of the Chinook Operational Conversion Unit, which had just completed converting all existing Mk1 Chinook pilots to the Mk2.

He was asked about the differences between the two marques and, in particular, about FADEC. It seems that many of the early problems experienced with FADEC were caused by Boscombe Down (BD) mishandling it (his word) by forcing an engine run-up or *'over-speed checks'*. It was felt that this *'back-stop of the FADEC system'* had to be proved on each flight. Later he suggested that Boeing had not anticipated such frequent checks. He himself had not experienced run-ups and had had no major problems with FADEC itself, only with systems that feed information to the FADEC. He denied that BD stopped flying their Chinooks during flight trials due to FADEC problems. Indeed he told the Committee that, the day after the accident, he had been called by the lead test pilot at BD, who made it clear that the grounding of their Chinook the day before the accident was in no way connected to the accident; it was to do with icing trials. Although he had told the Board of unforeseen flight-critical malfunctions associated with FADEC, he had not experienced any himself.

At the time of the accident, he had been aware of one incident involving a detached control pallet (he had since heard of more). However, he had not mentioned it in evidence because it was not flight-critical. When Lord Tombs suggested that detached parts could cause a jam, Morgan explained that the flight control system incorporated an anti-jam system, making the chance of jam *'relatively remote'*.

Asked about pilots suddenly finding themselves in cloud, Morgan explained the need to reduce speed to achieve the maximum rate of climb, to turn away from any known high ground and to continue to climb to safety altitude. He surmised that failure to do that indicated that the pilot had other pressures on him while being certain that he was not heading towards high ground. Either the pilot was unable to slow down or he was not concerned about the high ground.

Questioning turned to the navigation system. Morgan explained that, since the first Gulf War (Operation Granby), it had been upgraded from a Decca Navigator system to the combined GPS and Doppler system (TANS). This was because Decca had not provided coverage over the desert in the Gulf. He added that he had told the Board that, in his opinion, crews had become almost complacent and over-reliant on the accuracy of the GPS, starting to work to tolerances of tens and hundreds of metres. This was despite the fact that the manuals clearly warned crews not to rely on the GPS as the primary source of navigation. The reason was that it was believed that the Americans, who ran the system, could introduce errors to prevent enemies using the system to their advantage. Morgan explained that, although the TANS system did record height from the GPS, pilots used either the RadAlt or barometric altimeters to determine height.

Morgan claimed that, in 1994, the Flight Reference Cards for the Mk2 were complete and fully compliable (sic) and approved by the Handling Squadron at BD. However, they were constantly updated and some of the malfunctions covered were not user friendly. This required the crews to have a better than average level of knowledge of the system so as to understand what the Cards were telling them. The Cards had since been improved.

The Committee was somewhat concerned that, although the Board discussed many matters informally with Morgan, it only asked him three formal questions (on malfunctions, FADEC and Flight Reference Cards). How did it determine that many other matters were not relevant to the investigation? Morgan explained that Boards can recall witnesses if they think they have relevant evidence.

Finally, Lord Tombs wanted to know if the ground effect as the Chinook closed on the Mull would have lifted the front of the aircraft. Morgan told him that ground effect only occurred in helicopters below 15kt. At higher speeds, the downwash was swept behind the aircraft. At 140kt, an eighteen-tonne aircraft closing on a 30 degree slope would require a massive ground effect to alter its flight path. Nor would an aircraft travelling at such a relatively low speed produce much of a bow wave. Tombs noted Morgan's view but said that he had an alternative. Sarcastically, Morgan declared that he would be interested in the theory that Chinooks could avoid colliding with the ground simply because of an increase in the ground effect. Tombs said he was referring to the *'differential ground effect'*, but Morgan dismissed the idea.

The RAeS members' evidence

The Committee's next witnesses that day were the authors of 'The Macdonald Report' (see References and summary in Appendix Four), Ralph Kohn, Ronald Macdonald and Richard Hadlow, all fellows of the Royal Aeronautical Society (RAeS) and retired captains of commercial airliners, in the case of Hadlow after RAF service. Between them, they had some 60,000 hours flying experience, mainly in aeroplanes. Hadlow had some experience of flying single-rotor helicopters (Whirlwind and Wessex). In his opening remarks, Macdonald claimed that the Report, which Kohn had edited, was the work of a study group of the Flight Operations Group of the RAeS, formed to consider the findings of gross negligence against the pilots of ZD576. They had found it difficult to understand how the RAF reviewing officers had overturned the finding of the Board, which, he claimed, could not find *'a definitive cause'*. They thought that *'reasonable doubt'* did exist and Macdonald rehearsed all the factors which they thought *'played a part'* in the accident (all of them have been mentioned already).

Questioned about the metal particles found in the residual fluid of the boost actuator, Macdonald recalled his surprise at finding that this did not concern the investigators and that they did not attempt to find where the particles had originated. He alleged that subsequent accidents had been *'traced back to metal filings'*, but he gave no details. On FADEC, Macdonald explained why they mentioned it in the Report and, when the Chairman reminded him that nothing had been found to be wrong with the engines, pointed out that nothing had been found wrong with the American Chinook that rolled over. There was some discussion of the as-found positions of the flight controls, which the witnesses thought *'highly unusual'*, indicating a requirement to raise the nose of the aircraft and turn left. They did not understand why the aircraft did not turn left if that was what it was trying to do. They thought that the controls had become jammed and that turning left would normally be achieved by use of the cyclic stick. Kohn explained why they had commented on the E5 code found in the surviving DECU. He claimed that it had been the cause of the Wilmington incident and that this made them suspicious of it being found in the memory of ZD576's FADEC. He read an extract from a US Army report, a copy of which he had sent to the Committee, which claimed that *'CH-47D helicopters* [Chinooks] *are experiencing uncommanded oscillations, flight control movements and flight attitude changes that may be related to the performance of the upper boost actuators'*. Apparently, the US report associated these anomalies with metal contamination and moisture found in the lower control actuators, which it considered critical to flight safety. Asked about electric malfunctions, the witnesses described several accidents where these had occurred with fatal consequences. One involved a circuit break due to water ingress, and another an over-voltage. Pressed by Lord Brennan to point to post-crash evidence of malfunctions, Kohn admitted that the E5 code was their only such evidence. Hadlow emphasized that they had not sought to prove anything, only that *'reasonable doubt'* existed. In a subsequent note, he claimed that, since no one had produced proof that the crew were not obeying VFR rules, it is reasonable to deduce that they had seen the coast and would turn left. Doubt existed because they did not turn left. The weather over the land had little relevance to a crew flying VFR round the coastline. Asked about the Boeing simulation, Macdonald claimed that his experience was that, although the use of simulators (*sic*) had value, they are *'very inconclusive'*.[150] He could not say what percentage of power a fully raised collective would produce, but, in a subsequent note, he declared that it would give full power.

The yachtsman's evidence

The following day, the Committee examined yachtsman Mark Holbrook. He started by making a lengthy statement expressing his concern to have discovered that his evidence did not corroborate the other evidence on which Sir William Wratten relied. He considered that his evidence had not been collected with either diligence or professionalism and complained that even then he had not been shown pictures of a Chinook for comparison with his sighting. He wanted to emphasize that, at the time, the wind was constantly changing direction and strength, the latter varying from calm to 30kt gusts. This variability explained the variation in visibility in his evidence.

He told the Committee that, generally, visibility was one mile, but towards the Antrim coast was three to five miles (4.8–8km) and he stated that, although he could not see the lighthouse itself, he could make out the *building complex and white fence lower down*. Although low cloud clung to the Mull, he was sure that the pilots could have seen where the Mull was from the cliffs, beach and lower perimeter walls of the lighthouse complex. During questioning, he stated that, although he was located some two miles south-west of the lighthouse, he could see the perimeter wall where he thought the foghorn was located. It was only identifiable as a colour change through haze, but he was sure that the pilots would have been able to see it. He stated that the cloud clinging to the Mull, which moved up and down, did not extend out to sea. In describing the trawlers he encountered, he said that he had told the police that there was a St Andrew's cross painted on the superstructure of one of them. Consequently, he could not understand why the RUC was contacted; the trawlers must have been Scottish.

Robert Burke's evidence

The second witness that day was Squadron Leader Burke. He had been retired four years but had provided many documents to the Committee. He reported the unease felt at Odiham about the introduction of the Mk2. It was thought that neither the RAF nor

Boeing knew as much as they should about FADEC. He was asked about an incident at the Boeing factory in Philadelphia that he witnessed. A Chinook under ground test suffered an engine run-up to 108 per cent.[151] He also mentioned another incident where a Chinook suffered either a *'freeze or a run-down'* while hovering; he attributed this to a misunderstanding of FADEC by the Boeing test pilot.[152] Burke explained how he was told by his superior at Odiham to give no help in the investigation and not to speak to anyone about it. Consequently, he gave no evidence to the Board, nor to the FAI.

He was asked about a document he had prepared in response to what Dr Reid had told the HOC Defence Select Committee (see p. 126). He challenged Reid's claim that there had been only one Chinook accident before the Mull of Kintyre crash; there had been seven, although all to Mk1s and so not involving FADEC (see list on p. 183 and Appendix One). He could not recall whether or not anyone refused to fly Mk2 Chinooks, but he did recollect that relations between Odiham and Boscombe Down (BD) were *'very strained'* because of the limitations, especially after the accident. A ninety-minute briefing by a BD project team made things even worse. He alleged that, because BD would not fly their Chinook, he had had to fly it back to Odiham for minor servicing. He disagreed with Squadron Leader Morgan's assessment of the situation and listed several problems with FADEC, some of which, he alleged, could lead to loss of control. However he did not think that there was very much wrong with FADEC, just with the ground test procedures. The pilots lost confidence in it because the tests were leading to runaways and *'over temps'*. On control-system jams, Burke told of one he experienced in a Mk1 on the ground, but explained that the Mk2 had an anti-jam system. When the Chairman claimed that there had been an occasion when a control pallet became detached, Burke corrected him to point out that it was just *'the insert'* that had become detached. During discussion of the large number of allegedly faulty DECUs, Burke suggested that this was mainly due to bad electrical connections caused by frequent swapping of DECUs by technicians unfamiliar with the system. Of the possible engine malfunctions that might have occurred on ZD576's last flight, Burke thought that an engine freeze or a run-down was unlikely. A temporary runaway or a partial runaway up or RPM cycling were more likely; they would cause the aircraft to climb into cloud with a lot of vibration and yaw. Burke was asked why a pilot would continue towards a waypoint after identifying it, instead of turning early to cut the corner. He explained that the purpose of overflying a waypoint, especially after flying over sea, was to update the Doppler input into the TANS because the Doppler had problems over sea. Asked about the large 'rudder' input, he explained how the 'rudder' operated (see note 130) and suggested that the only reason for making the effort to do this (it is a heavy control) was to counteract a large yaw. On speed, Burke thought that the crew had planned to fly at 135kt airspeed, just below the Mk1 high vibration level, not the 150kt assumed by the Boeing simulation. He also found a discrepancy between the assumed rotor speed and that found by the AAIB. He thought the most likely cause of the accident was a control jam of some kind and went on to describe concern in the RAF about a DASH runaway. Finally, Burke exhibited a slide made from tracing one of Sir John Day's slides showing the cloud cover over the Mull relative to the flight path of the aircraft. Burke modified it to show cloud starting at the lighthouse so that it would have been visible to the pilots. He also showed another of Sir John's slides (a map of the route) to emphasize that the Chinook was not flying 'straight at the Mull'.

Squadron Leader MacFarlane's evidence

The Committee then took evidence from an anonymous Special Forces Chinook pilot who is referred to in the Minutes of Evidence as 'Witness A'. Because he revealed that he had given evidence to the FAI on his theory about a control jam as the cause of the accident, he can be identified as Squadron Leader Ian MacFarlane. It is not known why he was granted anonymity.

He gave the Committee evidence of various FADEC problems and uncommanded flight control movements, the latter on Mk1 Chinooks. Asked about options after the change of waypoint, MacFarlane stated that the crew could have left the decision to change track 'as long as they wanted'. He denied that the crew

159

could have been ignorant of their proximity to the Mull. The excessive 'rudder' position, he thought, could be either due to the aircraft being difficult to control or due to movement of the pedal during the crash. The latter could not be ignored. He was concerned to point out that the SuperTANS did not give simultaneous data for horizontal position and height; the Board had treated them as simultaneous. There was then some doubt about the SuperTANS giving the time for these readings. MacFarlane criticized the Boeing simulation for producing a cruise climb (150kt at 1,000fpm) which, he claimed, was impossible for a Chinook to attain without using emergency torque. At 150kt, it would only climb at 400fpm, a rate he had recently established in a test. They were either not doing 150kt or not climbing at 1,000fpm. Pressed, he opted for a speed of 130–135kt. Commenting on the fact that it was unclear whether or not the emergency power latches were reliable, MacFarlane explained that there would be no record if emergency torque (but not emergency power) had been applied.

Air Commodore Crawford's evidence

On 7 November 2001, the Select Committee met again to hear evidence, first from Air Commodore Peter Crawford, then retired. As a group captain and the OC RAF Odiham, he had made 'remarks' on the Board report.

He agreed that there had been concern about the Mk2, mainly because it could not be used to its full operational capabilities. Although he had flown the Mk2, he had not himself experienced any problems. Crawford explained his reasons for discounting major technical malfunction, including a control jam or an engine problem and he refused to accept Lord Tombs's claim that there was no evidence that the aircraft was serviceable before impact. The fact that the aircraft was climbing showed that the engines were working and the flare showed that it was under control. Asked about the embargo put on Squadron Leader Burke, Crawford related that, after finding a general debate about the crash going on in the officers' mess bar at Odiham, a discussion in which Burke participated, he told his commanders that such speculation should not be happening in a public place and that it should stop. Crawford explained how he concluded that Tapper, but not Cook, had to carry responsibility for the accident. As captain, Tapper was responsible for the *'degree of aircrew error'* involved. In another exchange with Lord Tombs, Crawford admitted that, although he may have phrased his conclusion *'rather clumsily'*, it was logical. Finding themselves in cloud, the crew should have turned away from the high ground. He did not understand why they had not.

More from Squadron Leader Burke

The Committee then recalled Squadron Leader Burke to hear his views on the mismatch between the rotor speed found by the AAIB (100.5 per cent) and that found from the Boeing simulation (91 per cent). The latter, with the collective lever fully up, indicated engines operating at maximum, perhaps at emergency power level. He contrasted this with the AAIB's finding that the engines were operating at an intermediate level. Burke criticized the simulation for assuming initial steady conditions, ignoring the possibility of the aircraft having control or engine problems. He had no confidence in the flight simulator at Farnborough being able to simulate the power requirements.[153] He would not say which rotor speed was correct, but was sure that the AAIB's findings were consistent with each other. There was further discussion of the effects of control jams. He declined to comment on a letter from his then superior at Odiham denying that he had ever forbidden Burke to discuss the accident.

More from the AAIB

The Committee also recalled Tony Cable and Ken Smart from the AAIB. Cable confirmed that, shortly after the accident, he had spoken to Squadron Leader Burke. He also confirmed that, on 15 August 1994, he had faxed Boeing, defining the parameters he had established from the crash site together with some other parameters supplied by the Board.[154] Boeing needed these parameters to model a flight path that would match what he had found.

Asked about the discrepancy in rotor speeds mentioned by Squadron Leader Burke, Cable explained how the multiple impacts involved would have cut off signals to instruments at different times and in an order that could not be established. If, as he thought, power was cut at the initial impact, there was time for indications to change before a later impact caused a mark on a particular gauge. He also recalled that the Boeing model did not accurately model the FADEC. Nevertheless, he was fairly satisfied that, for the purpose that the model was being used (to find gross manoeuvres over a very short time), the limitations did not make much difference. Questioned by Lord Tombs, Cable would not be drawn on choosing between 91 and 100 per cent (rotor speed) and thought that engine performance was not important in modelling the flight characteristics. Lord Tombs was not convinced and again attempted to get Cable to choose between rotor speeds. Cable emphasized that he had made difficult judgements based on thin evidence and professional experience. Ultimately, because Boeing could not model FADEC, Cable cast doubt on the 91 per cent rotor speed.

Ken Smart intervened to observe that some people had chosen to make more of Cable's evidence than he would himself. Without a flight data recorder, nothing was certain and he cautioned against seeing any one reading as accurate. He agreed with Lord Brennan that caution should also be exercised by those who concluded that there was no evidence of malfunction.

Questioned about whether or not the simulation indicated when the climb rate started, Cable explained that it assumed an infinite period of climb but ran for only one second at that rate before the specified control inputs commenced. The purpose was to try to assess the aircraft's behaviour in the following few seconds. In fact, good matches for the impact parameters were found at 2.9 seconds. Cable had to explain that the rate of climb of 4,670fpm was the instantaneous climb rate at the end of 2.9 seconds (not an average rate) and that the rate of climb was increasing. Emergency power was measured by the power turbine inlet temperature (PTIT) being exceeded for more than five seconds. This caused magnetic indicators to switch and a clock to start. Although these had been found unswitched, because the clock only registered whole minutes, Cable could not exclude the possibility that the crash had altered the indicator settings. The result was that it was unknown whether or not emergency power had been called. Questioned several times about pre-impact malfunctions, Cable emphasized that it was not possible to prove serviceability; he could not prove a negative.

More from the air marshals

Finally, the Committee recalled ACMs Sir John Day and Sir William Wratten. Although they appeared together, the questions were mainly addressed to Sir John. Day repeated his assertion that the negligence occurred before the waypoint change but denied that this necessarily meant that the crew intended to continue with the planned track. He had previously sent the Committee a paper with a map, to which he then referred.[155] The map showed the point, on the aircraft's actual track, where the crew may have got their first glimpse of the Mull, about 1km away. He stated that the aircraft continued for some eight or nine seconds before the waypoint change was made, at a distance of about 600m from the shore. At that point, the crew should have realized their danger and made a 30 degree-banked turn to the left if they wanted to continue flying VFR. Leaving it for even a few seconds would mean that the angle of bank would need to be about 60 degrees.[156] Sir John found it completely negligent to place the aircraft in such a dangerous position; negligent not to have turned when they first saw the shore, before the waypoint change. Sir John based these calculations on an airspeed of 135–145kt with a wind component of 25kt, or a ground speed of nearly 3 miles (4.8km) a minute (288kph).

The alternative hypothesis was that, at some point before the waypoint change, they went into cloud. Either this was voluntarily because they had decided to climb over the Mull, or it was involuntarily. Either way they should have taken immediate action to outclimb the Mull with a low-level abort while turning left away from the high ground. Instead, they carried on with a serviceable aircraft to make a waypoint change. This also was negligent. Sir William added three conclusions: the Board was fully justified in concluding that flight near the Mull required IFR; the pilots had adequate time and skill to have reached safety altitude by the vicinity of the Mull; and, by choosing to remain at low level in the vicinity of the Mull, the pilots did not discharge their duty of care.

Lord Tombs pointed out that, during the Committee's trip to the Mull, they had established that a 12 degree turn to port a few seconds after the point of waypoint change *cleared the land quite easily*. Sir John objected that they had a clear day and Sir William claimed that the Committee's Chinook was above 300ft (91.4m), which would have put ZD576 in cloud. Lord Brennan wanted to know how other investigators had missed the conclusion that appeared so obvious to the air marshals. Day thought there was little difference in the conclusions: even though Pulford called it pilot error, it was negligent to have selected an inappropriate rate of climb.

As the exchanges continued, it became evident that there was less and less understanding between the Committee and the air marshals. The latter repeatedly had to refute conclusions that members of the Committee put to them. In addition, some of the questions were so badly phrased and convoluted that it is surprising that the air marshals managed to answer at all. At one point, the Chairman put it to Wratten that he could not say that he had *'absolutely no doubt'* that there was no mechanical problem (*sic*). Calmly, Wratten replied that there was *'absolutely no doubt'* that there had not been one before the waypoint change and that anything that happened afterwards did not mitigate the negligence. Day agreed. Later, Lord Tombs suggested to Day that the conclusion that the pre-impact serviceability of the aircraft could not be verified was rather *'less than absolutely certain'*. Day cited the flare manoeuvre as evidence that, at that point, the aircraft was under full control and that the pilot was responsible for the flare after he or someone else got an indication of their danger. In addition, the matched engine power settings indicated that there was no runaway in progress.

Asked about MacFarlane's claim that a Chinook could not climb at 1,000fpm doing 150kt, Day revealed that a test on the simulator had shown that, at that speed, with full power (100 per cent torque) it could climb at 650fpm. At 135kt, it climbed at 1,150fpm. When he flew to the Mull, Day himself achieved 1,100fpm at 135/140kt. He agreed that 1,000fpm and 150kt were incompatible.

Lord Brennan wanted to know if the air marshals would have found the pilots negligent if evidence that the crash had been caused by a malfunction were found, even though this malfunction occurred after the point of waypoint change. Was that not very severe? Day likened this hypothetical situation to someone driving too fast in fog and colliding with a lorry because his brakes have failed. Wratten pointed out that he had already answered this question, but agreed that such a judgement would be severe.

There the hearings ended. The evidence had taken about twenty-five hours and thirty-six separate written submissions had been made to the Committee. Transcripts, with additional notes, were published with many other documents in HL Papers 25(i) and 25(ii) – see References. The public hearings on 27 and 28 September were broadcast live on the BBC's Parliament Channel; recordings of those on 15 and 16 October and 7 November were broadcast later on those days and also early the next morning.

The Select Committee's report

On 31 January 2002, the Select Committee published its report.[157] Its first conclusion was that Boeing's mathematical simulation could not be relied on as accurate. Then, since the simulation was the basis for the Board's conclusions that the Chinook was under control at the time of the final flare, there was insufficient evidence that this was the case. Because it was persuaded that pilots usually change track after making a waypoint change, it doubted that there was absolutely no doubt whatsoever that the pilots intended to overfly the Mull; indeed it thought the opposite (sic) 'a distinct possibility if not more likely'. Nor did it think that it could be said that there was absolutely no doubt whatsoever that some mechanical failure had not caused a loss of control. It thought that a serious control jam or un-commanded flight control movement could provide the crew with a considerable distraction. However, it was satisfied that the E5 code found in one of the DECUs had no relevance to the accident. Nor did it think that the faulty altimeter was relevant. Pointing out that it was not its role to determine the cause of the accident, the Committee nevertheless considered that, on the evidence presented to it, the air marshals were not justified in finding that negligence by the pilots caused the crash.

The Committee was surprised that Wing Commander Pulford was appointed to conduct the inquiry into such a serious accident when he had never before conducted any Board of Inquiry. It observed that the high standard of proof required to find negligence required that all other plausible explanations for the crash be positively excluded. It also declared that the absence of evidence of an event that might produce an explanation is not proof positive that it did not. On the FAI, it observed that, although it was not required to find as to negligence, the sheriff's inability to determine the cause of the accident meant that no facts emerged from which negligence could be inferred. Commenting on the House of Commons Defence Committee's report, it noted that Dr Reid's declaration (that negligence would have been deemed to have taken place had the crash not occurred) was not stated by either air marshal in their written remarks to the Board's report.

The Committee disputed five 'facts' claimed by Sir John Day: that the point of waypoint change occurred about twenty seconds before impact (it is based on a speed of 150kt and a straight track from the waypoint change to impact); that the crew started to flare the aircraft some four seconds before impact (it is based on assumptions in the Boeing simulation); that the crew had chosen to fly straight over the Mull (they thought the change of waypoint indicated otherwise); that the aircraft was in a cruise climb at a rate of 1,000fpm in the last twenty seconds; and that emergency power was not pulled (Sir John had agreed that evidence of this last may have been destroyed).

The Committee recorded that, on 7 January 2002, it had received a letter from the MOD telling them that the aircraft had been observed on radar in Northern Ireland about 7nm from Belfast VOR on its track of 027 degrees at 17:47. Since the crash occurred at 17:59:30, 35nm down track, its average cruising speed must have been in excess of 150kt ground speed.[158] The Committee wondered why this information had not been made available earlier, but (in any case) it thought that it threw no light on the speed at waypoint change. Nor did it believe that it supported the Boeing simulation; the equivalent airspeed of 125kt was below the minimum of 135kt considered by Boeing. Considering all the evidence on visibility, the Committee concluded that the crew had probably seen the Mull, or at least breakers on the shore, at or before the time the waypoint was changed and it noted that Sir William Wratten accepted this as a possibility. It concluded that the crew could have flown VFR at low level just off the coast of the Mull and below the cloud, noting that there was no evidence that the low cloud on the Mull extended over the sea.

The Committee concluded that there was no evidence to the required standard of proof that the aircraft was under control four seconds before impact; rejecting evidence from the simulation, it concluded that the evidence suggested otherwise. It was impressed by evidence that the *'enormous rudder input'* was unusual and inexplicable and also by the idea of a control jam. While rejecting the air marshals' verdict, the Committee ended by concluding that it would never be known why the aircraft flew into the Mull.

As a result of the report, Lord Chalfont wrote to Prime Minister Tony Blair, urging him to seek independent advice on the cause of the accident. Chalfont claimed that the air staff would *'simply provide the brief which they have adhered to for years'* and that the MOD had a conflict of interest. The issue had reached a critical stage, with a need for the air marshals' verdict of gross negligence to be set aside. He warned that, if it were not, his campaign might be *'stepped up'* and MPs and peers might raise the constitutional matter of whether the final say over what caused the crash should lie with officials or with Parliament.

The Government's response to the Select Committee's report

The Government's response was made in statements to both Houses of Parliament on the afternoon of 22 July 2002; in the Lords by Lord Bach, the Parliamentary Under-Secretary of State in the Ministry of Defence, and in the Commons (a little later) by Geoff Hoon, the Secretary of State for Defence. The statements reviewed the response and were identical. It was announced that the Government (MOD) had carefully considered the Committee's report and was placing copies of its response, together with copies of further work by Boeing, in the libraries of both Houses of Parliament (see References). Apart from a summary, the response deals with five aspects: chronology of the flight; alternative hypotheses; weather; Boeing's further work; and the standard of proof (the following summary is drawn from both the statement and the response).

Parliament was told that, based on a total journey time of *'just under 18 minutes'*, the average ground speed of the Chinook was 158kt, which was described as *'a high cruising speed for their crossing'*. This was based on deducting the time of an exchange with ATC at 16:42:24 UT from the time of the power down of the SuperTANS (16:59:36 UT).[159] From the evidence at the crash site and the position of the flight controls, it was concluded that the aircraft had flared in the final few seconds and that this indicated that the aircraft was under control at that point. It was claimed that these *'facts'* had not been seriously challenged by anyone. Further analysis by Boeing had shown that the aircraft could not have slowed to 80kt at the point of waypoint change (it would not have been able to accelerate from below 80kt and achieve the speed conditions necessary for the flare). Boeing also concluded that, although the aircraft slowed slightly as it approached the Mull, the increased wind speed in that vicinity maintained its ground speed. From the weather forecast, Boeing concluded that, until the waypoint change, the tailwind component was 9.2kt at the surface and 24.5kt at 2,000ft. The MOD reported that Boeing, after analysing data logged by the SuperTANS, discovered that the last steering command was recorded less than a second before impact. Taking account of tyre tracks and wind speed, Boeing derived a ground speed of 162.8kt on a heading of 017 degrees true. The MOD claimed that this was consistent with the ground speed derived from the last displayed *'distance to go'* (86.63nm) and *'time to go'* (32.8 min.) received from the steering command calculation. It was claimed that the difference between the above ground speed and the recorded ground speed of 150kt (*sic*) produces a derived instantaneous flight path angle of +23 degrees climb. Likewise, a similar comparison between the recorded and *'assumed'* airspeed produced an angle of +20 degrees. It was claimed that both these values correlated well with the AAIB's conclusions on probable flight path at impact. The MOD claimed that data from the SuperTANS, not originally available to Boeing, showed that, immediately prior to impact, the airspeed was 135kt. Boeing claimed that, in theory, a Mk2 can climb at a rate of 1,000fpm at 150kt (airspeed) without exceeding engine limits, although there is difficulty setting up and maintaining engine torque. It also claimed that the post-impact rotor speed on the rotor RPM gauge did not reflect the pre-impact speed and that, at 91 per cent, the coning angle of the rotors would be only 4.5 degrees, only 1 degree greater than normal for an aircraft of ZD576's weight.

For a control jam to have occurred, the aircraft would first have had to have been rotated nose down to an accelerating attitude, the power set to full, and the controls 'frozen' to such an extent that neither a heading change, nor a climb, nor a speed change, was possible. Moreover, this condition would have had to remain fixed throughout the significant period required to achieve the acceleration. To achieve these conditions, either simultaneous multiple failures would have had to have occurred to the pitch of the aircraft and frozen the controls, or the pilots would have had voluntarily to conduct at least some of the extraordinary control combinations needed. On the matter of a detached thrust balance spring and other inserts, it was stated that, because the controls were hydraulically powered, such a fault would merely have resulted in a change in the 'feel' of the controls, detectable by the pilots; the aircraft would still have been controllable and it was not credible that this could have caused the accident. The brackets were likely to have detached in the crash. Because of the turbulent conditions, the handling pilot would have had to make constant control inputs and adjustments that would have revealed any tendency to jam. The AFCS would also have been making minor control inputs. As a result, a catastrophic control failure could not have gone unnoticed. If it had occurred before the point of waypoint change, the crew would not have made the change. The fine metal slivers had been caught on the servo screens, where they did no harm, and the hydraulic fluid itself was found to be fit for use.

On the matter of negligence, it was stated that it did not depend on whether (or not) the pilots could see the Mull at the time of waypoint change. It could be concluded that, at some point, the aircraft entered cloud well below safety altitude. The issue was whether (or not), at the time they did so, the aircraft was fully under control (Bach and Hoon had already explained that the Government concluded that it had been). As they approached the Mull, the crew would have been aware that their visibility was about to reduce significantly. Had they been flying with the minimum visibility allowed for VFR, then, by the point of waypoint change, they would have seen the Mull and should have flown higher or turned away. It was negligent to fail to take avoiding action. Consequently it was regretted that, after reviewing all the alternatives, the Government could not posthumously exonerate the pilots.

The MOD noted the Committee's conclusion that the crew probably saw the Mull at or before the waypoint change and that they intended to fly around the Mull under VFR. It noted that there is no evidence for or against this idea, but claimed that, had the crew been able to see the Mull, they would have appreciated that they were displaced to the east and that they were perilously close to high ground (Sir John Day had made the same claim to the Committee).

The response made a comment on the incident in which a US Army Chinook inverted at 1,100ft and only righted itself 250ft from the ground. The US Accident Investigation Board suspected that the Forward Swivel Actuator (part of the Upper Boost Actuator) had jammed because of contaminated hydraulic oil[160], causing an uncommanded attitude change. The MOD concluded that no remedial action was required to the RAF's Chinooks, certainly not the Mk2s, which are fitted with an improved actu-ator that could not suffer from this problem.

The MOD concluded that the 4 degrees C isotherm over the Mull at the time of the accident was at 3,500ft and, therefore, that there was nothing to prevent the aircraft reaching safety alti-tude over the Mull, which they put at 2,400ft (731.5m).

Having noted the Select Committee's criticism of the Boeing simulation, the MOD had commissioned further work from Boeing. This was undertaken on a more advanced model known as BH-Sim (B-29), which fully reflects FADEC technical parameters and flight performance and a more realistic range schedule for the rotors (see Boeing's 2002 report, which also contains Boeing's comments on selected sections of the Select Committee's report). This work did not change any of Boeing's conclusions except to withdraw their claim that only first impact at 150kt airspeed met the specified response criteria—they now allowed airspeeds down to 120kt or below, but preferred 135kt which they adopted in a new flight profile (see p. 179).

In summing up, Bach and Hoon confirmed the verdict that the pilots were negligent, but the detailed response added the conclu-sion that the accident was a controlled flight into terrain.

After the statement in the Lords, there was a short (half-hour) question and answer session in which Lord Craig of Radley called for an end to unfounded attacks on the integrity and professional judgement of the two air marshals. Lord Chalfont, astonished by the Government's response, described the air marshals' verdict as *'manslaughter'*. The House was promised a full debate on the matter in the autumn. This occurred on 5 November 2002, on a motion that the House *'take note'* of it. However, Lord Chalfont proposed an amendment that would (instead) *'accept the report'* and call on the Government to *'set aside the finding of gross negli-gence against the two pilots'*. A five-hour debate followed, ending after midnight. Strong views were expressed on both sides, many supporting the Government and critical of the Select Committee, some lords even regretting that it had been established or that they had voted for its establishment. Some were concerned that this was only the second time (the first was twenty-four years earlier) that an amendment to such a motion had been proposed and they called on Chalfont to withdraw his amendment. He

171

refused to do that, but declared that he had no intention of bringing the matter again before the Lords. Lord Burnham made the interesting observation that the pilots must have wanted to overfly the lighthouse *'to check their navigation'*. Chalfont's amendment was lost by sixty-five to thirty-four, but a motion to note the report was agreed without a vote. This debate was broadcast on the BBC's Parliament Channel on 14 November 2002.

Chapter Nine

Review of the Evidence and Conclusions

Readers who have reached this point may feel somewhat over-whelmed and confused by the plethora of disputed data and conflicting views. How can sense be made of it all? Only by patient analysis and concentration on those data which emerge clearly from the fog. First, it is necessary to dispel some distractions.

Tracks and turns

There has been much confusion about tracks and turns. It seems that the track to the lighthouse was 020 degrees T and that, with a magnetic deviation of 7.8 degrees W, the compass track should have been 27.8 degrees M. Indeed, Tapper's HCS was set close to that, at 028M, although many, including Tapper himself, have referred to it as 027M. Cook, having to cope with a crosswind, had his HCS set to 035M, the heading he required to keep them on track for waypoint A. Near the waypoint, one of them, prob-ably Tapper, selected data for waypoint B (Corran), getting advice to turn left to obtain a heading of 025M, the actual track required being 020M. Even at that time, the aircraft was east of track, the bearing to waypoint A having drifted down to 018T (026M) and it was on a track of 022T (030M).

Over the Mull

There has also been confusion about flying over the Mull of Kintyre. Without qualification, this may suggest a flight from one side of the peninsula to the other, from the North Channel to Kilbrannan Sound. It may even be associated with the idea that the crew did not intend to turn left towards Corran, but intended to fly straight on over the lighthouse towards Machrihanish Airfield. Although few have proposed that, it needs to be pointed out that *flying over the Mull* refers to flying along a track plotted from waypoint A to waypoint B, along and over the high ground along the western edge of the peninsula between the Mull in the south and Machrihanish in the north. It is the alternative to turning left short of the lighthouse (or at the lighthouse if one could see it) and flying northwards parallel with the coast but keeping within sight of it. References to *'flying over the Mull'* without the above qualification have not been helpful.

The sheriff's conclusion

Another point of confusion has been the result of the FAI. Many appear to believe that the sheriff either rejected the RAF's judgement of negligence or they seize on his declaration that he could not say that there had been negligence (implying that this was a denial of that judgement). In fact, as the sheriff pointed out, because FAIs cannot attribute negligence, he refrained from doing so. Although his Determination rejects the MOD's explanation for the accident, it has no bearing on the air marshals' verdict of gross negligence.

Weather and visibility

At the time, a depression lay to the west of Ireland with an associated cold front moving east across Northern Ireland, bringing showers by early afternoon. Ahead of it, Scotland remained dry but cloudy with just a few light showers. The situation that the pilots faced is described by the aftercast (see p. 59), which tells of the very poor visibility on the Mull itself while visibility elsewhere varied from up to 2km below the cloud base to up to 10km at sea level.

By chance, a weather satellite took a picture of the area just one

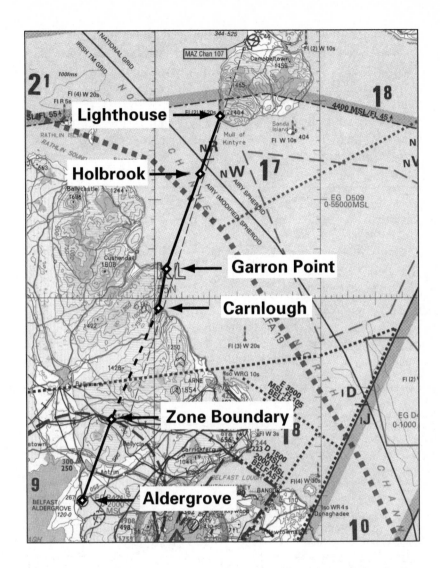

Part of the 1/500,000-scale aeronautical chart used by Tapper to plan the first part of the route to Scotland (LFC Sheet 3, Edition 34) to which has been added the route of ZD576 to the Mull of Kintyre (shown as a broken line where the exact route is uncertain). The diagonal broken line which passes close to the lighthouse is an isogonic line joining places where the magnetic declination was 7½° west in 1994. The original map is in colour. ©*Crown copyright.*

and a half minutes before the crash (see plate 2). It shows the cloud cover over a wide area of Ireland, Scotland and Northern England. The cloud was widespread, but it can be seen that it was patchy over the North Channel on the route taken by ZD576. This agrees with the yachtsman's report of thin cloud through which the sunlight was filtering. The patch of low stratus ends short of the Mull, which is hidden under higher clouds, as is any orographic cloud around the Mull.

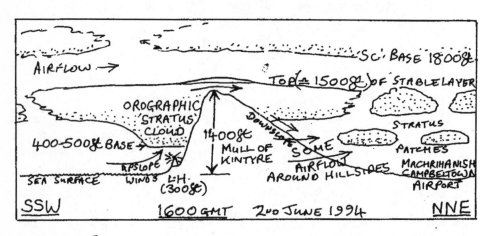

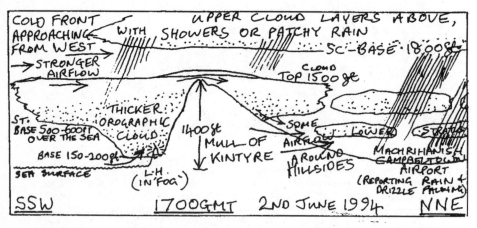

Schematic SSW to NNE cross-section (not to scale) of the weather around the Mull of Kintyre making use of all available observations (from Pike 2001b). The upper diagram shows the situation an hour before the crash and the lower one the situation at the time – illustrating how the weather was deteriorating. *Copyright: William Pike and* The Journal of Meteorology UK.

The weather at the time of the crash has been thoroughly discussed in the pages of *The Journal of Meteorology (UK)*, mainly by William Pike (see References). His conclusion was that the crew endeavoured to maintain VFR by flying just below the stratus at 500ft. He accepts that the crew could probably make out the shore of the Mull and perhaps part of the lighthouse before they found themselves in the orographic cloud around the Mull, which came down to about 200ft below the Chinook. Once in the cloud, they could see the Mull no more than the people on the Mull could see the aircraft. However, his schematic cross-section (opposite) shows that the orographic cloud would have cleared at about 1,500ft, above the highest peaks on the Mull, and would have broken up into patches north of the Mull. It also shows how the weather was deteriorating. The main cloud base was at 1,800ft.

During the FAI, it emerged that Holbrook's statement was not made until some weeks later, after Strathclyde Police had traced him. In a statement to them, he gave visibility as about 1 mile (1.6km), limited by haze, and that quite dense low cloud covered the Mull, following the contours behind and above the lighthouse two miles away. Although Holbrook explained this discrepancy to the House of Lords Select Committee, it has been used to claim that neither he nor the pilots could have seen the Mull at that time. In fact it is more likely that Holbrook saw the Mull than that he estimated visibility at a range lower than his distance from it. The coordinates that Holbrook gave to the Board are for a position that is about 2.1nm from the Mull, about 2.6nm from the lighthouse and about 0.5nm west of the Chinook's track. It is also about 9.5nm from the Antrim coast.

If the visibility at sea level was 2–10km, then it is understandable how Holbrook could see the Mull, Antrim and perhaps the lighthouse from his position. However, it seems that visibility higher up was not so good—no more than 2km at between 200 and 800ft and probably less. Consequently, if the Chinook was flying at 300–400ft, the crew might not have been able to see clearly for more than about 1km and they would not see the Mull until they came within that distance. At some point, they may have seen the shoreline below the fog hanging over the upper part of the Mull. With a Force 7 wind, there would be white foam crests on waves and breakers on the shore. Even the MOD appears to accept this possibility; Sir John Day told the House of Lords Select Committee that, if the pilots were flying in VMC, they would have seen the cliffs of the Mull as they approached.

The aftercast shows that the 4 degrees C level was at 5,000ft, well above the safety altitude around the Mull. However, the crew would not have known that. Seeing the air temperature at 9 degrees C, and assuming a two-degree C drop every 1,000ft, they would have calculated that the 4 degrees C level would be at 2,500ft, *below* the safety altitude.

The speed of the Chinook

This has been the subject of much speculation and various conclusions. The AAIB, understandably dealing only with the crash parameters, stated that the airspeed was recorded as 127.6kt (234.7kph) and that the GPS system recorded a ground speed of 150kt. The damaged GSDI jammed at 147kt (276kph). Because Boeing's simulation found a match for the AAIB's impact parameters only when it assumed an initial airspeed of 150kt, that (or 151kt) was accepted by the MOD, as has a ground speed of 174kt (based on a wind component of 24kt). Boeing's later review of their simulation showed that it had been skewed towards a high airspeed. They have since opted for an airspeed before control inputs of 135kt (see opposite), but allow that it could be as low as 130kt.

The average speed has also been variously estimated. Yachtsman Mark Holbrook told the Board (but not the FAI) that the aircraft was travelling *'somewhat faster than Sea Kings in level flight'*[161], which the MOD has pointed out is about 100–110kt (his own estimate was far lower than that and clearly wrong). At the FAI, the counsel for the relatives of Flight Lieutenant Tapper claimed that the aircraft's average ground speed was 150kt and the sheriff himself calculated it as 152kt. He also calculated that, assuming a tail wind of 24kt, the average airspeed was 128kt. Despite all that, in an apparent attempt to make the speed fit the Boeing simulation, the counsel for the

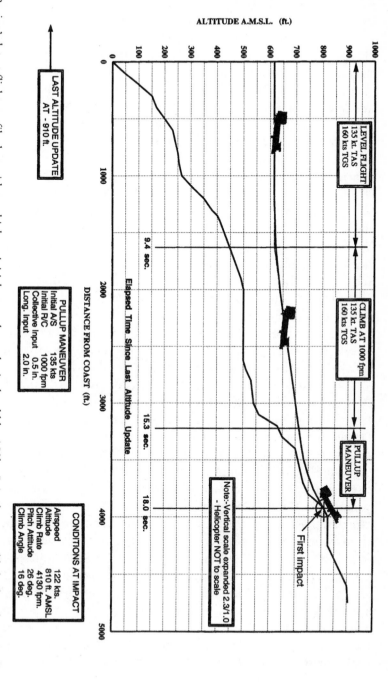

ALTITUDE A.M.S.L. (ft.)

LEVEL FLIGHT
135 kt. TAS
160 kts TGS

CLIMB AT 1000 fpm
135 kt. TAS
160 kts TGS

PULLUP MANEUVER

Note:- Vertical scale expanded 2.3/1.0
- Helicopter NOT to scale

First impact

9.4 sec.

15.3 sec.

18.0 sec.

Elapsed Time Since Last Altitude Update

DISTANCE FROM COAST (ft.)

LAST ALTITUDE UPDATE
AT - 910 ft.

PULLUP MANEUVER
Initial A/S   135 kts
Initial R/C   1000 fpm
Collective Input   0.5 in.
Long. Input   2.0 in.

CONDITIONS AT IMPACT
Airspeed   122 kts.
Altitude   810 ft. AMSL
Climb Rate   4130 fpm.
Pitch Attitude 26 deg.
Climb Angle   16 deg.

Boeing's latest flight profile, but with too high an initial ground speed – it should be 150kt. It is also more likely that the aircraft was climbing before landfall.

MOD at the FAI (Dunlop) insisted that, before the final flare, the aircraft had been travelling at 174kt ground speed and that, after it, the ground speed had been 150kt. This conclusion was accepted by the sheriff in his determination, despite his own different calculation and despite having challenged Dunlop's claim in the FAI (when he asked how the aircraft had come to accelerate). More recently, Boeing has calculated that the average speed was 158kt. This was based on the aircraft being identified on radar as '*7nm from the Aldergrove VOR . . . radio beacon*' at 16:46:24, described by the MOD as '*leaving the Aldergrove control zone*'. In fact, the control zone has nothing to do with the VOR. Nor does it appear to have been a radar identification; it was a VHF radio exchange in which the pilots were reporting that they had reached the Belfast control zone boundary (see p. 11). Worse, the zone boundary is at 9nm, not 7. Consequently, Boeing's calculation of the average speed is too high. It is not clear why the MOD left Boeing to do this simple calculation.

In their 2002 report, Boeing point out that the aircraft's ground speed just before impact can be calculated from the time and range to waypoint B being shown by the SuperTANS (it would have calculated these parameters from the aircraft's speed at the time). The result is 158.5kt[162] (or 162.6kt at power-down).

The average ground speed of the aircraft over the 42nm from Aldergrove to the Mull of Kintyre lighthouse is simply calculated from the departure time (16:42:46) and the time of impact (16:59:36), a total time of sixteen minutes and fifty seconds. This comes to 150kt (to the nearest knot).[163] When Boeing's error is corrected, their calculated average speed from the zone boundary to the point of impact comes back down to 150kt.[164] If the aircraft was blown along on average by a 24kt wind, we can also calculate that the average airspeed must have been about 126kt (higher if the wind speed was lower), little more than the typical cruising speed of a Chinook and close to the AAIB's stated airspeed at impact. Far from selecting a high speed, the crew appear to have selected a normal speed, below the 140kt airspeed, above which VFR require better visibility and greater separation from cloud. There also seem to be no grounds for claiming that the speed increased near the Mull. The only change would be the slight decrease in speed that resulted from the final flare. Nevertheless, this speed is not slow; the helicopter hit the hillside at about the top speed of a Formula 1 racing car.

If we accept this average ground speed as the speed for almost the whole journey, we can use it to check on the times at which the Chinook passed the two observers en route who gave times. It shows that the aircraft must have gone over Carnlough at about 16:50, within the time frame Ann Tyler gave (16:45–16:50). Yachtsman Mark Holbrook says it passed him shortly after 16:55. At that time, the aircraft was still 8nm from the Mull and over 9nm from the lighthouse. However, for every minute that passed, this encounter occurred another 2.5nm closer to the Mull. If he were 2.1nm from the Mull, then he must have seen the Chinook at about 16:58, quite likely if his friend had finished listening to the weather forecast at 16:55 and had, by then, emerged on deck. It might be argued that, with a higher wind speed over the North Channel, the aircraft was likely to have travelled faster over the water than over the land. However, any increase in speed over one part of the journey must be compensated by a lower speed on another. A lower speed over Antrim would mean that the aircraft would have passed over Carnlough a little later than recorded by Ann Tyler. This does not seem to be justified; the Chinook appears to have maintained a steady speed of 150kt ground speed throughout.

The House of Lords Select Committee rejected many of the air marshals' conclusions on the basis that the speed they assumed was not high enough. In fact, it was the Committee's mistake, in assuming too high a speed.

Malfunction

The accident in Wilmington in 1989 was to a Mk1 Chinook that, for testing purposes, had been fitted with an experimental FADEC engine control system. The unit inquiry (not a Board) that investigated found that the accident was caused by an error in testing procedure, specifically the disconnection of a vital connector. It turned out that it was also due to a fault in the FADEC software that allowed a catastrophic engine runaway when the signal from that connector was lost. In effect, it was due to an unfortunate combination of these two factors. The aircraft was seriously damaged, but not beyond repair and the FADEC software was later substantially rewritten before Mk2s were introduced into service. Consequently, allegations that the incident showed that FADEC is dangerous and might have contributed to the Kintyre crash are misplaced and specious. It is invalid to argue that, because an engine runaway occurred five years earlier in a Chinook on test when a vital sensor was disconnected and the software was not able to cope, this happened on the fatal flight of ZD576. The problems that Boscombe Down experienced appear to have been self-inflicted, in taking FADEC beyond its limits. As a result, BD unnecessarily alarmed Chinook pilots. Nor, as it turned out, were the CA Release restrictions necessary.

FADEC has not featured in any of the other Chinook crashes, all to Mk1s fitted with a hydro-mechanical fuel control system with a poor record for reliability. Although the particular FADEC system installed in the RAF Chinooks is unique to them, similar computerized fuel control systems are installed in US and Dutch Chinooks, all Airbuses, the Boeings 767 and 777, Concorde and aircraft of the Queen's Flight.[165] Consequently, such an engine control system is not inherently unsafe and it has not been implicated in any aircraft accident. Nor, once the software was rewritten, has the RAF FADEC given further trouble. It is inherently unlikely therefore that the FADEC had anything to do with the accident. The House of Lords Select Committee accepted that neither the E5 code found in one of the FADEC's DECUs nor the faulty altimeter were relevant to the accident.

Excluding the Wilmington incident, of the eight other Chinook accidents (see table opposite and reports in Appendix One), only two were definitely attributed to a technical fault and in neither case were there any fatalities. In only one fatal case were mechanical faults discovered which could have caused the accident. However, in the case of ZD576, no mechanical fault was found. Crew error has been identified as the cause in all the fatal accidents except for one, the cause of which could not positively be determined.

Much has been made of the fact that the AAIB admitted that it could not exclude the possibility of pre-impact damage or faults

RAF Chinooks lost in crashes

Date	Location	Cause	Fatalities
14 November 1984	Hampshire	Technical Fault	Nil
13 May 1986	Falkland Islands	Human Factors (Aircrew)	3
27 February 1987	Falkland Islands	Not Positively Determined	7
6 May 1988	Hannover [sic]	Human Factors (Aircrew)	3
24 July 1989	RAF Odiham	Non Service Control*	Nil
25 July 1989	Falkland Islands	Non Service Control*	Nil
15 October 1991	RAF Odiham	Technical Fault	Nil
2 June 1994	Mull of Kintyre	Human Factors (Aircrew)	29

From the HOC Defence Committee's Report *Lessons of the Chinook Crash on the Mull of Kintyre* (Fourth Report Session 1997/98).

* Indicates a cause or contributory factor which was outside the RAF's control, e.g. a problem arising out of air management such as an air traffic control error or a technical difficulty arising out of a contractor's error.

with some systems in ZD576. Those convinced that the accident was caused by some mechanical fault, that somehow distracted the pilots at the moment when they should have been turning or made it impossible to turn the aircraft, have seized on this admission as evidence that there was such a fault. However, absence of evidence is not evidence of absence (nor evidence of presence). If a mechanical component is found to be damaged from the impact, but it could have been faulty or damaged before the impact, *and there is no way to distinguish between these two alternatives*, it cannot be assumed that the damage was pre-impact. Claims that there was a pre-impact fault need to be based on direct evidence of such a fault. The complete absence of such evidence suggests that there was no such fault and that the aircraft was completely serviceable when it crashed. There is also the evidence of an attempt to avoid collision (see below).

Boeing explain the 77 per cent left 'rudder' by pointing out that the impact of the right front of the aircraft with terrain sloping to the left is likely to have forced the right pedal aft, consequently forcing the left pedal forwards.

Many of the MOD's critics claim that the Boeing simulation did not match with either the wreckage or the impact marks.[166] They appear to have overlooked the fact that the simulation was based on Tony Cable's assessment of the wreckage and the impact marks, not the other way about. Furthermore, the simulation can be no better than Cable's assessment. If he has made any mistakes about the impact parameters, they will carry over into the simulation making it difficult or impossible. Despite the difficulty Boeing experienced in matching Cable's parameters, the evidence for a flare in the last few seconds remains convincing, and logical. If the aircraft were under control, then an emergency pull-up is only to be expected. Nor is it likely that, after normal radio communications up to five minutes before the crash and a normal selection of data for the next waypoint only twenty seconds before the crash, a serious control fault developed and then cleared itself after just seventeen seconds, three seconds before impact. As was pointed out at the FAI, the chance of this happening is very remote and must be discounted. Some also claim that, if there had been such a flare, lighthouse keeper Murchie would have heard a change in the sound of the aircraft.

Since the engine house was between him and the aircraft at the time, it is unsurprising that he did not report such a change. Also, the fog would have muffled all sounds. This is not a sustainable argument against a flare. In their 2002 report, Boeing suggest that, because of the speed of events, the witnesses on the Mull would not be able to distinguish between the sound of violent manoeuvre and that of the crash itself.

Computer Weekly's interest in the whole affair is somewhat mysterious. One would imagine that a computer trade journal would be interested on account of some problem with computers on the aircraft, those which control the engines or the navigation computer, or both. However, CW has been unable to point to any defect known to be present in either of the computer systems at the time. It certainly could not point to any computer defect responsible for the crash. It is hard to see how knowledge of historical problems with FADEC would have changed anything. Consequently, one has to conclude that CW was merely exploiting public interest in the accident and, in particular, the campaign to exonerate the pilots. Its report has not helped to explain the accident.

In relation to several claims, including CW's, that the aircraft's engines were not operating at full power at the time of the crash, it should be pointed out that, while the AAIB report concluded that the engines were operating at about 70 per cent of maximum power, it suggested that they may have relaxed from maximum when relieved of the load from the rotors, seconds before the final crash which involved the engines themselves. In other words, the as-found state of the engines was not necessarily any guide to their performance just before the crash. Boeing have since pointed out (in their 2002 report) that the flare would have put a demand on the engines that they would be unable to meet immediately (accounting for the 91 per cent RPM at first impact). This impact is likely to have severed the drive to the forward rotor, diverting more power to the aft rotor, which would then accelerate (accounting for the cockpit display showing 100.5 per cent). Then, if FADEC continued to operate, it would reduce engine power to 100 per cent, so explaining why the engines were found to be at an intermediate power setting.

Sir John Day's claim that the pilots would have pulled

emergency power if faced with a control restriction (except for yaw) assumes that they knew that they might otherwise hit the rising ground, which he states was *'predominantly to their right'*. However, if they believed that their cruise climb would easily carry them over the lighthouse and onto the track for Corran, they cannot have feared hitting the ground. Why would they pull emergency power to clear ground that they already believed was well off to their right? Moreover, if a control restriction froze the controls for the cruise climb, surely that climb would continue and there would be no need for emergency power. In fact there is no evidence for a control restriction or the application of emergency power, albeit the latter was probably applied in the last three seconds, but leaving no record.

The crew's intention

When the sortie was being planned, Kingston and Trapp were willing to undertake it, even though it was on their scheduled rest day. So why did Tapper and Cook take it when they had been flying all morning and were in danger of running over their daily limit by doing so? No answer to this question appeared until Tapper's father gave evidence to the House of Lords Select Committee. Kingston had less experience on Chinooks and was accompanied by a navigator, not another pilot. Tapper was concerned about them getting into difficulties with an aircraft which (allegedly) he and Cook distrusted. In an emergency, Trapp would be little help to Kingston, who may not have had enough experience to cope. It seems that Tapper felt that it was safer for his experienced crew to undertake the sortie to Scotland. There was also the attraction of a change from the boring routine 'bus runs' of normal Northern Ireland operations. It was a chance of a change of scenery. As the senior pilot, Tapper could *'pull rank'* and insist on his crew taking the mission. However, he appears to have ignored the time problem, not telling Stangroom that the schedule required ten and a half hours' flying. Did he think that he could get that down to eight hours? The evidence is that it was impossible.

Did they intend to return to Aldergrove that evening? Although the Board came to no conclusion, there is much evidence that they did. When Cook's brother Chris called the officers' mess in Aldergrove to ask to speak to him (after he had heard about the crash), he was told that, although he was not there, he had booked a late dinner.[167] In addition, the crew's request for a weather forecast gave the expected return time as 21:00 GMT and Stangroom told the Board that JATOC expected the Chinook to return that evening. Evidently, they expected to return that day. Having consumed five hours forty minutes in the morning troop movements and anticipating taking one hour thirty-eight minutes to get to Inverness, only forty-two minutes would be left to get back to Aldergrove before the eight-hour limit expired. However, with a following wind and at an average speed of 150kt, the journey to Inverness might take only one hour eighteen minutes (arriving about 19:00), leaving about one hour to return. Allowing for refuelling in Inverness, they might indeed expect to be back by 22:00, the end of normal working hours. Whether or not Tapper called SRAFONI for permission to exceed the limit on the return, he would have been reprimanded. Was this of no concern to him?

It has to be assumed that Tapper entered the coordinates for the lighthouse (as he thought) aware that Kingston and Trapp had intended the turning point to be to the west of it, not over it. Indeed, he told Wing Commander Stangroom that it (the Mull lighthouse) was his point of entry into Low Flying Area 14 and that it was one of his turning points. It is unfortunate that Tapper did not enter the exact coordinates for the lighthouse; he could have obtained them from an Admiralty list[168], but perhaps the RAF does not use Admiralty data. Instead, he estimated them from a chart. In doing so, he made a slight error in the wrong direction.[169] An error to the west would perhaps have saved the aircraft. However, Tapper cannot have known of this error and may have assumed that he had plotted the lighthouse more accurately than he did. Nevertheless, he did know that the waypoint was at or near the lighthouse and that it had been planned that they should turn somewhere to the west of it. But did his crew agree with that plan? Or did they always plan to overfly the lighthouse? If so, why would they do so? An answer to this question was given by Squadron Leader Burke to the

House of Lords Select Committee. He was asked why a pilot would continue towards a waypoint after identifying it, instead of turning early to *'cut the corner'*. He explained that the purpose of overflying a waypoint, especially after flying over sea, was to update the Doppler input into the TANS because the Doppler had problems over the sea. Indeed, the CA Release had reported that the Doppler is subject to 'degraded performance over water' and this was confirmed by the Racal report.[170] Evidently, the GSDI has difficulty tracking drift over a moving surface. The CA Release also advised that the accuracy of the GPS system could not be guaranteed 'to any level' and that it should not be relied on as the sole navigation aid.[171] The evidence is that Tapper at least distrusted the accuracy of the SuperTANS. If the crew were aware of these deficiencies, they would have tried to minimize them by updating the SuperTANS with accurate position data whenever possible. To do so, they needed to be at a known position and the only available position as they neared land was the Mull of Kintyre lighthouse, which they identified with waypoint A. In fact, the Doppler had drifted about 300m to the right and the GPS had a left error. The only other reason for not skirting around the Mull was that it would cost them time. Since the change of track was only about 7 degrees, there was not much of a corner to cut.

Consequently, the crew's intention appears to have been to use the SuperTANS as a general guide to the lighthouse and then, when it was sighted, to fly as close as possible to it to update the Doppler. Their expectation was that, with the waypoint plotted close to the lighthouse, they would come upon it at landfall. However, as it turned out they were faced with the problem of cloud around the Mull. Could they update the Doppler without even seeing the lighthouse?

As Group Captain Crawford and others have pointed out, the selection of the next waypoint indicates an intention to turn very shortly onto a new track for Corran. Indeed, the selection of waypoint B indicates that the lighthouse had been seen and identified. Until the change of waypoint, the distance and time to waypoint A was shown on the SuperTANS. Consequently, they would have known how long it would be until they were over the waypoint (lighthouse). From about this point, the aircraft

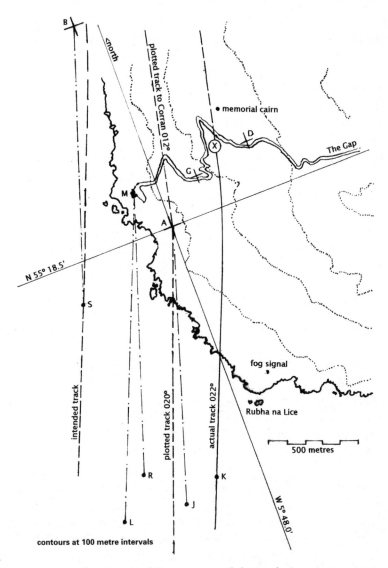

Sketch map of the area around the crash site

A = waypoint A
B = where the crew probably thought waypoint A was
D = the Doppler plot at powerdown
G = the GPS plot at powerdown
J = SuperTANS plot at leg transfer
K = Most likely position of aircraft at leg transfer

L = where the MOD thought the crew thought they were at leg transfer
M = the Mull of Kintyre Lighthouse
R = where the sheriff thought the crew thought they were at leg transfer
S = where the crew probably thought they were at leg transfer
X = the initial impact point

appears to have begun a climb of about 1,000fpm. The Board recognized that the *lack of a significant change of track and a ROC of around 1,000fpm in the period after the waypoint change, appear to support the theory that the crew elected to climb and overfly the Mull of Kintyre on track for Corran*.[172] If the crew believed that the 4 degrees C level was some 300ft below safety altitude, they could not follow regulations and abort to safety level when they entered cloud. However, they could climb steadily to clear the high ground they knew to be underneath the track to Corran. The direct track to Corran from the lighthouse lay over a small hill 948ft (289m) high and, a little further north, over the west flank of Cnoc Moy at about 1,350ft (411.5m). Indeed, if they had been on track for the lighthouse and turned when they reached it, this climb would have given clearance of those obstacles. According to Sir John Day's flight profile, by four seconds before impact, before the emergency flare, they had already reached 665ft (202.6m). Assuming that they would have reached 730ft (222.5m) by the time they were over the lighthouse, and assuming a continued rate of climb of 1,000fpm on the track for Corran, they would have cleared the 948ft hill by 1,046ft (318.8m) and the western flank of Cnoc Moy by 1,455ft (443.5m), when they would have been at about 2,800ft, coincidentally the safety altitude for the first leg, but above where they believed the 4 degrees C level to be. They might also have emerged from the cloud around the Mull. So perhaps they intended to level out at 2,500ft, still over 1,000ft above any ground on the route to Corran. Alternatively, perhaps they expected clear air at 2,800ft, in which case the 4 degrees C limitation would not apply. Since 1,000ft clearance is required for IFR flight, it can be argued that the crew were intent on flying under IFR. After that, they may have hoped to see the ground again and return to VFR. Since the rules allowed a crew to transfer to IFR and reach safety altitude in a cruise climb if they have sufficient warning that VMC will be lost, it can be argued that this was exactly what they were doing, albeit they entered cloud before reaching safety altitude and feared to reach that altitude because of the icing limitation. An advantage of a cruise climb over a maximum power pull-up would be that the air temperature could be closely monitored so that the crew would know the rate of temperature fall and how

190

near they were to the 4 degrees C level. We now know that it was about 5,000ft and that the temperature was still 8 degrees C at 3,000ft. The crew would have found that they could have climbed to safety altitude, where the temperature would have been at least 7 degrees C. They may also have been conscious of a regulation that prohibited the use of full power (torque) to achieve maximum rate of climb (except in an emergency). The normal maximum rate of climb was 3,000fpm. A cruise climb at 1,000fpm was easier on the engines, and perhaps on the passengers.

It has been claimed that a rate of climb (ROC) of 1,000fpm could not be achieved with an airspeed of 150kt and that it would need to come down to 135kt. In fact, the Chinook was travelling at a lower speed than that and so can quite easily have achieved a ROC of 1,000fpm.

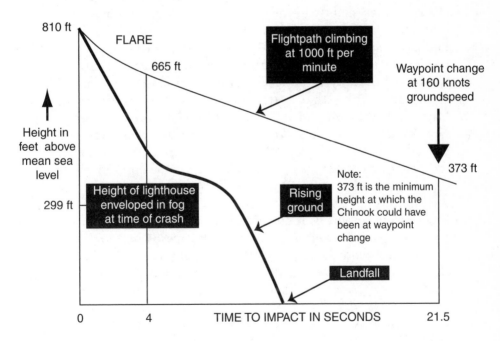

A reconstruction of Sir John Day's calculated flight path with an IAS of 135kt (GS of 160kt). However, at 150kt GS, the waypoint change must have occurred 22.8 second before impact at a minimum height of 351ft.

191

What went wrong?

To answer this question, it is necessary to establish what is known (or believed) before speculating on what is not known. If Holbrook could see the Mull when the Chinook passed him, then it is quite likely that the crew also saw it, albeit, because their visibility was less than his, a little later. At their height, visibility might have been no more than about 1km, as assumed by the air marshals. On the track they were flying, the shoreline is about 1,200m from the point of impact and, at their speed (150kt), would have taken 15.5 seconds. With 1km visibility, they cannot have seen the shoreline until about 28.5 seconds[173] before impact. The change of waypoint occurred about six seconds later, when they were only about 600m from the shore.[174]

The SuperTANS records that, from the change of waypoint, the Chinook took a track of 022 degrees T, or had already changed to that track. In other words, the crew appear to have changed track slightly to the right; nor do we really know how long they had been on that track. This needs to be explained. Pulford's explanation for the 022 degrees track (that it was the result of manoeuvring over Northern Ireland) is unconvincing. As it approached Kintyre, the helicopter was very close to its planned track, indicating that, after the eastwards excursion at Carnlough, the crew had regained their track before crossing the North Channel. Boeing's further study (June 2002) observes that, instead of turning 7 degrees left for waypoint B (as expected after the waypoint change), the Chinook turned in the opposite direction on to a track of 22.22 degrees T, nearly 3 degrees right of the initial route and nearly 10 degrees right of the direct route (track) to waypoint B. It concluded that this indicated that the crew *made a conscious decision, for some reason, not to follow the directed route to waypoint B*. Later, emphasizing that this change was not the result of drift (it was into the wind), it states that *the real issue that should be addressed with respect to the aircraft horizontal flight path is why this right turn was made*. Because the new course was almost aimed at the TACAN beacon at Machrihanish and the TACAN Control Unit was found set to the channel for that beacon, Boeing suggested that the crew might have decided to make a transition to IFR using the beacon for direction. However, they noted that this track would take the helicopter over the highest points in the local terrain. Apparently unconvinced by their own suggestion, Boeing still regarded the change of track as *'unexplained'*.

What also needs to be explained is the track they were on when they crashed. The AAIB's evidence is that the aircraft crashed on a track of 012 degrees T, which is exactly the track required for waypoint B. Does this not indicate that they had already turned? Since they were actually past the waypoint when they crashed, it is logical to assume that they had indeed turned near the waypoint and were already on the track for Corran. This would mean that they must have approached on an even more easterly track. Strangely, the MOD's maps show the actual track parallel to the intended track (020 degrees T). Consequently, if it is assumed that the change of track occurred near the waypoint, the track flown must have been as shown on the sketch map (see p. 189). The crew must have thought that they were on track to the waypoint and changed track when they thought they were over it, updating the Doppler at the same time.

All that is needed now is an explanation for the turn towards the Mull.

Misidentification

Sir John Day told the House of Lords Select Committee that the nearest land on their actual track was a *'small headland with a little rock island just sitting off it'* (he was sure that they could have seen it in VMC). He did not name the headland, but it is Rubha na Lice. Nor did Sir John mention that, just above the cliffs at this point, there is a fog signal station. Holbrook thought that the foghorn (*sic*) he could hear was located at the lighthouse. In fact, the compressed air foghorn there is rarely used and was not in use at the time of the accident. What Holbrook heard was an 'air chime', electric-powered horns mounted (at the time) in the walls of a building about a mile south of the lighthouse at Rubha na Lice (see plate 9). Hector Lamont told the FAI that the air chime was sounding periodically that day and that it had to be on when visibility fell below four miles. Holbrook told the House of Lords Select Committee that he only identified the lighthouse from his position some 2nm south of it by the slight change of colour in haze. Since the fog signal station was nearer to him than the lighthouse, it cannot be certain that what he saw was the lighthouse; it might have been the fog signal building, which is also white and which he should have been able to see in addition to the lighthouse and even more clearly. However, he reported seeing only one building. Nor can it be certain that the crew did not mistake the fog signal building for the lighthouse. The Board rejected the idea that the crew mistook their position relative to the Mull because it could not envisage circumstances where this illusion would be so compelling for the crew not to have reduced speed. Pulford told the FAI that the Board had even considered the possibility that the fog signal had been mistaken for the lighthouse, but rejected that for the same reason (not slowing down). It is not clear why the Board thought that failure to slow down ruled out misidentification; there was no evidence that aircraft slow down on identifying waypoints. With unrestricted visibility, the crew would have been able to see both the lighthouse and the fog signal station and know which one to aim for. However, with restricted visibility the crew would see the shore and the fog signal station first and, more importantly, not be able to see the lighthouse 1km further away.

If the crew saw the fog signal building, but only as a white patch on the hillside (see plate 10), and concluded that it was the lighthouse, this can explain why they changed waypoint and track towards it. It lay slightly to starboard, perhaps convincing them that waypoint A itself lay a little further north just off the coast (but see below). This meant that the lighthouse was safely to their right and that they were clear of high ground. However, as they climbed they entered dense cloud and must have lost sight of the shore and the fog signal station. Now they were flying blind with no point of reference. Holding their track to update the Doppler as near as possible to the lighthouse, they may actually have changed track when the face of the Mull loomed up in front of them. The sketch map shows, as point 'S', where the crew may have believed they were when they changed waypoint.

It can be objected that Tapper could not have accepted the fog signal as the lighthouse because waypoint A, which he thought

194

was near the lighthouse, was then indicated by the SuperTANS to be roughly twice as far away as the fog signal building. Moreover, the lighthouse itself is much larger than the fog signal building. However, if visibility was poor and he saw the fog signal through mist or fog, it could have appeared both larger and further away than it really was. There is evidence that, in mist or fog, size is overestimated by a factor of about 1.2 and distances are overestimated by factors of between 1.4 and 2.1 (on average about 1.8).[175] At the waypoint change, the fog signal was about 650m away. If the mist or fog caused it to appear 1.8 times further away (1,170m), it must have seemed to be nearly the same distance as waypoint A, perhaps convincing Tapper that it really was the lighthouse.

The air marshals, perhaps referring to the information provided by the SuperTANS, concluded that the crew could see that they were off–track to the right. This overlooks the probability that the crew deliberately deviated from track after concluding (wrongly) that the waypoint was displaced slightly west of the lighthouse and that they were trying to correct its location. If they wanted to update the Doppler accurately, they needed to be closer to the lighthouse. By the time they reached the coast, they were about 270m to the right of the plotted track to waypoint A on a track of 022 degrees T. If they had previously been on track 020 degrees, then it can be calculated that the deviation must have occurred about 4nm back.[176] Did they spot the Mull from that distance and see a need to veer right? Or were they already on a track parallel to the plotted one but shifted slightly to the right because they had not completely eliminated the entire excursion to Carnlough? It is likely that the crew saw the Mull well before they were able to identify the lighthouse (as they thought).

Already it is obvious that, although Tapper had plotted waypoint A fairly close to the actual position of the lighthouse, a displacement that, in good visibility, would not have mattered, the eastward displacement, combined with the slight displacement in the GPS system, had put the aircraft on track that brought them to landfall over the fog signal instead of over the lighthouse. A more accurate plot of the waypoint and less error in the GPS should have brought them to a landfall at the lighthouse, as they expected.

195

If this hypothesis is correct, the critical mistake was misidentification of the waypoint. With restricted visibility through patchy stratus, it cannot have been easy to make the identification. Eventually they must have seen the shoreline just below the cloud over the Mull. Perhaps they were looking for a headland with two small offshore islands, as at the lighthouse, the one on the right somewhat larger than the one on the left. Both Tapper and Cook were familiar with the Scottish islands and the coastline of western Scotland. In particular, Tapper had previously visited the helicopter landing site at the lighthouse. Consequently, they may have remembered these islands as markers for it. Unfortunately, there is a similar headland at Rubha na Lice, also with two small offshore islands, again with the larger one on the right. Sight of a white building above the cliffs could only confirm the identification and lead the crew to conclude that it was the lighthouse, steering nearer to it to update the Doppler. However, they must have lost sight of the coast almost immediately as they flew into cloud. Sure of the identification and their position, they began a climb designed to give them 1,000ft clearance on a track close to the lighthouse and over the edge of the Mull. At the same time, they made a turn for Corran and updated the Doppler as they passed where they thought the lighthouse was. However, within a few seconds of making the turn, they must have seen a hillside some 300m ahead and/or the RadAlt warned them of rising ground and, too late, they realized that they had made a mistake. An attempt to climb and turn away proved inadequate.

The cause of the accident and conclusions

The Board concluded that the cause was the selection of a rate of climb that was *'inappropriate'* and *'insufficient to secure adequate terrain clearance on the track being flown'*. This statement of the obvious explains nothing. Since they crashed, the rate of climb must have been inadequate. Some assume that the crew were intent on flying over the hills of the Mull ahead of them continuing on the track they were following. If that was their intention, then of course they had not climbed high enough. However, why would experienced SHF pilots choose a rate of climb that was inadequate to clear the hills they must have known lay ahead? The chairman of the Board (Pulford) told the FAI that the crew might have thought that they were further from the Mull than they were. This was an attempt to justify the slow rate of climb; clearly, it might have been appropriate if they had started to climb earlier than they did. However, they would have known their distance from the waypoint (from the SuperTANS). Pulford also suggested that the crew might have thought that the Mull was to their right, instead of dead ahead. Evidently the crew did believe this, but it suggests a navigation error, which the Board had already rejected. Consequently, no one explored the implications of this idea or asked why the crew should have had this conviction.

As in so many accidents, there are many contributory causes. While the primary cause appears to have been misidentification of a waypoint, several contributory causes can be identified.

It may have been a mistake for Tapper to insist on taking the sortie near the end of his crew's shift, especially when he was bound to exceed the time limit and so break regulations. But he also broke regulations in not outbriefing the 230 Squadron Duty Authorizing Officer, in failing to make a written report of a faulty gauge and an alleged anomaly in the SuperTANS's recognition of GPS satellites (which he misread) and in ignoring the CA Release warning about sustained low-level flight. Most seriously, he broke regulations in not climbing to safety altitude (or as near it as the icing limitation allowed) on entering IMC. Was Tapper's relaxed attitude to regulations a contributory cause? There was evidence that SF pilots do not always follow the rules. Failing to follow the correct procedure for transition to IFR on entering cloud was, as the air marshals have repeatedly pointed out, a major breach of regulations (but not of IFR) and the reason they accuse the pilots of gross negligence (but why not the whole crew?). There can be no doubt that, had the crew flared and climbed the aircraft to safety altitude the accident would not have occurred. Even if the aircraft had climbed earlier to where the crew thought the 4 degrees isotherm was (2,500ft), a crash would have been avoided. However, here there appear to be two mistakes: failure to climb immediately to safety altitude *and* a misidentification of a waypoint. One or the other on its own would not have resulted in CFIT; it was the combination that was fatal.

Another subsidiary cause was Tapper's slight error in plotting the position of the lighthouse. Perhaps it was usual to make such plots approximate on the basis that the plotted position would be within sight of the actual position and the crew could adjust their track accordingly. The mistake was to rely on it when sight of the waypoint had been lost or when the wrong identification had been made.

Sir John Day referred to the aircraft being 280m *'to the right'*, but that was the distance by which waypoint A was thought to be south-east of the lighthouse. That distance is uncertain but constitutes only part of the difference between the track to the lighthouse and the actual track. The sketch map shows that, when the aircraft crashed, it was on a track that is about 450m to the east (right) of the track to the lighthouse, the impact point being about 500m from the lighthouse. About half of this displacement was due to Tapper's mislocation of the lighthouse. Some was due to the GPS system locating the aircraft slightly west of track. However, some can have been due to the crew steering east to put them nearer to where they thought the lighthouse lay. If the crew thought that they were some 200m west of the lighthouse, then they were actually displaced some 700–800m to the east.

Flying close to high ground is always risky. Some rescue helicopters have crashed in clear weather when too close to hills. In poor visibility, it is very dangerous. It can be argued that the crew were being careful to identify the lighthouse and improve the accuracy of their navigation equipment before proceeding on the next leg of their journey. They continued only when they were confident that they had identified the lighthouse. However, their confidence was misplaced and, with hindsight, can be seen as over-confidence. It cost them their lives and the lives of twenty-five other people. It was a mistake to fly without much margin for error in an area close to high ground. Malcolm Spaven described the crew's flight plan as *'fail-deadly'* navigation. So it turned out. Spaven also criticized the self-authorization permitted to the pilots and the RAF's complacency in not recognizing that their procedures needed review and that lessons could be learned. He feared that another such accident could occur.[177] Pulford told the FAI that, if experience and capability prevented accidents, there would be *'less* [fewer] *accidents'*. Wratten made the same point in his article in *Pilot* (see References). It has also been pointed out that recent military aviation history is littered with cases where extremely experienced aircrew using state-of-the-art equipment have made fundamental airmanship errors that have resulted in the loss of aircraft and lives. Examples are the RAF Hercules which flew 'level and straight' into the floor of Glen Loch in 1993[178], the RAF Nimrod filmed two years later as it flew into Lake Ontario and, a few years earlier, the loss of almost the entire USAF Thunderbirds aerobatic display team as they flew into the ground just after levelling out after a loop. There have also been several well-publicized crashes of two Russian aircraft flown by test pilots at air shows and the disaster involving the Italian aerobatic display team at Ramstein (Germany). In all these cases, the cause was pilot error.[179] More recently (26 March 2001), two experienced USAF pilots flew their serviceable F15s into Ben Macdui in the Cairngorms Mountains in Scotland. Of the forty-three RAF aircraft accidents that occurred during the five years from 1992 to 1996 (inclusive), the MOD attributed twenty to 'Aircrew Error', albeit, in four cases, the cause was not positively identified and, at the time (May 1998), three were still under investigation.[180]

IFR and safety altitudes are clearly designed to prevent CFIT. They allow for an aircraft being somewhat off its track and/or too low. However, pilots with navigation equipment that keeps them on track and a RadAlt might see safety altitude as un-necessary. If they are on track, they know their height above the terrain beneath and slightly ahead. This can be confirmed at any time by the RadAlt. Perhaps this crew thought like that. Alternatively, perhaps the knowledge that they could not reach safety altitude without risking an icing problem kept them below it. It is obvious why Tapper had his RadAlt warning system switched off (it would have been sounding all across the North Channel). However, both pilots should have noticed the fall in radar altitude at landfall.

The pilots flew into the hillside because they were not aware of their proximity to it. In that respect, it is similar to the crashes of Wessex HC.2 XT667 of 18 Squadron on 25 April 1968 and of Sunderland W4026 of 228 Squadron on 25 August 1942, which killed the then Duke of Kent. In both cases, the pilots were blamed and, although the crash of XT667 was simply explained, the crash of the Sunderland has never been explained properly.[181] CFIT is the most common cause of weather-related fatalities in UK airspace (Pike 2001a) and between 1992 and 2002, commercial jets met with 43 CFIT accidents worldwide, an average of four per year.[182] The Flight Safety Foundation issues a checklist for airlines to evaluate the risk and take action to reduce CFIT accidents. While this does not apply directly to the RAF, it is notable that high risk factors include lack of radar coverage, lack of an air traffic control service, IMC, flight crew duty at maximum, altitude change, and a lack of ground-mapping radar on the aircraft or radio altimeters for both captain and pilot with a full 2,500ft range. All these factors apply in this case and show that there was a very great risk of CFIT.

The crew's mistake is an example of *'the false hypothesis'* described by Allnutt (Hurst 1982). Expectancy was very high that they would see the lighthouse and perhaps the (old) foghorn above the cliffs with two small islands just below. In fact, they must have been very anxious to see it; they desperately wanted to identify the waypoint before continuing with the sortie. For this reason, they too readily identified what they wanted to see.

It is very likely that the crew failed to flare to safety altitude before entering cloud because they wanted to identify the lighthouse. It is ironic therefore that they crashed *because* they did this, misidentifying the waypoint. If they had abandoned the attempt to see the lighthouse and climbed to safety altitude, they would not have crashed. The accident was the result of an unwise and unnecessary attempt to refine navigation.

We can also draw conclusions about subsequent inquiries. It has already been suggested that Pulford was too young and inexperienced to handle such an important Board of Inquiry. However, it has also been suggested that those officers who control the findings of Boards of Inquiry should not be those engaged in management and command responsibility for the aircraft and personnel involved (the PAC and Batey 2001). Nor does the sheriff escape criticism. In their determinations, sheriffs conducting FAIs are required to state what reasonable precautions might have prevented the death or deaths and point to any *defect in a system of working* that contributed to the death or deaths. During the FAI, while counsel for the relatives of Flight Lieutenant Tapper (Aiden O'Neill), claimed that it was impossible to say what precautions might have prevented the accident or what defects in any system of working might have contributed to the accident, counsel for the relatives of the remainder of the deceased (Colin Campbell) merely observed that it could have been prevented if the aircraft had slowed down, turned away or been at a higher level. Surprisingly, the sheriff himself made no recommendations in this respect, not even referring to the two counsel's comments or explaining why he made no recommendations. Perhaps this was because the FAI did not hear from anyone prepared to criticize RAF procedures; certainly, the RAF witnesses would not do so. Sheriff Young could have recommended that the RAF reconsider self-authorization by pilots, that it more closely supervise a crew's working hours and that only senior officers should decide which crew should undertake which sortie. He also could have recommended a review of the procedure for inadvertently entering IMC flight and that the RAF avoid transporting many VIPs in one aircraft. Even without being able to determine the cause of the accident, it should have been obvious that different 'systems of working' might have prevented the accident, or at least reduced its severity.

The House of Lords Select Committee's marathon effort deserves some comment. The Committee appears to have relished the opportunity to question some of the country's most senior air force officers and bring them to account. The Committee's hostility was very evident, as was their prejudice against the MOD. However, this did not excuse the occasional brusqueness, verging on rudeness. Lord Tombs in particular was very aggressive and occasionally insulting. As an engineer, but not an aviator, he appears to have taken upon himself the role of technical expert for the Committee. Unfortunately, his confidence in his mastery of the technical aspects was often misplaced. The Committee's unfortunate condemnation of the air marshals' verdict appears to have been based on a wilful misunderstanding

201

of their case and a preoccupation with the idea that the aircraft suffered a mechanical malfunction. It ignored the fact that no evidence of a malfunction was found and it drew many erroneous conclusions (such as that the displacement of waypoint A from the true position of the lighthouse was partly due to *'a technical error in the TANS'*). The outcome justifies the fears expressed beforehand by the House of Lords Liaison Committee.

It is now clear that the MOD's explanation (that this CFIT was due to the selection of an 'inappropriate rate of climb') is wrong and that Sheriff Young was right to reject it. The MOD was also wrong to dismiss a navigation error. Even though the MOD is right to point to the failure to climb to safety altitude, the primary cause appears to be misidentification of the waypoint. There are therefore grounds for recalling the Board so that it can revise its conclusion and ask Boeing to revise its simulation with the correct airspeed. It might also conclude that the crew made an 'error of judgement' in that respect, although not perhaps in neglecting to climb to safety altitude. The FAI should also be recalled to consider a navigation error as the cause of the accident. Likewise, the House of Lords Select Committee needs to consider the evidence for such an error and, perhaps, modify its criticism of the air marshals. It failed to point out, or perhaps even recognize, that, even if the air marshals were not justified in accusing the crew of *'gross negligence'*, the crew might still be guilty on a lesser charge, such as an *'error of judgement'*. By making so much of the possibility of mechanical error, for which there was no evidence, the Committee lost sight of the main point and gave the impression that the pilots were not to blame in any way, so encouraging the 'Mull of Kintyre Group' and the pilots' families in their campaign. It also claimed, as have others, that the cause of the accident would never be known. If this means that a credible explanation would never be found, this book disproves that notion.

Appendix One

Military Aircraft Accident Summaries of accidents to Chinook helicopters (RAF)

Text and layout reset without correction; not a facsimile.
Copyright Ministry of Defence.

 MINISTRY OF DEFENCE

Military Aircraft Accident Summaries

MAAS 24/85
12 November 1985

AIRCRAFT ACCIDENT TO ROYAL AIR FORCE CHINOOK HC1 ZA 676

Date:	14 November 1984
Parent Airfield:	RAF Odiham, Hampshire
Place of Accident:	Near Micheldever, Hampshire
Crew:	1 Pilot Instructor, 2 Student Pilots, 1 Crewman Instructor, 2 Student Crewmen, 1 Passenger
Casualties:	2 Major Injuries

CIRCUMSTANCES

1.   The Chinook was on a training flight which included landing and taking-off from small areas surrounded by trees. Simulated failure of

one of the aircraft's 2 engines was also practised. After taking off from a confined area, the helicopter had started the transition into forward flight, just above the level of trees, when the pilot instructor reduced power on No 2 engine to simulate its failure. The No 1 engine should have applied compensating power automatically but it failed to respond and the aircraft was unable to maintain level flight. It descended into the trees before striking the ground and rolling over. Two of the crew sustained major injuries but were quickly flown to a local hospital by another helicopter that had been flying close to the scene of the accident.

CAUSE

2.   Loss of power in the No 1 engine was caused by a failure in the fuel system which starved the engine of fuel at a time when the No 2 engine was producing insufficient power for flight. Subsequent trials proved that the pilot instructor had insufficient time to increase power on the No 2 engine and so fly the aircraft away before it struck the trees.

SUBSEQUENT ACTIONS

3.   The aircraft was totally destroyed. All practice single-engine flying by RAF Chinook aircraft was stopped and a study was conducted to determine how single-engine training requirements could be met whilst ensuring complete safety if the other engine failed. As a result, changes have been made to single-engine training procedures and training has restarted.

Issued by: Public Relations
Ministry of Defence
Main Building
Whitehall
London SW1A 2HB
01-218 3253/3254 (Royal Air Force)

MINISTRY OF DEFENCE

Military Aircraft Accident Summary

Aircraft:	Chinook HC1 ZA715
Date of accident:	13 May 1986
Parent Airfield:	RAF Mount Pleasant
Place of accident:	West Falkland
Crew:	2 pilots, 2 crewmen – 12 soldiers
Casualties:	3 fatal, 3 major, 5 minor and 4 slight injuries

[19/88]
[9 December 1988]

Circumstances

1.   Shortly after 0815 hours on 13 May 1986 the crew of RAF Chinook ZA715 were tasked to return some troops that had been on exercise to their base located at the southern end of West Falkland. A direct route was chosen which involved the aircraft overflying a section of high ground just short of their destination. The weather was bad and included snow showers, strong winds and low cloud. At about 0840 hours radar contact with the Chinook was lost and repeated radio calls to the aircraft were unanswered. Overdue action was taken and an airborne Hercules was diverted to search. An intermittent signal from a Personal Locator beacon was detected and it became apparent that the aircraft had crashed into gently sloping ground about 40 feet below the crest of a saddle feature, some 4 miles short of its destination.

2.   A Chinook flew to the crash site and the crew found the majority of the aircraft's cabin structure intact, but that the forward parts of the cabin and cockpit were badly crushed.

3.   All the personnel in the aircraft were knocked unconscious by the crash. One soldier subsequently regained consciousness and was able to free some of his colleagues and administer first aid to the aircraft's captain who had been badly injured in the crash.

4.   An intensive evacuation operation was mounted involving 6 British military helicopters together with medical and engineering staffs. The conditions were increasingly severe with movement hampered by blizzards and winds of up to 70kts.

5.   Three personnel died as a result of the accident, a crewman shortly after the crash and the co-pilot and a soldier during transit to hospital.

Cause

6.   No evidence was found of any technical defect which could have led to the accident. It was concluded that the most likely cause was that the air crew had become victims of a phenomenon known as "white-out" whereby a combination of cloud, precipitation and a snow-covered land surface merge and cause spatial disorientation. In severe conditions, such as experienced, it is also not uncommon to encounter false horizons and it is possible that the aircrew mistook the crest of the saddle for a layer of cloud. The situation was probably compounded by strong gusts of downdraughting air on the Chinook.

Subsequent Actions

7.   Considerable publicity has been given to the problems of disorientation and visual illusions since they can affect operations in all aircraft. Specific operating procedures for flying in snow conditions have been adopted by Chinook crews.

MINISTRY OF DEFENCE

Military Aircraft Accident Summaries

2/89

March 17, 1989

AIRCRAFT ACCIDENT TO ROYAL AIR FORCE CHINOOK HC1 ZA721

Date:	27 February 1987
Parent airfield:	Royal Air Force Mount Pleasant
Place of accident:	Falkland Islands
Crew:	2 pilots, 1 crewman, 4 test recorders
Casualties:	7 fatal

CIRCUMSTANCES

1.   On 27 February 1987, Chinook HC1 ZA721 was prepared for a full flight test following a minor servicing and a structural repair. Ground runs and hover checks had been completed satisfactorily the previous day. In addition to the normal crew, the helicopter carried 4 technical NCOs: 2 operating the rotor-tune equipment, 1 under instruction on the rotor-tune and 1 recording engine vibration data.

2.   The helicopter took off, transitioned and climbed west along the runway, turned right and passed north and east of the runway before continuing outbound to the south east. The aircraft flew south easterly at normal cruise speed at heights reported as between 300 and 700 feet. Shortly afterwards, from straight and level flight on a north westerly heading, the nose began to dip at a moderate rate until the aircraft assumed a very steep, possibly vertical dive. A short, unintelligible radio transmission from the Chinook was recorded on the Air Traffic Control tape and the aircraft hit the ground immediately afterwards some 6 kilometres south east of the airfield. An eyewitness at the Air Traffic Control centre initiated the rescue services and on arrival at the crash site it was immediately apparent to the Search and Rescue helicopter crew that the aircraft had disintegrated on impact and had been almost totally consumed by a subsequent fire. There were no survivors.

CAUSE

3.   Little evidence could be obtained from the brief and garbled final radio call, and eyewitnesses were only able to report seeing the aircraft tilt nose down and fly into the ground. However, during the course of its investigation the Inquiry was able to eliminate operating and natural hazards, engine/major structural failure as well as disorientation and air crew error as possible causes.

4.   Examination of the wreckage showed that the aft Longitudinal Cyclic Trim Actuator (LCTA) clutch had failed, preventing the LCTA from extending once retracted. Flight loads could not have caused the LCTA to retract; therefore it was most likely to have been retracted either automatically on take-off or manually by the pilot whilst following the flight test schedule. However, the effects of a failure of an aft LCTA to extend from fully retracted would have been easily contained by the pilot unless something, such as another flying control defect, prevented him from so doing. Simulator experiments showed that, under such circumstances, the estimated impact speed of 150 kts could be achieved from a height of 700 ft if the starting speed was about 120 kts.

5.   The forward swivelling upper boost actuator (UBA – a form of hydraulic flying control jack) showed an extension of 180mm which is less than expected under the circumstances. When the actuator was dismantled it was found that, during manufacture, the controlling spool valve had not been locked to the threaded input control rod. Moreover, the internal bore of the spool had been machined at an angle to the spool axis so that transverse G loads caused by vibration could turn the spool, screwing it along the control rod. When dismantled, the spool was found to be displaced along the rod by 1/10 turn from the normal position. The Inquiry determined that spool valve displacement of 1/2 to 2 turns from the normal position would result in a very slow rate of extension of the actuator, tending towards a jam at 3 1/2 turns.

6.   Following practical tests the Inquiry decided that if the pilot had applied a rapid control input, in response to some unidentified nose down pitch attitude change, at a moment when the spool valve was considerably displaced along its control rod when the UBA could have jammed with an extension of about 180 mm. The failed aft LCTA position would then have produced a flight path resembling that

reported by eyewitnesses. Thus the Inquiry considered that a possible cause of the accident was jamming of the forward swivelling UBA by spool migration with LCTA malfunction as a likely contributory cause. However, the valve position found after the impact was inconsistent with this cause and prevented the Inquiry from attributing the accident conclusively to it.

7.   Due to lack of evidence the Inquiry could not completely discount a number of other possible causes. These included disconnection or failure of a control run, hydraulic return line blockage, loose article hazard and crew incapacitation or psychological problems.

SUBSEQUENT ACTIONS

8.   All RAF Chinook UBA spool valves were inspected as soon as the condition of the valve on ZA721 became known. All new valves are now inspected upon receipt.

9.   Consideration is being given to the fitting of an ADR and Crash Locator Beacon to the aircraft. Action is in hand to obtain a full Design Authority hazard analysis of the flying controls and associated systems.

Issued by: Public relations (RAF)
Ministry of Defence
Main Building
Whitehall, London SW1A 2HB
Tel: 01-218 3253/3254

MINISTRY OF DEFENCE

Military Aircraft Accident Summary

Aircraft:	Chinook HC MK1 ZA672
Date of accident:	6 May 1988
Parent Airfield:	RAF Gutersloh, Germany
Place of accident:	Hannover International Airport
Crew:	1 Pilot, 1 Navigator, 2 Crewmen
	1 Pilot Supernumery Crew
Casualties:	3 Fatal, 1 Major, 1 Minor

[19 December 1988]

Circumstances

1.   On 6 May 1988 Chinook ZA672 was flown from Gutersloh to Hannover to position for a static display at the International Airshow to be held the following day. After landing on the runway the crew obtained clearance to taxy. A "follow me" vehicle led them towards the airport main terminal and indicated that the aircraft was to be parked between a line of static military aircraft and 2 passenger aircraft access walkways, Piers 9 and 10. Some distance short of the final parking area, the guide vehicle broke away leaving the aircraft to proceed on its own. However, the crew were concerned about the size of the designated parking area and the aircraft was stopped.

2.   A crewman descended from the Chinook and was advised that towing equipment was available. However, he was concerned that the aircraft's rear rotor was obstructing the busy main taxyway and, although aware that 2 RAF groundcrew were on hand to marshal the aircraft, he elected to marshal the Chinook forward himself. The 2 RAF marshallers on their own initiatives, and without direction by the crewman, subsequently positioned themselves to check rotor clearances either side of the aircraft. As the Chinook moved forward slowly and cautiously, the crewman moved to the left-hand side of the

210

aircraft to assess the clearance with Pier 9 which he estimated to be 12–15 feet. This partially obstructed the view of the 'safety-man' on that side. Believing that the crewman had taken over responsibility for monitoring blade clearance, the 'safety-man' turned away and went to indicate the aircraft's final parking position. The crewman then returned to the front of the aircraft and proceeded to guide the aircraft past Pier 10, unaware that an optical illusion was leading him to believe that good separation existed between the rotors and the pier when, in fact no such clearance was available. The illusion was caused by the raised and horizontally protruding configuration of the piers which did not provide a clear vertical reference for judging rotor clearance unless the observer was in line with the end of the pier or was standing under the edge of the rotor disc.

3. When the Chinook was abeam Pier 10 its front rotor struck the underside of the walkway and the aircraft started to rock violently. It then reared up, nose first, until the fuselage was almost vertical before falling to the left and coming to rest on top of Pier 10. Debris was scattered over a wide area and some people in the vicinity were injured. Several nearby aircraft sustained damage. A major fire developed at the back end of the fuselage which spread rapidly throughout the whole length of the aircraft. Rescue services arrived within 2 minutes but the fire was not finally extinguished for some 35 minutes. Three of the crew were fatally injured and 1 sustained major injury. The aircraft was totally destroyed.

Cause

4. The rotor impact occurred because the Chinook was taxied into a very confined space without the crew being aware of the acute dangers they faced.

Subsequent Actions

5. Disciplinary action has been taken against the captain of the aircraft. Studies are to be set in hand to examine the need for formal ground marshalling instruction for helicopter crewmen and to investigate all aspects of Chinook captaincy training. The possibility for introducing a minimum rotor clearance for ground taxying helicopters is to be reviewed.

Claims for compensation

6.   As a result of the accident a number of claims have been made which are presently being processed.

MINISTRY OF DEFENCE

Military Aircraft Accident Summaries

19 July 1990

10/90

AIRCRAFT ACCIDENT TO ROYAL AIR FORCE CHINOOK HC1 ZA678

Date: 24 July 1989
Parent Airfield: Royal Air Force Odiham
Place of Accident: Odiham Airfield
Crew: One pilot, one co-pilot, one
                                  crewman and four groundcrew
Casualties: Two slight injuries

CIRCUMSTANCES

1.   On 24 July 1989, Chinook HC1 ZA678 was prepared for an air test following a Minor Servicing during which the aft drive transmission had been changed. The air test was to comprise a series of ground runs with the rotors turning followed by a flight test. In addition to the three aircraft crew members, four groundcrew technicians were detailed to assist; their duties were to record vibration levels and, if necessary, carry out adjustments to the aircraft systems.

2.   The ground runs were carried out without incident. The pilot then hover-taxied the aircraft towards a grassed area where cross-wind hover checks were to be conducted. During the hover-taxi, the groundcrew sitting in the rear of the cabin heard an unusual whirring noise, lasting for about two seconds, coming from the vicinity of the aft transmission. However, the noise did not recur and the crew proceeded to hover check.

3.   The Chinook HC1 is fitted with a number of systems to warn the crew of an incipient failure of critical components in the transmission system. One of these – the centreline transmission chip warning light – was noticed by the co-pilot to flicker faintly during the hover check.

The air test was therefore terminated. As the aircraft started to hover taxi back towards the dispersal area, there was a second flicker of the chip warning light and the crewman reported that wispy smoke had been seen behind the aircraft. The captain, therefore, immediately initiated a running landing onto the grass, but before the landing could be completed, a loud bang was heard, and the aircraft fell to the ground and performed a ground loop.

4.   During the ground loop, the front rotor head, transmission and pylon broke away from the aircraft and debris was flung in all directions. The aircraft came to rest in an upright position with the roof of the cockpit missing and the rear pylon assembly bent at an angle of about 70 degrees to the vertical. The aircraft was evacuated quickly and only slight injuries were sustained by the crew.

CAUSE

5.   The accident was caused by the incorrect assembly of the aft transmission input thrust bearing by an agency outside Royal Air Force control. The transmission then failed the first time it was subjected to normal loads in flight, resulting in the desyncronisation of the rotor systems and subsequent collision between the aft and front rotors.

SUBSEQUENT ACTIONS

6.   The aircraft was beyond economical repair. Procedures have now been introduced to prevent the incorrect fitment of transmission input thrust bearings, and a claim for compensation is being pursued against the agency that undertook the assembly of the aft transmission.

Issued by: Public Relations(Royal Air Force)
                                    Ministry of Defence
                                    Main Building
                                    Whitehall
                                    LONDON SW1A 2HB

                                    Telephone(071)218-3253/4

MINISTRY OF DEFENCE

Military Aircraft Accident Summaries

33/90
17 December 1990

AIRCRAFT ACCIDENT TO ROYAL AIR FORCE CHINOOK HC1 ZA717

Date:	25 July 1989
Parent Airfield:	Royal Air Force Mount Pleasant
Place of Accident:	Mount Pleasant Airfield
Crew:	One pilot, one co-pilot, one crewman and two groundcrew
Casualities:	Two slight injuries

CIRCUMSTANCES

1.   On 25 July 1989, Chinook HC1 ZA 717 was prepared for an air test on the airfield at RAF Mount Pleasant following scheduled maintenance during which the aft transmission assembly had been changed. The air test was to comprise a series of ground runs followed by a flight test which was to include a hover check. In addition to the three aircraft crew members, two groundcrew technicians were detailed to assist with the flight. Their duties were to measure vibration levels and record technical data.

2.   The ground runs were completed without incident. The pilot then took off and hover-taxied the aircraft a distance of about 250 metres to a clear area to perform the initial part of the flight phase.

3.   The Chinook HC1 is fitted with a number of systems to warn the crew of an incipient failure of critical components in the transmission system. Shortly after the pilot established the aircraft in the hover, the co-pilot saw one of these warning systems – the transmission low oil pressure caption – illuminate and he noted that the aft transmission oil pressure was well below normal. He warned the pilot, who initiated a descent for an immediate landing. However, before the aircraft could be landed, the co-pilot noticed a second warning on the Caution and Advisory Panel and one of the technicians heard a high pitched

screech followed by a loud bang from the rear of the aircraft. The aft rotor blades then began to slow down and collide with the front blades and debris was seen to fall from the rear of the aircraft. Shortly afterwards, the aircraft hit the ground and rolled onto its Port side. At some stage during the impact sequence, the aft transmission and most of the aft pylon became detached from the aircraft.

4.   All occupants were able to evacuate the aircraft safely. The pilots were uninjured, whilst the occupants of the cabin received injuries which were only slight.

CAUSE

5.   The accident was caused by the incorrect fitment of the aft transmission input thrust bearing. The transmission then failed the first time it was subjected to normal loads in flight, resulting in the desynchronisation of the rotor systems and subsequent collision between the aft and front rotor blades.

SUBSEQUENT ACTIONS

6.   The aircraft was beyond economical repair. Procedures have now been introduced to prevent the incorrect fitment of transmission input thrust bearings.

MINISTRY OF DEFENCE

Military Aircraft Accident Summary

MILITARY AIRCRAFT ACCIDENT SUMMARY
PUBLISHED BY THE MINISTRY OF DEFENCE
AIRCRAFT ACCIDENT TO ROYAL AIR FORCE
CHINOOK HC MK1 ZA675

Date:	15 October 1991
Parent Airfield:	Royal Air Force Odiham
Place of accident:	Royal Air Force Odiham
Crew:	Two pilots, two crewmen
Casualties:	Nil

CIRCUMSTANCES

1.	During the evening of 15 October 1991, the crew of Chinook HC Mk1 ZA675 was conducting a series of night flying exercises on the airfield at RAF Odiham. Twenty minutes into the sortie, whilst the aircraft was hovering, one of the crewmen in the cabin saw a shower of burning liquid coming from the rear cabin roof. He alerted the Captain who made an emergency radio transmission and landed immediately. The crew completed the shut down checks and evacuated the aircraft without difficulty. A fierce liquid fire continued to burn in the rear pylon area of the aircraft causing extensive damage until the fire service brought it under control.

2.	The subsequent technical investigation revealed that chafing had taken place between an electrical cable connecting the No 2 generator to its busbar and the steel braided utility hydraulic pump pressure hose. The cable had become chafed down to its conducting core. Arc erosion of the hose had melted the braiding strands and caused a number of pin-hole sized punctures to develop through which a mist of hydraulic fluid escaped under pressure. The mist was ignited by further arcing.

CAUSE

3.   The cause of the accident was the ignition of hydraulic fluid as a result of chafing between the utility hydraulic pump pressure hose and the exposed core of the electrical cable connecting the No 2 generator to its busbar.

SUBSEQUENT ACTIONS

4.   The aircraft is undergoing repair at a maintenance facility. An improved routeing and cleating plan is being developed for Chinook HC Mk1 pipes, hoses and cables.

[5 May 1993]

MILITARY AIRCRAFT ACCIDENT SUMMARY

PUBLISHED BY THE MINISTRY OF DEFENCE

AIRCRAFT ACCIDENT TO ROYAL AIR FORCE

CHINOOK HC Mk2 ZD576

Date: 2 June 1994
Parent Station: RAF Odiham
Place of Accident: Mull of Kintyre, Strathclyde
Crew: 4 (2 Pilots, 2 Air Loadmasters)
Passengers: 25
Casualties: All 29 persons on board killed

CIRCUMSTANCES

1.   On the afternoon of 2nd June 1994, Chinook HC Mk2 ZD576 departed RAF Aldergrove, Co Antrim, on a low-level flight to Fort George, Inverness with four crew and 25 passengers on board. At approximately 1800 hours, after an apparently uneventful, direct transit across the North Channel of the Irish Sea, ZD576 crashed into rising terrain on the southern tip of the Mull of Kintyre. Weather conditions in the area were bad with poor visibility and low cloud. The aircraft was destroyed and all 29 persons on board were killed.

CAUSE

2.   There were no eyewitnesses to the crash nor Accident Data Recorder information to assist the Board of Inquiry with its investigation. Nevertheless, there was sufficient evidence to eliminate as possible causes: major technical malfunction or structural failure of the aircraft prior to impact; hostile action; or electromagnetic interference with navigation equipment. Therefore, the Inquiry focused on the crew's handling and operation of the aircraft.

3.   The pilots of ZD576 were operating the aircraft under Visual Flight Rules (VFR) at the time of the accident and had sole responsibility for maintaining safe clearance from terrain. Moreover, the Inquiry was able to confirm that, prior to impact, ZD576's navigation equipment had been functioning accurately. The Inquiry, therefore, considered all plausible factors and scenarios which might explain the

219

apparent breakdown in the pilots' awareness of their proximity to the high ground, and their failure to take appropriate action to avoid it. Ultimately however, the Inquiry concluded that none of the possible contributory factors would have been compelling enough to have prevented this experienced flight deck crew from maintaining safe flight, either visually at low-level or, if conditions were below VFR minima, on instruments above Safety Altitude and under Instrument Flight Rules (IFR). The Inquiry therefore concluded that the cause of the accident was that the two pilots had wrongly continued to fly towards the high ground of the Mull of Kintyre below a safe altitude in unsuitable conditions. This constituted a failure in their duty to operate the aircraft safely; regrettably therefore, it was concluded that both pilots had been negligent. The two Air Loadmasters were absolved of blame.

SUBSEQUENT ACTIONS

4.   Subsequent analysis concluded that no practical, additional crashworthy design features would have saved any of the persons on board in the circumstances of the accident. A thorough review of training, flying standards and supervision within the RAF Support Helicopter Force has since been carried out; this has not revealed any deficiencies that might have contributed to this accident. It is planned to fit both Accident Data Recorders and Cockpit Voice Recorders to RAF Chinook helicopters in 1997/98.

[15 June 1995]

Appendix Two

Schedule of witnesses as they appeared at the FAI:

DAY 1 (8 Jan 1996)
> David Thomas Murchie; lighthouse keeper, NLB
> Marjorie Black; pathologist
> Hector Lamont; lighthouse keeper, NLB
> Kenneth Banks; journalist
> Jeanette Harriet McFarlane; pathologist
> Marie Therese Cassidy; pathologist
> Sinead Swift; air traffic controller
> Peter Venezis; Prof. of forensic medicine

DAY 2 (9 Jan 1996)
> Mark Burton Holbrook; amateur sailor
> Anne Llewd Tyler; housewife
> Graham Anderson; Detective Constable, police
> Russel Glenn Ellacott; holidaymaker
> Janet Joyce; Detective Chief Inspector, police
> James Durward; Chief Inspector, police
> Leonard Warren; Scenes Of Crime Officer, police
> Michael Moffat; Scenes Of Crime Officer, police
> John Coles; Flight Sergeant, RAF

DAY 3 (10 Jan 1996)
> John Coles (recalled)
> David Anthony Guest; Corporal, RAF
> Steven Richard Clark; Senior Aircraftman, RAF
> Christopher Albert Valente; Chief Technician, RAF
> Ian James Kingston; Flight Lieutenant, RN

DAY 4 (11 Jan 1996)
Ian James Kingston (recalled)

DAY 5 (12 Jan 1996)
Ian James Kingston (recalled)
David James Carruthers; Chief Technician, RAF/Boeing
Darren Stephen May; Propulsion Engineer, RAF
Peter Polidano; Flight Sergeant, RAF (in 1994)
Duncan George Trapp; Flight Lieutenant, RAF

DAY 6 (16 Jan 1996)
Rodger Edward Wedge; Group Captain, RAF
Anthony Neville Cable; Senior Inspector, AAIB

DAY 7 (17 Jan 1996)
Anthony Neville Cable (recalled)

DAY 8 (18 Jan 1996)
Anthony Neville Cable (recalled)

DAY 9 (19 Jan 1996)
Anthony Neville Cable (recalled)

DAY 10 (22 Jan 1996)
Anthony Neville Cable (recalled)
Geoffrey Lee Young; Flight Lieutenant, RAF
David Lawrence Prowse; Squadron Leader, RAF
John Richard Denis Mellor; Master Air Crewman, RAF
Hamish Miller; Flight Lieutenant, Air Traffic Controller,
    RAF

DAY 11 (23 Jan 1996)
Donald Devine; Wing Commander, Air Traffic Controller,
    RAF
Michael Edward Lee; Squadron Leader, Senior
    Engineering Officer, RAF
Michael Stangroom; Squadron Leader, RAF

DAY 12 (24 Jan 1996)
Barry Mark North; Squadron Leader, RAF
Andrew Douglas Pulford, Wing Commander, RAF
(President of the MOD Board)

DAY 13 (25 Jan 1996)
Andrew Douglas Pulford (recalled)

DAY 14 (26 Jan 1996)
Andrew Douglas Pulford (recalled)

DAY 15 (29 Jan 1996)
Carl Morrell Scott; Flight Lieutenant, RAF
Ian James McKechnie MacFarlane; Flight Lieutenant, RAF

DAY 16 (30 Jan 1996)
Ian James McKechnie MacFarlane (recalled)
Andrew Douglas Pulford (recalled)

DAY 17 (1 Feb 1996)
Closing submissions

DAY 18 (2 Feb 1996)
Closing submissions

Sheriff Sir Stephen Young's Determination

1   Chinook MkII helicopter ZD576 was delivered to RAF Aldergrove on 31 May 1994. It had recently been the subject of a mid-life update by its manufacturers, Boeing Helicopters.

2   The operation of ZD576 was subject to the terms of the CA Release issued by the Controller Aircraft who is responsible to the Secretary of State for Defence. The CA Release, which may be amended from time to time, certifies the airworthiness of the type of aircraft to which it relates within the particular limitations set forth therein. At the material time ZD576 was subject to limitations in respect of weight and icing clearance.

3   On 2 June 1994 in the late afternoon ZD576 was tasked to carry a group of 26 passengers from RAF Aldergrove to Fort George near Inverness. In the event only 25 passengers went on the flight.

4   The crew of ZD576 for the flight to Fort George were Flt Lt Tapper (captain), Flt Lt Cook (co-pilot) and MALM Forbes and Sgt Hardie (crewman).

5   Before departure of the flight the crew obtained from the Met Office at Belfast International Airport up-to-date terminal area forecasts and actual observations which covered their planned route to Fort George. The forecast for the Machrihanish area was that visibility in general would be 7,000 metres in haze with the scattered cloud base at 1,200 feet and the broken cloud base at 3,000 feet and that temporarily between 1400 and 2100 GMT the visibility would be 4,000 metres with the broken cloud

base at 500 feet. In addition there was a 30 per cent probability that between these times the visibility would be reduced to 500 metres in fog with the broken cloud base at 100 feet. The actual observations taken at Machrihanish at 1416 GMT indicated that the visibility was 4,800 metres in haze with the scattered cloud base at 200 feet and the broken cloud base at 800 feet.

6   The journey to Fort George was planned by the crew to be flown under Visual Flight Rules (VFR) at low level on the way out and at medium level on the return to RAF Aldergrove.

7   Before departure the crew left with an operations clerk at RAF Aldergrove copies of three sections of a 1:500000 scale map on which had been recorded details of the planned route to Fort George including tracks, distances, estimated times and safety altitudes for each leg of the sortie.

8   The planned route was to fly from RAF Aldergrove to the lighthouse at the Mull of Kintyre, thence to Corran near Fort William and thence up the Great Glen to Inverness and Fort George. On the first leg to the lighthouse the track was shown as 027°M, the distance 42 nautical miles (nm), the time 21 minutes and the safety altitude 2,800 feet.

9   During pre-flight procedures, the crew entered five waypoints into the aircraft's RNS252 SuperTANS computer. Waypoint A was entered as N55° 18.50 W005° 48.00 which was a point approximately 280 metres south east of the Mull of Kintyre lighthouse. Waypoint B was entered as a point near Corran.

10   In due course the 25 passengers boarded the aircraft and at 1642 GMT (1742 BST) a member of the crew reported to Aerodrome Control at Belfast International Airport that the aircraft was lifting and departing.

11   At 1643 GMT a member of the crew reported to Approach Control at the airport that the aircraft was outbound on a course [track] of 027°M at low level. At 1646:14.06 a further report was received from the aircraft to the effect that it was at the airport zone boundary (approximately 9 nm from the airport) flying VFR. These reports were all routine and unexceptional.

12   During the flight Flt Lt Tapper occupied the left hand seat in the cockpit of the aircraft and acted as non-handling pilot while Flt Lt Cook occupied the right hand seat and acted as handling pilot. MALM Forbes acted as No 2 crewman at the front of the cabin while Sgt Hardie acted as No 1 crewman at the rear.

13   At about 1750 BST the aircraft was observed flying at low level over Carnlough on the Antrim coast and out over the North Channel in the direction of the Mull of Kintyre.

14   At 1655:14 GMT a member of the crew called the Scottish Air Traffic Control Centre (Military) at Prestwick in the following terms: "Scottish Military, good afternoon, this is F4J40" (which was the aircraft's callsign). This was not an emergency call. For reasons which are not known the call was not answered. Nor was it repeated. No further radio communications were heard from the aircraft.

15   At the time or shortly after this call was made the aircraft was observed flying below the cloud base at a height between 200 and 400 feet and at a point about 2 nm south west of the Mull of Kintyre lighthouse. It was in straight and level flight and heading in the direction of the land-mass of the Mull at a steady speed.

16   At this time cloud and hill fog extended over the land mass from approximately the base of the lighthouse building (at 250 feet above sea level) to at least the summit of Beinn na Lice (1404 feet) which is situated a little under 1 nm east of the lighthouse.

17   When the aircraft was about 0.81 nm from the position entered into the SuperTANS for the lighthouse (waypoint A) on a bearing of 018°T a member of the crew manually changed the waypoint displayed on the SuperTANS (which was in Tactical Steering mode) so as to give steering, distance and time to go information to Corran (waypoint B).

18   This change of waypoint was made when the aircraft was approximately 400 to 500 feet above sea level.

19   After the change of waypoint the aircraft flew towards the land mass of the Mull on an ascending track of 022°T (which was approximately two degrees to the right of the

226

track which the crew had planned to follow from RAF Aldergrove to the lighthouse and nine degrees to the right of the planned track from the lighthouse to Corran).

20   A few seconds after the change of waypoint (and about 15 to 18 seconds prior to impact with the landmass of the Mull) the aircraft was at a height of 468 plus or minus 50 feet above sea level.

21   At some stage the aircraft entered Instrument Meteorological Conditions (IMC). This required the aircraft to transfer to flight under Instrument Flight Rules (IFR), and in particular to climb at least as high as the calculated safety altitude for that leg of the route, namely 2,800 feet.

22   At a point in time some 2.9 seconds before the initial impact, the aircraft was climbing at a rate of approximately 1,000 feet per minute and at an airspeed of approximately 150 knots. To this speed there fell to be added a tailwind component of approximately 24 knots which resulted in a groundspeed of approximately 174 knots.

23   At that point in time large aft and left cyclic and collective control inputs were made in the aircraft which resulted in a final cyclic flare before the aircraft struck the ground. During this final flare the aircraft travelled approximately 812 feet over the ground, increased its rate of climb to approximately 4,670 feet per minute and climbed approximately 128 feet. In addition the flight path angle increased to 20° above the horizontal and the nose of the aircraft was pitched up to about 31° above the horizontal.

24   The distance between the point where the change of waypoint was made and the initial impact point was about 0.95 nm.

25   The aircraft initially struck a rocky outcrop on the side of Beinn na Lice at a point 810 feet above mean sea level and approximately 0.28 nm east of the Mull of Kintyre lighthouse.

26   At the time of the initial impact the aircraft was travelling at a groundspeed of approximately 150 knots on a track of approximately 012°T. It was banked some 5 to 10° to the left with a yaw angle of less than 10°.

27   Upon initial impact much of the fuselage undersurface of the aircraft and rear end was torn off and the right and lower area of the cockpit damaged.

28   The aircraft then travelled almost 200 metres airborne while sustaining fuselage strikes from rotor blades and executing extreme violent manoeuvres. It impacted the ground inverted and broke into two major pieces which tumbled a short distance, shedding the aft pylon and both engines. Fuel tanks on both sides were ruptured at initial impact and extensive ground fire initiated, severely damaging much of the remains.

29   The time of the initial impact was approximately 1759:30 BST on 2 June 1994. All the occupants of the aircraft were rendered unconscious at once and died more or less instantaneously.

30   The names of those who died, and the cause of death in each case, were as follows: [list follows]

31   The wreckage of the aircraft was subsequently examined in very considerable detail by Mr Cable, a Senior Inspector of Air Accidents (Engineering) with the Air Accidents Investigation Branch (AAIB) of the UK Department of Transport, assisted by various colleagues and other personnel from Boeing Helicopters, a number of component manufacturers and the RAF.

32   Fire damage to the wreckage of the aircraft was consistent with the effects of the accident. No evidence of explosive effects or pre-impact fire were [sic] found.

33   The completeness of the aircraft at impact could not be positively verified but no evidence was found to suggest pre-impact separation of any part.

34   The groundspeed and drift indicator of the aircraft was probably registering 147 knots groundspeed at, or very shortly after, the initial impact.

35   Engine condition and the available evidence of instrument indications and control settings in the aircraft suggested normal operations of both engines at the time of the accident.

36   Fire damage prevented assessment of the functionality of No.1 DECU and had destroyed its memories of the

operating program and exceedances and fault history.

37   The No.2 DECU remained partially functionable [*sic*], with deficiencies that were consistent with the effects of impact damage.

38   The No.2 DECU memories showed that the operating program and constants had not altered since delivery, that no abnormal exceedances or faults had been detected over its life and that no faults had been detected on the last flight.

39   HMA internal settings confirmed correct operation for most HMA elements and indicated power levels that possibly reflected aircraft manoeuvre effects.

40   Thorough assessment of most flight control hydraulic system components of the aircraft was possible and revealed no signs of pre-impact failure or malfunction. Available cockpit indications indicated that both systems were providing normal pressure at impact.

41   Available evidence indicated normal AFCS operation.

42   Available evidence precluded major pre-impact loss of electrical supplies but indicated that all electrical systems had probably de-energised almost immediately on initial impact.

43   No signs of pre-impact malfunction of the transmission or rotor systems were found.

44   Almost all parts of the flight control mechanical systems of the aircraft were identified, with no evidence of pre-impact failure or malfunction, although the possibility of control system jam could not be positively dismissed.

45   Most attachment inserts on both flight control system pallets had detached, including the collective balance spring bracket that had previously detached from the aircraft's thrust/yaw pallet, with little evidence available to eliminate the possibility of pre-impact detachment.

46   The method of attaching components to the pallets appeared less positive and less verifiable than would normally be expected for a flight control system application.

47   The aircraft's radar altimeter receiver was excessively sensitive, probably a pre-existing condition that was

mainly the result of incorrect adjustment. The fault had the potential for causing erroneous height indication but a previous flight test result indicated that this was unlikely, provided the antenna environment for the aircraft was similar to that for the test.

48   The radar altimeter receiver's excessive sensitivity would have increased the maximum indicated height error build-up in circumstances where the terrain closure rate exceeded the system's tracking capability.

49   A detailed investigation of possibly relevant technical aspects of the accidents [sic] was made. The pre-impact serviceability of the aircraft could not be positively verified but no evidence was found of malfunction that could have contributed to the accident, with the possible exception of the radar altimeter system fault.

50   The aircraft was not fitted with either a cockpit voice recorder or an accident data recorder. Had these been fitted it is likely that they would have led to the recovery of important evidence relevant to the circumstances of the deaths and, more particularly, the cause of the accident.

The Macdonald Report

In April 2000, three members of the Royal Aeronautical Society (RAeS) published a report on the accident.[183] The RAeS itself had neither commissioned nor endorsed the report and refused to publish it. The Society claimed that air safety was outside its remit.

The report, which consists of only fifteen A4 pages, was aimed at addressing the accusation of gross negligence against the pilots by questioning whether or not there could be any doubt about the cause (the charge relied on there being no doubt). Naturally the report dwells on the technical problems experienced by Chinook helicopters, most of which has already been reviewed in Chapter Six, and claimed that *'something must have happened to force the aircraft straight into the side of the Mull'*. It also reviewed the uncontested events of the day, including commenting that the level of training received by the pilots was unacceptable for the carriage of VIP passengers and that the idea that any of the crew had suffered from hypoglycaemia through lack of meals on the day of the accident could be discounted. The report claimed that the aircraft had accelerated from 140kt to 150kt (airspeed) at the critical time and asked why that happened. The report did acknowledge that the change of waypoint indicated that the crew were aware of their position. Commenting on engine overspeeds, the report claimed that they result in *'a sudden climb of the sort performed by ZD576 before it crashed'*.

Attached to the report are eleven appendices, some of them poor photocopies of various public and private documents. One appendix consists of fourteen pages of a precognition by a Chinook pilot the authors identified only as 'WITNESS J', who subsequently gave evidence to the FAI on behalf of the family of Flight Lieutenant Tapper. Because 'J' was the designation given to this witness by the sheriff in his Determination, he can be identified as Flight Lieutenant Carl Scott. Other appendices included a copy of some pages from *Flightfax* (December 1998) which spotlighted a safety performance review of Chinooks and some mishaps, some accounts of the crash of a US Army Chinook on 7 March 1996 which was attributed to pilot error, a copy of part of the 1/500,000-scale route planning map, a copy of a letter from Air Chief Marshal Sir Michael Graydon to Captain Kohn supporting the RAF's verdict, an extract from the evidence given to the FAI by Flight Sergeant Coles, a copy from Hansard of part of the House of Lords debate on 1 November 1999, a copy of a memorandum from the Electronic Assessment Section at Boscombe Down to MOD Procurement on 3 June 1994 about the Textron Lycoming 'White Paper' on the Chinook FADEC and a copy of a report on a repair carried out to the balance-spring mounting bracket in the collective channel of ZD576 on 11 May 1994 at RAF Odiham.

Three supplementary reports were later issued, two described as 'addenda' and one described as an 'appendix'. The first discussed the weather at the time of the accident, emphasizing that, although there was dense fog on the Mull itself, this did not mean that the crew could not see the Mull as they approached. Consequently, the opinion of the reviewing officers (that the weather over the Mull was a contributory factor in the accident) was questionable. Although the aircraft certainly entered cloud, the reason it did so *'has yet to be explained and must remain imponderable'*. A summary of a precognition made by a Royal Navy weather forecaster was included; he supported the idea that the crew could have seen the area of the lighthouse. The second discussed the possibility of uncommanded flying control movements caused by high frequency radio-induced electromagnetic interference. It claimed that it is widely believed that a call was made or received by one of the passengers on the Chinook close to the time of the accident and that this was not thoroughly investigated by the RAF. It suggested that other sources of inter-ference could be an infrared jammer or radar from ships, including trawlers and Royal Navy vessels. The report empha-

232

sized that the use of a TETRA mobile telephone could have adversely affected the operation of one or more of the electronic systems on the aircraft. It seems that, when someone from the CAA's Policy Section spoke to Pulford about this, he replied that only one telephone could have had any effect, but he did not elaborate. All the mobile telephones found at the crash site were removed by security personnel. The third supplementary report is a copy of a CAA report on interference from portable telephones.

The RAeS group also prepared a special report for Lord Jauncey on accidents and technical faults in Chinook helicopters. It listed the incidents shown on p. 183. It also lists the several FADEC related faults and other failures on ZD576, including (provocatively) one which the group assumes to have occurred on the day of the crash. Likewise, lists of hydro-mechanical assembly faults, FADEC-related warnings and associated faults, electrical faults, and uncommanded flying control movements on Chinook Mk2s include one each assumed to have occurred to ZD576 on the day of the crash. There is also comment on electromagnetic interference and what little is known of problems with the US Army Chinooks, with lists of incidents.

The Upside-Down Chinook

The report on the incident released by the US Army Safety Center under the US Freedom of Information Act is 3cm thick. Consequently, this is a summary.

The incident involved a CH-47D Army helicopter (a Chinook equivalent to the RAF Mk2), serial no. 84-24156 which departed Truax Field, Texas, at 10:50 on 11 April 1997 for Mathis Field, San Angelo. It was refuelled there and departed for Amarillo at 13:45. At about 16:58, it was flying near Tulia at 4,450ft AMSL (1,100ft AGL) at 140kt, when the nose pitched down and yawed left. The pilot applied aft right cyclic and right pedal but the nose-low attitude increased and left yaw continued even with full right pedal application. The aircraft then entered a left roll, smoothly for 90 degrees but 'snap roll' to the remaining 270 degrees. It lost about 850ft altitude in the full left roll, after which it returned to upright in a right yaw of about 90 degrees. The crew initiated and completed a precautionary landing to an open field, touching down with about 32ft ground roll, and shut down the engines. The aft main rotor blades then struck the fuselage as they coasted down. The cost of repairing the damage, including replacing the entire power train, was put at $11.6 million.

An Aircraft Accident Investigation Board was appointed on 11 May 1997. The initial investigation report (USASC 97-305 dated 2 June 1997) revealed numerous components with minor and major defects which could have caused the uncommanded oscillations and flight control movements. These included a gouge and a dent in one of the caps of the forward swivelling boost actuator and a locking ring not properly torqued. There was also metal in the directional selector valve cavity which could have caused a jam. The most critical defect was excessive corrosion in system 2 of the pitch and roll ILCAs.

A supplementary investigation report (USASC 97-305 dated 3 December 1997) found water contamination of approximately 20 per cent in the hydraulic fluid in both upper boost actuators. The permitted level is only 300 ppm (0.0003 per cent). Barium and zinc were also found in the fluid.

It was recommended that immediate and positive action should be taken regarding the upper boost actuators and ILCAs since these are critical to flight safety.

References

Official documents (in chronological order):

The Marine Observer's Handbook (1995): 11th edition. Meteorological Office, HMSO.

Transcript of the Fatal Accident Inquiry, Paisley, 1996 (author's corrected copy on CD-ROM, which is also available in the National Library of Scotland); uncorrected original is in Paisley Sheriff Court.

Lessons of the Chinook crash on the Mull of Kintyre, House of Commons Defence Committee, Fourth Report (HC 611), The Stationery Office, London, 13 May 1998.

Government Responses to the Fourth, Fifth and Sixth Reports from the Defence Committee of Session 1997-98 (HC 1109), The Stationery Office, London, 21 October 1998.

Ministry of Defence: Accepting equipment off-contract and into service, House of Commons Committee of Public Accounts, Forty-fourth Report (HC 319), The Stationery Office, 2000.[184]

Ministry of Defence: Acceptance of the Chinook Mk2 Helicopter, House of Commons Committee of Public Accounts, Forty-fifth Report (HC 975), The Stationery Office, 1999–2000.

Proposal for a Select Committee on the crash of Chinook helicopter ZD 576 on the Mull of Kintyre on 2 June 1994, House of Lords Liaison Committee 2nd Report, 2000-01, HL Paper 67.

Treasury Minute on the Forty-fourth and Forty-fifth Reports

236

from the Committee of Public Accounts 1999–2000,
pp. 9–13 (Ministry of Defence, Acceptance of the Chinook
Mk2 Helicopter), March 2001 (Cm 5078).

*Report of RAF Board of Inquiry; Statement of Air Accidents
Investigation Branch; Oral evidence September 2001.* Select
Committee on Chinook ZD 576, House of Lords Select
Committee, House of Lords Paper 25(i): The Stationery
Office, 2001.

*Oral evidence Oct-Nov 2001; Written evidence; Sheriff's
Determination and note.* Select Committee on Chinook ZD
576, House of Lords Paper 25(ii): The Stationery Office,
2002.

Report from the Select Committee on Chinook ZD 576. House
of Lords Paper 25(iii): The Stationery Office, 2002.

*The Government's Response to the Report from the Select
Committee on Chinook ZD 576, House of Lords Session
2001-02 (HL Paper 25 (iii))*, 22 July 2002, including an
annex: *Review of RAF Chinook Accident 2 June 1994 –
Further Work Undertaken by Boeing Helicopters*, June
2002.

Independent publications and articles:

Hurst, Ronald and Leslie (eds.), (1982): *Pilot Error, The Human
Factors*, St Albans, Granada.

MacDonald, Ron[ald] (with Richard K.J. Hadlow and Ralph
Kohn), (2000): *Royal Air Force Chinook Mark 2 Accident,
Mull of Kintyre, Strathclyde –Scotland 2 June 1994*, ('The
MacDonald Report') with three appendices: *Notes relating
to weather at the time of the accident*, 2 September 2000;
Electromagnetic Interference, 12 March 2001; and *A Study
of Interference Levels in Aircraft at Radio Frequencies used
by Portable Telephones* (a copy of a UK CAA report dated
2 May 2000, ref: 9/40:23-90-02), 12 March 2001.

——(2001a): *RAF Chinook Helicopters – Accidents and
Technical Faults* (A Special Report for Lord Jauncey of
Tullichettle).

——(2001b): 'The crash of the RAF Chinook HC2 helicopter ZD

237

576 on the Mull of Kintyre, 2 June 1994', *J. Meteorology, U.K.* Vol. 26, No. 261.

——(2002): 'Reply to article by Mr W. S. Pike and letter from Mr D. Pedgley regarding the Mull of Kintyre helicopter accident', Ibid, Vol. 27, No. 266.

Mitchell, Ian (ed.), (1999): *RAF Justice: How the Royal Air Force covered up software problems while blaming the dead pilots in the 1994 crash of a Chinook helicopter.* (A Computer Weekly Investigation), Reed Business Information.

Pike, William S. (2001a): 'Weather notes on 2 June 1994 with particular reference to the Chinook helicopter accident on the Mull of Kintyre', *J. Meteorology, U.K.* Vol. 26, No. 259.

——(2001b): 'A further note on the weather on 2 June 1994, the day of the Chinook helicopter disaster', Ibid. Vol. 26, No. 261.

——(2001c): 'A reply to points raised by Captain Ralph Kohn regarding the Mull of Kintyre helicopter accident on 2 June 1994', Ibid, with comments by David Pedgley.

——(2001d): 'Further remarks about the weather of the Mull of Kintyre', Ibid, Vol. 26, No. 264.

——(2002): 'A reconstruction of the helicopter accident on 2 June 1994, with historical note on nine other aircraft accidents on the Mull of Kintyre since 1941', Ibid, Vol. 27, No. 266.

Ramsden, J.M. (1999): 'The Mull of Kintyre Chinook crash', *Pilot,* October.

——(2002): *Chinook Justice: A Plain Person's Guide,* 4th ed. 25 pp. private.

Ross, H.E. (1967): 'Water, fog and the size-distance invariance hypothesis.' *British J. of Psychology,* 58, 301–13.

Slessor, Tim, (2002): *Ministries of Deception,* London, Aurum Press.

Wratten, Sir William, (2000): 'Why those Chinook pilots were "grossly negligent"', *Pilot,* August.

Notes

1   'Mull' means promontory, in this case the southernmost tip of the Kintyre peninsula.

2   Both parties acknowledged the basis for this agreement, but did not necessarily agree. The families of the pilots did not admit liability.

3   Irish Republican Army, a terrorist organization wanting union with the Irish Republic.

4   Now the Police Service of Northern Ireland.

5   Hereinafter referred to as 'the Board'.

6   AP3207, Ch. 8, App. G, para.9.

7   Negligence is defined as 'The omission to do something which, in the circumstances, a reasonable person would do, or doing something which . . . a reasonable person would not do, or would do differently . . . When related to flying an aircraft, . . . a breach of duty to take care, or in other words carelessness in a matter where care is demanded . . .'. Negligence must be defined by degree, as either 'minor' or 'gross' or constituting recklessness or disobedience.

8   The Scottish equivalent of an English coroner (also a public prosecutor).

9   A sheriff is a judge in a Scottish all-purpose court.

10   The highest civil court in Scotland.

11   The Government's chief lawyer in Scotland and now a member of the Scottish Executive.

12   By Martin Bell on 12 July 2000 and James Arbuthnot on 26 July 2004.

13   *The Last Flight of Zulu Delta 576.*

14 *Sunday Herald*, 3 December 2000.

15 This is the altitude in any particular area at which an aircraft would be clear of any ground or obstruction.

16 'Why the MoD must pardon the Chinook pilots', *Sunday Herald*, 10 February 2002.

17 www.chinook-justice.org

18 027 was actually the magnetic track; to maintain that track with the wind conditions given by the tower and an airspeed of 140kt, the 'heading' would have to have been 030 magnetic.

19 VFR: below 140kt air speed, visibility must be at least 1km with cloud no lower than 250ft. Above 140kt, visibility must be 5km with 500ft clearance between cloud and the 50ft minimum ground clearance.

20 VHF Omnidirectional Radio.

21 Lord Rathcavan in the House of Lords on 1 November 1999.

22 Lord Rathcavan, as above.

23 In his statement to the Board, Holbrook indicated that McLeod had missed the weather forecast.

24 In his statement to the Board, he gave his position as N55°16'20", W5°50'20".

25 She later became Mrs Gresswell.

26 *Mull of Kintyre* by Wings (1977). Sir Paul McCartney still has a small estate in Kintyre, but not near the Mull.

27 A Royal Navy pilot who has since left the services.

28 Now a wing commander.

29 Special Forces are trained for unconventional warfare behind enemy lines, especially reconnaissance of targets for attack by other forces, sabotage or attacks on key targets, support of opposition forces and guerrilla groups, freeing hostages, capturing key individuals or weapons and counter-terrorism.

30 In written evidence to the Defence Committee, Malcolm Spaven questioned the suitability of the route chosen.

31 Mk1 Chinooks could go to −6 degrees C. In clear air, all Chinooks could fly down to −10 degrees C.

32 A rapid change in pitch angle of the aircraft, either to slow down or to climb quickly.

33   Instrument Flight Rules: aircraft must be at least 1,000ft clear of highest obstacle.

34   A 'waypoint' is a term peculiar to the computerized navigation equipment installed in Chinooks and is the aiming point of a route or part of a route where a change of direction is required.

35   The seven/eight hours flying limit in Northern Ireland was imposed because of the high flying rate in Northern Ireland, which led to cumulative fatigue in the crews. The normal limit in the UK is ten hours.

36   Safety altitude is calculated by looking for the highest obstacle in a strip 10nm (18.4km) either side of the planned route and at both turning points. If this obstacle is below 3,000ft (914m), 1,000ft (305m) is added and the total rounded up to the next 100ft multiple. If the obstacle is between 3,000 and 5,000ft (1524m), 2,000ft (610m) is added and again rounded to the next 100ft multiple.

37   In IFR flight, the minimum safety altitude in the UK outside controlled airspace is 3,000ft except for take-off and landing, unless specially cleared by the MOD (*Military Flying Orders*).

38   Wrongly calculated by Tapper as 5,800ft (1,768m).

39   120kt also makes calculation of transit time easy; time in minutes is the distance in nautical miles divided by two.

40   If the aircraft weighed 11,000kg, and the people on board and their luggage weighed 2,894kg, with a full load of fuel the total mass was only 16,894kg.

41   Since retired.

42   Tapper had completed these tasks in fifty minutes less than the allocated time.

43   The journey to Inverness would be within the eight hours extension. But Tapper could not return that day without extension to ten hours, not even travelling at the aircraft's top speed of 155kt (285km/h).

44   Since the Chinook was not required for duty until 16:00 the next day, there was time for it to return during the next morning.

45   The lowest authorized height for low-level operations for

transit flying with two pilots on the flight deck is 50ft (15m). In daylight, anything below 500ft (150m) is classed as 'low-level'. Tapper booked the low-level flight with the Military Air Traffic Organisation (MATO) in London and planned to fly at about 100ft (30.5m).

46   Tapper could also have booked into the *night* low-flying system, where helicopters are permitted by making special arrangements to ensure that they not in conflict with any fixed-wing aircraft.

47   'CA' stands for 'Controller Aircraft', an organization that approves the airworthiness of an aircraft entering RAF service. The 'CA Release' document sets out the parameters of the airworthiness approval, including any conditions or limitations on how the aircraft is to be flown.

48   The crash of RAF Chinook ZA721 on 27 February 1987 in the Falklands (see Appendix One).

49   Form 700 is actually a fairly large book containing a number of sheets.

50   Pre-flight checks are followed by pre-start-up checks, after-start checks, pre-taxi checks, pre-take-off checks, after-take-off checks and finally a channel check of the automatic flight control systems. There are further checks on landing.

51   Now a squadron leader.

52   An 'outbriefing' is an RAF procedure in which the departing captain gives a Duty Authorizing Officer details of an imminent sortie.

53   The RAF organization with responsibility for convening and advising Boards of Inquiry and generally pursuing flight safety in the Air Force.

54   Now part of the Thales group.

55   Apparently Racal had not previously realized that flight data could be extracted from their equipment.

56   A correction to indicate at what level the conditions at 247m that day would have corresponded to in the standard atmosphere (1013.25mb at sea level at 0 degrees C).

57   Yaw is rotation about a vertical axis of the aircraft.

58   Banking is rotation about the longitudinal axis of the aircraft.

59 The local magnetic deviation was found to be 9.5 degrees west of the OS Grid, which was itself three degrees west of true north.

60 A Doppler radar which shows the speed over the ground and drift left or right from the track set.

61 Torque is a turning effect or moment.

62 This is the component along the aircraft's track of a 30kt (15m/s) wind blowing from 170 degrees true (just east of south).

63 TANS stands for Tactical Area Navigation System.

64 The SuperTANS is not a flight data recorder and was not intended for this purpose.

65 The Racal report stated that the drive to the Steer Meter indicated a command to make a fourteen-degree left turn.

66 The amount by which magnetic north differed from true north at that time in that area.

67 Now Air Chief Marshal Sir John Day, recently retired as Air Officer Commanding-in-Chief Strike Command and Commander Allied Forces in North-Western Europe.

68 Now a group captain and station commander at RAF Odiham.

69 Now a wing commander.

70 Later DERA, part of which has since been privatized as 'QinetiQ'.

71 i.e. How recently they flew the aircraft, and whether they met the rules governing how often you have to fly a particular type to remain qualified to fly it without having to undergo a check flight or further training.

72 Cable had noted an indication that this gauge had been reading abnormally high, but he could not exclude the possibility that the reading resulted from the crash. In any case, the gauge was on the Maintenance Panel, behind the pilots. The Board's conclusion seems unjustified.

73 See the report on the crash of ZA715 in Appendix One.

74 Night Vision Goggles: training at night with special goggles, which enable pilots to see in the dark.

75 Defined in the RAF Flight Safety Manual as 'An honest mistake accompanied by no lack of zeal ... where a person, through no fault of his [sic] own, and while exercising the

degree of skill which can reasonably be expected makes an inappropriate response . . .'

76   Now an air commodore, retired.

77   It is not clear that this was Crawford's conclusion.

78   Then Air Officer Commanding-in-Chief Strike Command and Commander Allied Forces North-Western Europe. Now retired.

79   After retiring and in the face of criticism, Sir William defended his decision in a letter to *Pilot* (August 2000).

80   A weather summary written in retrospect.

81   'Annexe B' to Sir John Day's paper to the House of Lords Select Committee and shown in the reconstruction on p. 191.

82   Drizzle is defined as 'precipitation in which the drops are very small' (<0.5mm). *Marine Observer's Handbook.*

83   D/IFS(RAF)/140/30/94/1.

84   A public official who holds office under the Crown and who usually possesses both medical and legal qualifications.

85   The Fatal Accidents and Sudden Deaths Inquiry (Scotland) Act 1976.

86   The Scottish legal term for the officer who prosecutes in criminal cases in local and inferior courts. Sometimes abbreviated to 'fiscal'.

87   The headquarters in Edinburgh of the Scottish public prosecution system.

88   Sir Stephen Stewart Templeton Young, Third Baronet of Partick. In 2001 he was appointed Sheriff Principal of Grampian, Highlands and Islands.

89   Presumably Squadron Leader David Morgan of 240 Operational Conversion Unit, later 27(R) Squadron.

90   See schedule in Appendix Two.

91   Now a squadron leader.

92   The principle that, in explaining a thing, no more assumptions should be made than are necessary. Sometimes 'Ockham'.

93   In fact, Pulford's evidence was that left yaw could have altered the track and that nothing prevented applying full power to increase the climb rate.

94 Ian H. B. Carmichael: *Sudden deaths and fatal accident inquiries: Scot's law and practice*, 2nd ed. (Edinburgh 1993)

95 In fact, the White Star Line had only claimed that its ships *Olympic* and *Titanic* were designed to be unsinkable 'as far as it is possible' (*The Herald*, 4 Aug 2002, p. 4).

96 A chief judge in Scotland, supervising ordinary sheriffs in a sheriffdom and hearing some appeals.

97 There had been no conflict in his evidence to the FAI.

98 In fact $(2.5 \times 150)/60 = 6.25$nm (11.5km).

99 This is true until shortly before impact, when the Chinook was almost exactly windward of the lighthouse.

100 Previously recorded as 0.81nm (1.5km).

101 028 was not the track for waypoint B.

102 Nevertheless, he had exonerated Forbes and Hardie.

103 There is no evidence that he ever visited the site of crash.

104 *RAF Justice* (see Mitchell in References). The title is a pun on the phrase 'rough justice', leading one Scottish journalist mistakenly to refer to it by that title.

105 Now a wing commander.

106 In the USA, Chinooks are operated by the Army, not the Air Force.

107 EDS-Scicon found 485 anomalies after examining less than 20 per cent of the program, at which point it abandoned its analysis. Fifty-six of the anomalies were categorized as 'category one'. A claim against Boeing was settled in favour of the MOD in 1995 but the claim against Textron-Lycoming went to arbitration.

108 The MOD later found his report on this incident (14 Dec 1993) but declared that it was not caused by a FADEC software failure.

109 Later the MOD reported that it was not a FADEC fault.

110 March 1998.

111 In fact, only four were in the UK, one was in Germany and three were in the Falkland Islands. The ninth was the Wilmington incident in the USA. See list in Chapter Nine and reports in Appendix One.

112 11 April 1997 (see Report in Appendix Five).

113   Lewis's own account can be found in the US Army Safety Center's *Flightfax* (May 1998).
114   Now Lord Mayhew of Twysden.
115   The MAAS reproduced in Appendix One.
116   The statement continued to deal with compensation.
117   Bruce George, Crispin Blunt, Julian Brazier, Menzies Campbell, Jamie Cann, Harry Cohen, Michael Colvin, Jimmy Hood, John McWilliam, Laura Moffatt and Dari Taylor.
118   Flight Data Recorders (usually called ADRs or CVRs).
119   Some information from the memorandum is incorporated in the summary of the hearing below.
120   The Committee reported this as '8 other accidents . . . all involving *Mark-1* aircraft [their italics]'. The eight included the only Mk2 accident.
121   In its report, the Committee expressed this as a requirement that the MTBF 'would not exceed 5,500 flying hours'. In fact this is a lower, not an upper limit.
122   Under the warranty, Textron Lycoming repair and/or replace components free of charge. They also supply extra spares if required.
123   British Nuclear Fuels plc.
124   This is a confusion of VFR and IFR.
125   *Lessons of the Chinook crash on the Mull of Kintyre* (see References).
126   The 'Chinook Five': James Arbuthnot, Menzies Campbell, Martin O'Neill, Robert Key and Crispin Blunt.
127   Now Lord Robertson of Port Ellen, erstwhile Secretary General of NATO.
128   'Chinook FADEC – The New Evidence'.
129   2,000lbf may have been intended, which = 8.8kN, or 2,000pdl = 276.5N.
130   Chinooks do not have a conventional rudder; the effect of a rudder is achieved by tilting one rotor to the left and the other to the right.
131   See References. The document also deals with two other matters raised by the Defence Committee.
132   Since knighted.

133 Answers dated 25 May 2000, but none relevant to the accident.
134 Baron Chalfont.
135 Baron Gilbert of Dudley, etc.
136 One of the functions of the House of Lords Liaison Committee is to consider requests for ad hoc committees.
137 Baron Bowness of Warlington and Croydon.
138 Baron Brennan of Bilbury.
139 Baron Hooson.
140 A former judge in the Scottish Appeal Court.
141 Baron Tombs of Brailes.
142 Clause 55 of the Board's report.
143 These bearings are all magnetic.
144 Published with the Committee's report (HL Paper 25(i)).
145 In a footnote, Cable appears to express doubt about his previous conclusion on the emergency flags.
146 *Disciplinary Proceedings in Aircraft Accidents,* 16 February 1995.
147 'Mist' is when visibility is over 1km; below that it is 'fog'. (*Marine Observer's Handbook*).
148 Taken by Tony Gresswell.
149 Colonel Hodgkiss explained to the Defence Committee that this can have been due to flying so low that lock on a satellite was lost and that the pilots should have switched to the Doppler.
150 He appeared to confuse the use of simulators with the mathematical simulation produced by Boeing. It is not clear that the Committee understood the distinction.
151 The US handling pilot says that Burke himself may have triggered this run-up by leaning on a beep switch.
152 Neither the MOD nor Boeing could find a record of this incident.
153 Confusion between the mathematical simulation and the simulator.
154 An extract from the fax listing the parameters was published with the Committee's Minutes of Evidence (HL Paper 25(ii)).
155 Annex A on p. 157 of HL Paper 25(i).
156 The bank angle (θ) is related to the radius of the turn (R)

and the airspeed (V) by the formula: $R = V^2/g \tan \theta$, where g is the acceleration due to gravity. The MOD states that a turn of about 50 degrees would have been required to avoid the landmass.

157 HL Paper 25(iii).
158 In fact these data indicate an average ground speed of 168kt (possibly 144kt airspeed).
159 The exchange referred to is the same occasion which the Select Committee had been told was a radar identification 7nm from the Belfast VOR.
160 Boeing's 2002 report states that a US Army report (USASC 97-305 Supplement, see Appendix Five) describes contamination by barium, chlorine, zinc and water. It also points out that ZD576, with only fifty-seven flight hours, was unlikely to have had the same degree of contamination as the US CH-47D with 4,606 flight hours and that this explanation pales when compared with the CFIT causal chain established by the Board.
161 Revealed in the MOD's response to the HoL Select Committee, p. 22.
162 86.63nm/32.8min.
163 $42 \times 60/16.84 = 149.6kt$
164 $33 \times 60/13.2 = 150.0kt$
165 Slessor, pp. 71 and 99.
166 e.g. Slessor, p. 77.
167 'Gross negligence' by Eamonn O'Neill in the *Scotsman Magazine*, 3 May 2000.
168 Admiralty List of Lights Vol. A (NP74) gives them as N55° 18.6'; W005° 48.1'.
169 Not necessarily 280m; uncertainties mean that it can have been anything between 150 and 300m.
170 HoL Paper 25(ii), p. 123.
171 GPS typically drifts 1nm per hour.
172 Clause 56 of its report.
173 2200m/77.1m/s = 28.5s
174 At 150kt, the change of waypoint must have been made 22.8 seconds before inpact.
175 Ross 1967 (see References).
176 270m/0.0349rad = 7,736m (4.1nm).

177 'Chinook crash report should do more than attribute blame', *Scotsman*, 21 June 1995.

178 A Board of Inquiry concluded that this accident was likely to have been caused by a stall.

179 A.W. Reid, in a letter to the *Herald*, 17 June 2002.

180 Annex A to the Defence Committee's Fourth Report (see References).

181 Letter from J. Lewis-Rice in *Air Forces Monthly* (April 2000).

182 Data from the Flight Safety Foundation.

183 Macdonald, Ron, et al (see References).

184 Much of the evidence in this report is also published in the 45th report.

Index

icing limitation, 24–5, 46, 55–6, 77, 93, 101, 116. 190–1, 197

JATOC, 23, 97, 187
Jauncey of Tullichettle, Lord, 137, 142–5, 149, 233
Jenner, AVM Tim, 122
Joint Air Tasking Operations Centre, (see JATOC)
Jones, Michael, QC, 64, 67, 71, 91ff

Key, Robert, MP, 126
Kingston, Ian, 22–5, 27–8, 30, 67, 150, 186–7
Kohn, Ralph, 155–6, 232

Lamont, Hector, 15–17, 19, 193
Lewis, Bric, 115, 150
Liaison Committee, (HOL), 136, 202
low-level flight, 29–30, 49, 55–7, 72–3, 77–8, 86–7, 102, 143, 164,
    167, 197

'Macdonald Report', 138, 155, 231ff
Macdonald, Ronald, 155–6
MacFarlane, Ian, 67–70, 73, 77, 80, 83–5, 89–90, 94–5, 97–8, 127,
    159–60, 164
Machrihanish, (see RAF Machrihanish)
mean time between failures, (see MTBF)
Miller, Hamish, 19–20
Mitchell, John, QC, 63–4, 66, 69, 72ff
Moonie, Dr Lewis, MP, 133
Morgan, David, 63, 66, 117, 145, 153ff
MTBF, 122
Mull of Kintyre Group, 135, 202
Mull of Kintyre lighthouse, 13–17, 137, 180, 188,
    chosen as waypoint A, 25, 67, 92
    error in location, 42, 48, 72, 187
Murchie, David, 15–18, 80, 99, 184

negligence, 1–3, 6, 57, 75–6, 78, 81, 91, 103, 120–1, 124, 132–3,
    139–42, 145, 147–9, 151–2, 155, 163–7, 170–1, 174, 197, 202

O'Neill, Aidan, 64, 67, 74ff, 81, 84, 86, 88, 90–1, 113, 201
Oughton, John, 132
outbriefing, 32, 44, 46, 52–4, 72

Parkinson, Rex, 34, 138
Paton, Revd John, 5
Perks, Malcolm, 110, 112, 125–6, 129–30, 132